Scribes and Schools

LIBRARY OF ANCIENT ISRAEL

Douglas A. Knight, *General Editor*

Scribes and Schools

The Canonization of the Hebrew Scriptures

PHILIP R. DAVIES

WESTMINSTER JOHN KNOX PRESS
LOUISVILLE, KENTUCKY

All scripture quotations are the author's translation unless otherwise marked.

Book design by Publishers' WorkGroup
Cover design by Kim Wohlenhaus

First edition

Published by Westminster John Knox Press
Louisville, Kentucky

This book is printed on acid-free paper that meets the American National Standards Institute Z39.48 standard. ∞

PRINTED IN THE UNITED STATES OF AMERICA
98 99 00 01 02 03 04 05 06 07 — 10 9 8 7 6 5 4 3 2 1

Library of Congress Cataloging-in-Publication Data

Davies, Philip R.
    Scribes and schools : the canonization of the Hebrew Scriptures / Philip R. Davies. — 1st ed.
        p.   cm. — (Library of ancient Israel)
    Includes bibliographical references and indexes.
    ISBN 0-664-22077-0
    1. Bible. O.T.—Canon.   2. Scribes, Jewish.   I. Title.
II. Series.
BS1135.D38   1998
221.1′2—dc21   97–39684

Contents

Foreword

The historical and literary questions preoccupying biblical scholars since the Enlightenment have focused primarily on events and leaders in ancient Israel, the practices and beliefs of Yahwistic religion, and the oral and written stages in the development of the people's literature. Considering how little was known about Israel and indeed the whole ancient Near East just three centuries ago, the gains achieved to date have been extraordinary, due in no small part to the unanticipated discovery by archaeologists of innumerable texts and artifacts.

Recent years have witnessed a new turn in biblical studies, occasioned largely by a growing lack of confidence in the "assured results" of past generations of scholars. At the same time, an increased openness to the methods and issues of other disciplines such as anthropology, sociology, linguistics, and literary criticism has allowed new questions to be posed regarding the old materials. Social history, a well-established area within the field of historical studies, has proved especially fruitful as a means of analyzing specific segments of the society. Instead of concentrating predominantly on national events, leading individuals, political institutions, and "high culture," social historians attend to broader and more basic issues such as social organization, conditions in cities and villages, life stages, environmental contexts, power distribution according to class and status, and social stability and instability. To ask such questions of ancient Israel shifts the focus away from those with power and the events they instigated and onto the everyday realities and social subtleties experienced by the vast majority of the population. Such inquiry has now gained new force with the application of various forms of ideological criticism and other methods designed to ferret out the political, economic, and social interests concealed in the sources.

This series represents a collaborative effort to investigate several specific topics—politics, economics, religion, literature, material culture, law, intellectual leadership, ethnic identity, social marginalization, the international context, and canon formation—each in terms of its social dimensions and processes within ancient Israel. Some of these subjects have not been explored in depth until now; others are familiar areas currently in need of re-examination. While the sociohistorical approach provides the general perspective for all volumes of the series, each author has the latitude to determine the most appropriate means for dealing with the topic at hand. Individually and collectively, the volumes aim to expand our vision of the culture and society of ancient Israel and thereby generate new appreciation for its impact on subsequent history.

The subject of canonization provides an excellent example of the ways in which sociohistorical perspectives can make distinct and crucial contributions. Previous debates about the rise and significance of authoritative scriptures have tended to be preoccupied with theological, literary, and religious issues, and the apologetic interests of the respective interpreters have played no little role in their judgments. In this book, Philip R. Davies moves the discussion to a quite different and very pragmatic level—the social circumstances lying behind canonization: Which social groups would have had the training, the authority, the financial backing, and the longevity to write and preserve literary texts? How might the very manner of preservation—the writing materials, the cataloging, the storing—have influenced the selection and arrangement of texts? How was the variety of religious and political interests accommodated—or not—in the process? Why, in fact, did the move to canonize arise at all during the latter centuries of the first millennium B.C.E., especially in the political milieu of colonialism and the cultural milieu of Hellenism? Were there any earlier stages during which, in effect, previous canonical texts emerged? And can this gradual, complex process account for the multiple texts and arrangements that eventually became authoritative for diverse Jewish and Christian groups? In addressing such questions, the author presents a closely developed argument on the basis of meticulous analysis of biblical and nonbiblical texts, especially the Dead Sea scrolls. His thesis amounts to a clear challenge to conventional assessments of canonization and will henceforth need to be engaged whenever the subject is discussed.

Douglas A. Knight
General Editor

Preface

The writing of this book took place largely during a sabbatical semester granted by the University of Sheffield in the winter of 1996. That it could have been written in a relatively short space of time owes much to the advice and support of a number of colleagues. I must first mention the editor of the Library of Ancient Israel series, Douglas Knight, who invited me to contribute this volume, and has provided not only excellent editorial help and advice but also the kind of personal and intellectual support and stimulation that many other scholars, to my certain knowledge, have also enjoyed. It is always a particular pleasure to write for a close and valued friend. I am also grateful to Jon Berquist, formerly of Westminster John Knox Press. I have appreciated his help both professionally and as a fellow scholar, and his work on the Second Temple period has been valuable in the writing of this book.

I also want to mention my Sheffield colleague John Rogerson, with whom I have shared other writing projects, and who donated a good deal of his very precious time to read and correct a draft of this book and contribute a large number of valuable comments. It is quite probable that even now he knows more about canon than I do. To Loveday and Philip Alexander I also owe thanks for advice on matters rabbinic and classical (and much else), while Wilfrid Lambert has been characteristically generous in assisting me with understanding Akkadian canonizing, and Alan Millard with problems of literacy. Avigdor Horovitz was also very helpful, especially in alerting me to Haran's recent book and discussing problems of canon over e-mail. Also, to David Gunn I owe the term "serious entertainment" as applied to biblical literature.

With Jacob Neusner I shared a stroll and a conversation in New Orleans, in which he warned me about the difficulties of dealing with Jewish canonizing. I have written the book anyway, but not without a great deal of reflection on his research and borrowing of his ideas. Finally, I must thank my friends in Copenhagen who have continued to try to persuade me that the Hebrew scriptures are entirely Hellenistic in origin. If they have given up on this, I hope they will see in these pages that I am by no means totally unpersuaded.

Introduction

To understand a problem is not to answer it, nor is answering it necessarily the same as understanding it. Indeed, I have often introduced lectures by remarking that scholarship exists to create problems and not to solve them.

There is a serious truth behind this jocularity. Students—and perhaps some other readers as well—may tend to look to textbooks for answers. But scholarship, and especially when it deals with the past, is *not* about answers: it is about problems. Most of what we assert about the past is not "knowledge" in the sense that we can claim it as reliable fact. It is a conclusion which data, method, and reasoning have led us to assert as knowledge. That knowledge is only as good as the method, argument, and reasoning that produced it. And knowledge is always provisional.

Education, then, is not the assimilation of facts, something that computers are increasingly able to do better than we are. It is about the manipulation of facts into understanding, using reason and, sometimes, imagination and instinct. It is not always about finding the answer, but about learning how the answer should be sought. This lesson is particularly valuable in the area of biblical studies, which deals with literature that is understood by many people to be a book of definitive "answers," whereas its "answers" are really matters of interpretation and selection on the part of readers (including scholars).

The first thing to be said on the subject of canonizing the Hebrew scriptures, then, is that there is too little data. There is also too much "knowledge." We "know" that the "Hebrew scriptures" were "canonized"—or do we? What do we mean by "Hebrew scriptures"? And what does "canonized" denote? Is there a "Hebrew canon"? A "Jewish canon" even? What exactly *is* the problem we are dealing with? How far does it involve the data, and how far the way we approach the data before we even examine it? For no scholarship ever approaches a set of data without an agenda of some sort, or at least some prejudices and preconceptions.

A good deal of this volume is taken up with arguing and exploring, rather than "presenting the facts," which is partly because the "facts" are rather few, and many of them do not mean a lot, or they can be interpreted in many ways. It is also because what we know about the past is not a matter of what facts we can amass about it (in the case of Jewish canonizing these have been assembled over and over again and can easily be acquired). Rather, we can know only what we can establish (and insofar as we can establish it) by argument. I have tried to explain my own presuppositions and method of working in such a way that I do not pretend to be "objective" or better informed than anyone else. I also offer a conclusion only insofar as I can argue for it. In particular, in chapters 6–9 I have engaged in detailed exegesis of texts because reading texts is a fundamental skill of biblical studies and it is by such reading that we enjoy much of what we claim as "knowledge." Knowledge is not given *by* texts but acquired through interpretation *of* them.

A word about the religious dimension should be included, for most readers of this book will encounter "canon" as a religious category, and may well be studying it in a religious context. Religious and historical approaches to scripture are different. If scriptures are evidence of dimensions of reality beyond what can be empirically known to all humans, then these by definition lie beyond the capacity of history, which must deal with what is publicly accessible and can be rationally explained. Secular treatments of religion are often dismissed as "reductionist," meaning that they reduce phenomena to categories that suit them (e.g., religion to psychology or society). However, religious explanations can equally be accused of reducing social and psychological phenomena to the influence of transcendental forces and all phenomena, and the connection between them, to divine plans. All scholarship aims to reduce the inexplicable to the explicable. The differences lie in what one is prepared to accept as explanation and how far one is able to universalize the kinds of explanations one accepts. Many people accept as fact things reported in their Bibles that they would simply not believe if they saw them today with their own eyes.

As an explanation of what is, or was, or can be, "real," history is in no way intrinsically superior to religion or science. But neither is it inferior: it does have its own integrity, which must be respected. From the historical perspective, scriptures arise and become canonized not because of supernatural processes or self-evident truths imposing themselves, but as the result of individual decisions and social processes. As the eminent Wilfred Cantwell Smith has stated, "scripture is a human activity."[1] Study of the history of scripture, of canon, is not a religious discipline, nor a theological one. There is, of course, no reason why historical and religious explanations or analyses of scripture need conflict with each other. All that matters is that they do not try to answer each other's questions. A major obstacle facing a historian of Jewish canonizing is the canon itself. For the Jewish scriptural canon is divided into three sections: law, prophets, writings, and each of these three contains both descriptions of its own composition and hints of its own composition. It incorporates, as well as claims to be words of a deity, direct claims about how its contents came into existence; but it also undermines these claims because its account is not univocal—because it sometimes contains more than one version or explanation.

These two characteristics of this canon, its religious authority and its historical ambiguity, generally point in different directions, toward affirmation and toward doubt. Biblical scholarship has on the whole believed itself to be following the doubts, as it has constructed an account of canon formation that deviates from the main canonical presentation: thus, for instance, no scholars believe that the ten commandments were given as written to Moses on Sinai. But scholarship still rehearses the story of Ezra and his lawbook and clings, if less tenaciously, to the notion of a learned Solomon patronizing scribal schools. These stories are more plausible, because they do not entail gods writing with their fingers on tablets; but plausibility does not mean truthfulness. Religious faith can usually entertain doubt without damage, though it is doubt that assails faith and not the other way round. But for the historian, doubt is not an ethical or existential attribute. It is—at least, that is my own definition—part of a method by which some kind of truth can be gained. All "faith" for a historian is bad faith, and we have no business "believing" anything. Belief is not a method for reaching the truth we want to express: evidence, inference, and probability are. Since canons function as sources of truth and objects of belief, the confrontation between canon and historian *ought* to be somewhat antagonistic. And so it shall be, in this book at least. There are plenty of other books in which a Jewish or Christian canon is a Good Thing. But ethical stances on the contents of canons are really quite irrelevant to exploring their origins.

Finally, while I was delighted to accept the invitation to contribute to the Library of Ancient Israel, I was aware that I could say little about "ancient Israel," especially having written a book arguing that what passes for "ancient Israel" is a scholarly figment. I maintain that view (and will develop it in the following pages)—which means that I shall be concentrating on a period of time that I would certainly be happy to name the "biblical period" but which falls outside the "classical" age of the Israelite and Judean monarchies. The view taken in this book is that monarchic Israel and Judah and their "traditions" are a creation (though not necessarily entirely from nothing) of a later society and do not correspond to any society that occupied Palestine in the Iron Age.

But that "Israel," though it never existed as it is described, lives in the pages of a canon. This book, then, is not about how ancient Israel produced its canon, but rather about how a canon produced "ancient Israel." But whether or not this thesis convinces, it is in any case the problem that matters, not the solution.

CHAPTER 1

The Dimensions of Canon

DEALING WITH "CANON"

Study of the "Hebrew" or "Jewish" canon confronts a number of conceptual problems which, despite a good deal of recent work,[1] persist here and there:

1. The concept and the role of canons within the system of rabbinic Judaism, and in particular the "scriptural" or "biblical" canon (the terms "scripture" and "Bible," problematic in themselves, will be discussed in chapter 2). Here the concept and evaluation of "canon" has been dependent too much on the Christian model of a closed and authoritative list.

2. The inherited view of pre-rabbinic Judaism as having been, throughout its development, a unitary phenomenon, with a single line of evolution, and thus, implicitly, with a single canonizing process, leading to a single canon.

3. The assumption that the scriptural canon provides clear and reliable evidence of its own history. In a good deal of scholarship there is a lack of critical reflection, leading to a view of the origins of the rabbinic canon that cannot be supported by adequate arguments. (The problem here, as everywhere in biblical scholarship, is that while strong arguments are always expected when the historicity of bits of the canon is questioned, it rarely seems to be acknowledged that arguments are also needed for accepting the historicity of any part of it.)

4. The teleological fallacy: that within the process of formation of a canon lie the seeds of the final canon itself, so that we tend to write a history of canonizing from the canon backward, rather than forward, as if the inevitability of the given canon were taken for granted. One obvious example of this is to divide the history of canonization into the rabbinic-Masoretic divisions of "torah,"

"prophets," and "writings," without considering that different groupings may have been in force at earlier stages.

These problems, which will be considered in the next chapter, arise to a great extent from the nature of canon itself. For canon is a Janus-like phenomenon, facing backward through the process of canonizing that brought it into being, but also forward in exerting a "canonical" influence on subsequent study of it. Biblical scholarship, after all, is largely conducted within or among communities for whom that canon is in some way definitional. Any history of canonizing, then, that we construct, though supposedly dealing with the backward-looking face, is being composed under the forward-looking gaze of a final, definitive, and authoritative canon, which has helped to shape not just Christian communities, and not just the discourse of biblical scholarship (note the term carefully!) but also Western culture. Historical study can represent a threat to that authority, and indeed, so-called "historical critical scholarship" has been accused (see chapter 2) of failing to do justice to the "canonical dimension," as if the business of the historian were to justify the end product rather than account for it.

For canons lie uneasily with historical investigation. History is about human decisions, about change, about design, but also about accident. History shows how things might have been different but were not. What is more threatening, the view of history prevalent today sees all histories as narratives rather than as objective representations of a "real" past. Culturally literate historians now recognize all accounts of the past as being inevitably partial and ideological, designed to advance some particular point of view, and often to use the past as a means of controlling the present. No history, since it has to take the form of a narrative, can ever represent objective truth about the past. An important task of current historical scholarship is to demonstrate precisely this, and, without dissipating notions of a past in which things actually did happen, as well as using evidence and argument to retrieve these data, to critique and deprivilege stories about the past which claim to represent objective truth and command assent: stories which deny their own relativity or subjectivity but impute these to all other accounts.

And precisely such mechanisms are characteristic of canons, especially the Jewish and Christian canons that contain so much "history." This history is believed in by many people precisely because it is canonical, and therefore authoritative. After all, how else is a canonical history authoritative except by being true? This problem has, of course, been recognized and tackled by biblical scholarship, but very often by transferring the "truth" to some other category.

Within biblical scholarship, it is rarely asked whether or not "canon" is a good thing; where the matter does get an airing, the answer is almost invariably a ringing affirmation. Yet an ongoing controversy about whether or not canons do or should exist is raging in the field of English literature.[2] Some critics are saying that the notion of "canon" is no more than an attempt by educational (we could read "ecclesiastical") fascists to administer control of one's culture ("religion") and one's society, to preserve the values of a powerful few against the interests of the less powerful many. Others counter that excellence cannot be relativized and must be recognized, and that canons do and should exist because they testify to the *self-authorizing* nature of excellence. This book is not the place to offer an opinion on this controversy: but an awareness of such debates, of the pervasive power of canons to shape cultural perceptions, should not be ignored. At the very least, though, the idea that canon is an exercise in human cultural engineering, an exercise in power and control, an outcome of human decision making, should never desert the historian of Jewish (or Christian) canons.

Canons, after all, tend to represent themselves (or be represented) as signs of eternal, *transhistorical* values. Whether freezing forever a glorious culture or encoding the eternally valid words of a transcendent deity, they seek to defy or overcome the processes of history, in which cultures age and decay and in which languages shift the meanings of words. Between the perception of a permanent ideal reality and that of a constantly moving flux (between, we could say, Heraclitus and Plato) we are all caught, affirming at some time both one and the other, seeing eternal values behind the transience of our own historical experience (historians especially need to invoke some kind of universal and eternal principles such as providence, human nature, or laws of social behavior), but recognizing the inevitability of translating any such reality into concrete historical languages and periods (for history must also be about the particular).

THE ORIGINS AND
MEANING OF "CANON"

A *historical* definition of canon is a good way to begin a history of canonization. Although chapter 3 will include a study of Greek canonizing, it may be useful under the rubric of "origins" to sketch briefly the classical sources from which the word "canon" derives, and, as most scholars would agree, from which also derives the notion of canon inherited by Christianity and indeed by Jewish predecessors in Alexandria. We tend nowadays to think of canons as religious literature, but we owe the word to a civilization that did not itself produce any religious canon.[3] Literally, the Greek word *kanōn* signifies a straight rod (as, for example, in Homer), and it was perhaps the implicit quality of "straightness" that led to its connoting not just a physical ruler (such as a carpenter would use for measuring) but an abstract standard (as we might nowadays say "yardstick"). Thus, *kanōn* was accordingly used by Greeks to refer to the rules by which poetry or music could be composed, or geometrical shapes measured: thus, for example, in the middle of the fifth century B.C.E., the title "canon" was given to two textbooks dealing with sculpture. The apparently curious connection thus established between artistic creation and "canon" remained in Greek culture into the Hellenistic period, and the notion of a perfect work of art as representing the ideal, to be studied and copied, is fundamental to the Greek concept of canon. For the perfect work is itself a "canon" because it both enshrines and demonstrates the "rules" or the "art" in question (the eternal, as against the ephemeral). And since for Socrates and his circle, goodness was the supreme art (and knowledge the way to it), the good man can, as Aristotle says, be a "canon" of human nobility.

Canons in the classical world could thus be individual works, though collections of such works could also become canonical. Why works should be collected at all is, of course, an important issue in understanding the evolution of actual canons and thus of the usage of the word. Archives, libraries, and schools are important in this regard, because archives are about collecting and cataloging for future reference, while schools use textbooks or exemplars, and libraries instill the notion of something worth preserving, fostering the appreciation and dissemination of literature—and hence of the kinds of judgment and respect for standards that "canon" enshrines. Nevertheless, individual works or collections of works could still, however, be created in the Greek and Hellenistic world specifically as canons, and such works could cover a range of topics, whether art, medicine, technology, or philosophy. These canons are neither exclusive nor closed. The notion of a determinate set of books as forming a canon, which is fundamental to the Christian concept, may have originated in the treatment in Hellenistic schools and libraries of Homer, Herodotus, and Thucydides as perfect exemplars of their art, from which it follows that the determination of genuine, as opposed to false, works assigned to these authors was an important issue, as was also the establishment of a reliable text.

It was, indeed, probably under the influence of the scholars of the Alexandrian library, who used the word "canon" of collections of ancient authors, that the Christian notion of a canon derives. But it added a dimension to the classical usage that Western civilization has inherited: of a *closed* set of *religiously authoritative* books, their authority being divine rather than human because of their being presented as either "word of God" or inspired word of the apostolic generation: in either case guided by the Holy Spirit. The canonicity of these works does not rest on their being exemplary achievements of human culture. The Western Christian canon is exclusive and all-embracing, bound in a single volume (a "Bible"), and tends in some forms of this Christianity to be held to be the sole source of Christian doctrine. But even outside the church, so dominant is this Christian canon that it has also come to control modern dictionary definitions. Thus, the *Oxford English Dictionary* offers: "the collection or list of books of the Bible accepted by the Christian church as genuine and inspired," which is only then extended to "any set of sacred books"; Chambers' Dictionary offers "the books of the Bible accepted as the standard or rule of faith by the Christian church: the recognised genuine works of any author";[4] while Webster includes the following: "an accepted or sanctioned list of books."

Hence, our modern use of the word "canon" has moved some way beyond its classical origins. Yet, if we want to approach *Jewish* canonizing from a historical perspective, we must ask ourselves what "canon" might mean in terms of Jewish writings, and return to the definitions that governed the earlier age. Indeed, we must go even further than the classical origins of the word "canon." For even though the word (or its equivalent) may not have existed, a process of canonizing is also clearly at work in both Mesopotamian and Egyptian cultures, and it is important to place Jewish canonizing historically in the wider context of the great literary cultures to which the classical world was also indebted. Millennia before the Greeks learned to write, the civilizations of the Tigris-Euphrates and the Nile valleys had produced highly complex bureaucratic systems in which the art of writing was indispensable. This in turn necessitated a society of scribes, and over time this society defined and replicated itself through a body of literature that served as a kind of genetic blueprint of its own values and worldview, its theoretical and practical philosophy. By means of its own educational system and the constant copying and refining of this corpus, the Mesopotamian and Egyptian civilizations produced—alongside the much more numerous but transient administrative literature that paradoxically has survived where so much creative literature has been lost—works that we would call canonical, even in the Greek sense.

THE CANONIZING PROCESS

The topic of this book is not canons directly, but the processes that generate them: canonizing. Canonizing generates all kinds of canons which, as the process continues, can assume different shapes over time or between different groups. The production of a single closed list of authoritative writings is not the inevitable end product of this ongoing process. Canonizing, however, is an inevitable by-product of a consciously literary culture. Before the age of mass production of books (i.e., printing), the accumulation of a literary corpus involved many stages: composition, copying, editing; but also classifying, collecting, and archiving, since the growth of a corpus depends on its physical preservation. The equation being made in this book, which is fundamental if the thesis is to be understood, is that *copying and archiving are the very stuff of canonizing*. A work does not become canonized by being included in a formal list: that is a final flourish. A work becomes canonized (a) by being preserved by copying until its status as a classic is ensured; and (b) by being classified as belonging to a collection of some kind. Scrolls *can* be canons in their own right, but multiple scrolls need to be archived: that means labeling and storing in a sort of order. That means collecting. The result is various canons, groups of classic texts or classic collections on scrolls.

A written document in the ancient world generally had a very short life. Unless written on stone or maintained by unusual climatic conditions, in order to be preserved it had to be copied, as it did, of course, in order to be distributed. The development of writing seems to have occurred for economic reasons, in order to enable the collection of taxes or the recording and listing of property or to verify transactions. It is a function of the development of an economic system. The earliest texts are administrative, and these were copied for an archive, where they were carefully preserved. They were of value for consultation and needed to be classified for retrieval. Such texts are called "documentary." Literary texts, on the other hand, are not preserved as records to be consulted but as cultural artifacts, whose contents contain the stories, philosophy, laws, or prayers that furnish the social reality. As with the society itself, these texts are living and organic: they may be copied with reasonable fidelity, but they may also be altered by editing, supplementing, or combining with other texts. We have plenty of evidence to show that copying was rarely exact and often highly creative.

The fate of documentary texts and literary texts is basically different, even though they were sometimes archived together. Literary texts are *transmitted*—at least, those that survive. Transmission is a selective process: some literary works are copied; some not—at least in principle, for those *not* copied are lost and we cannot be certain. Some texts are rewritten and copied more than others. As this process takes place, some texts become more familiar, more ancient, and more respected. Such works become quoted, and influence other works. In other words, some texts become what we would call "classic." "Classic" works constitute a canon, even when that canon is not formally listed. The listing of such works can come about in a number of ways: there is cataloging, necessary both for administrative archiving and for the maintenance of libraries of literary works. There is also *curricular* listing, in which certain texts form the basics of an educational syllabus. And there is also *scholarly* listing, in which genuine works of a certain type or author are distinguished from those judged to be inauthentic or inferior. These processes of discrimination and of formal selection constitute the core of the "canonizing process," and what they produce are canons.

Thus, canonizing comprises a sequence of stages from the creation of texts, through transmission, and discrimination to formal lists. Though one stage tends to lead naturally to another, so that we can speak of a sequence of processes, even when the production of final canonical lists does not result, we can, and should, speak of a canonizing process. The *notion* of a canon can be present without any written definitive list (as it does in our own day). Indeed, the actual drawing up of formal canons is only a final stage in the entire process. For even before such lists are created, canons are created on shelves and in boxes, where literature of a certain kind or a certain value is grouped together physically. The tendency to issue canonical lists is in fact typical of a "postclassical" age anxious to preserve in writing the values of a culture that in reality is gone. In such circumstances we see a conscious effort to define and promote the study of a body of work. Such canons can have a long afterlife. The English public school educational system until very recently continued to treat the study of "the Classics" (Greek and Latin) in very much this way.

The "literate society" in which canons develop will, of course, differ over time and place, and even in societies of universal literacy, it is not the society as a whole that determines the canons of the future. Those who teach, pursue, and debate about the canon of English literature do not represent British or American or Canadian or Australasian society, far less English-speaking peoples as a whole. They represent a culture, or cultures, within a culture. The same is true of the canonizing of popular music. Literary canons in the ancient world emerged in a specific (sub)culture, that of the "scribal" class. "Scribe" and "scribal" are not always ideal terms for this society, but it has the advantage of underlining the connection between economic activity and literary culture. Religious canons were also not the product of the body of adherents of a religion, but of those (rabbis, bishops) who identified themselves as the leaders and definers of the value of their "society" (their "religion"). All canonizing is elitist in conception and authoritarian in implementation. Canonizing may commence by trying (not even explicitly) to create a culture; but it typically ends by dictating a culture through the medium of a fixed list of what is and what is not canonical. It is thus an entirely open question whether or not fixed, closed, and authoritative canons are a good thing at all. Perhaps it depends on how they are used. But typically they are imposed.

The role of canons in furthering cultural identity is a good example of both their benefit and their harm. Against the value of canons in preserving cultural identity and cultural pride must be weighed the danger of chauvinism, the neglect and lack of respect for other canons, and indeed the use of canons in the process of colonizing. To take an obvious recent example, the English language and the British political system have been introduced as the perfect models for a civilized society, and local elites educated (often in Britain) in the English canon. This situation leads (deliberately) to an interiorizing of a cultural history as well as a cultural value system that is at odds with that of the colonized culture and reinforces in a colonized society just that kind of separation of elite and nonelite cultural strata from which the canonizing process itself typically derives. This example also illustrates two of the ways in which the authority of canon is imposed: not only by political coercion, but by the cooption of indigenous elites. Cultures and societies may resist canons, or even ignore canons, but while canons remain mechanisms of control, and their definition and transmission in the hands of the elite, they will exercise an attraction on any who seek admission to that elite. In Foucauldian terms, a canon *itself* should be seen as a locus of power, facilitating cultural hegemony. The power of the Bible, for example, is quite blatantly invoked by preachers as a means of personal authority over their congregations, or even of political authority over national constituencies. Of course, its power resides in the willingness of people to recognize its canonicity and not in any intrinsic authority that its exploiters may seek to invoke as a disguise for their own ambitions.

Canonizing and authority are thus inseparable. The making of canonical lists requires some more direct exercise of *authority* for their installation than is needed for the development of a body of classic literature. In a modern school, teachers or higher educational authorities have the ability to recommend and enforce a syllabus. But outside of a school context, canonical lists may yet be created by acts of will. In the ancient world eminent practitioners of a skill (such as the Greek sculptor Polycletus) or eminent authorities (such as Cicero) attempted, with greater or less success, to declare a canon. Religious authorities typically do so in the name of the relevant deity. Thus, while such authoritative lists depend on a previous notion of canonicity and the accumulation of classic literature, the making of a fixed canon is not automatic. As with the canonizing process, a certain kind of social structure is needed to achieve it.

The final preliminary observation about canonizing is that canons, notional or inscribed, are not unilayered. Some works can be more firmly "canonical" than others. Let us take the example of the rabbinic-Masoretic scriptural canon:

here there are three divisions, one at least of which was at one time a canon in itself (torah). The Torah (the five books of Moses) also enjoys a higher degree of authority than the rest of the Jewish scriptural canon, and sometimes the entire Jewish scriptures are called "Torah." In the Christian scriptures, the New Testament is in a similar sense more "canonical" than the Old, providing the key to its "correct" understanding, abrogating many of its statements.[5] Thus, the notion that a canon differentiates strongly between authorized and unauthorized, authoritative and non-authoritative, inside and outside, is only true up to a point. Neither within nor outside canonical boundaries is there equality. Canons do not grow up with rigid boundaries, and the creation of such boundaries does not eliminate gray areas either within ("law" versus "gospel," "torah" versus "prophets") or on the edges (the "apocrypha") of the canon.

THE EFFECTS OF CANON

In chapter 3 a little more will be said about the post-canonizing process with respect to "canon(ical) criticism." But a few general comments may also be useful here. Canons never do succeed in freezing a culture or a religion, though many religious authorities seek to use canons in this way. Even when a canon is formally closed, the processes of linguistic and cultural change and the ongoing business of commentary ensure that the canon can have its meaning redefined again and again without that fact being explicitly acknowledged or the authority of the canon undermined. While appearing to represent stasis in form of fixed texts, fixed contents, or fixed values, canons are in fact constantly being reinterpreted. Texts are translated, contents are hierarchized, and values are redefined. The fluidity of the canonizing process is transformed by a fixed canon into a fluid hermeneutical process, at least in the cases of Judaism, Christianity, and Islam. (Whether and to what extent other religions have "canons" is disputable.)

Despite the possibilities for flexibility, canons *can* be a mechanism by which authority is indirectly exercised, the canon functioning as an instrument of institutional authority. A relationship between canon and power is not hard to discern. As Gerald Bruns puts it:[6]

> The whole point of canonization is to underwrite the authority of a text, not merely with respect to its origin as against competitors in the field— this, technically, would simply be a question of authenticity—but with respect to the future in which it will reign or govern as a binding text. . . . From a hermeneutical standpoint, in which the relation of a text to a situation is always of primary interest, the theme of canonization is *power.*

Instead of being recognized as the result of conscious human choice, a means for the exercise of human power, canons can be presented and accepted as self-authorizing. This is especially true of religious canons, though advocates of the canon of English literature sometimes suggest that canonical works "establish themselves" by their own virtue. The same was also true of many ancient canons, where the canonical work was held to embody perfection and thus to authenticate itself (rather than authenticate the judgment of the critic; Plato rightly opposed this tendency).

There are several possible manifestations of this "intrinsic" authority. One is internal coherence. Just as codices imparted a material unity and thus created bibles, so canons can (though they do not *necessarily*) impart a kind of unified essence to works that began the canonizing process as disparate. In the case of the Christian canon, the listing of which was attended by authoritarian doctrinal considerations, one may be driven to formulate conscious or unconscious criteria for exclusion or inclusion. Consistency among the contents, and conformity with one's own prejudices, are two obvious criteria. The result may be in some cases that a canon becomes more than the sum total of its parts.[7] Instead of being a *collection,* a canon can be regarded as a single statement or system (even a single book, a "bible").

Another way in which authority is invested in a canon is by the ascription of an authoritative authorship. Homer was once credited with more than he had written: in Mesopotamia and Egypt, canonical writings were sometimes assigned to eminent figures, and in both Jewish and Christian canonizing, works have had a tendency to gravitate toward authors of appropriate distinction. Attribution of divine authority to canons is a particularly dramatic instance of this mechanism, and although it is sometimes supposed that attribution to authorities is a canonizing device, in the case of canonized books it is very frequently a *post-canonizing* move, affirming the already existing canonized status of a work. The majority of Jewish and Christian pseudepigraphic works were never inside a canonizing process: indeed, they are parasitic on it.

OUTLINE OF AN APPROACH
TO JEWISH CANONIZING

To write a history of canonizing in (Israel and) Judah is difficult, because we know too little about the history of the societies in question. The approach taken in this book has three stages: first, to survey the ways in which canons were formed in Mesopotamia, Egypt, and the Greek and Hellenistic worlds, and the variable factors. From this the preliminary comments made earlier can be expanded and the social factors that operate in such development clarified.

Then we must review the history of Israelite and Judean society in its entirety, noting the features relevant to a canonizing process. Here the problem of the "canonized history" will present itself. I think it is methodologically imperative that we discount the "canonical" status of the canonized sources, because their canonicity does constrain the historian to credulity. Rather, the history that the canon tells must be itself analyzed as part of the canonizing process. Finally, we can make some suggestions, from a study of some parts of the Jewish scriptural canon (and of other works once canonized), as to the history of canonizing in Judaism. What will be resisted, however, is an attempt to cover every canonized work or to give a complete account. Pleasing as such an account would be, the reader is not served by being peddled the delusion that we can know how it all happened. Nor, indeed, is the reader served by the implication that from the historian's point of view it matters greatly which books finally were listed in a particular canon and which were not—or why and why not, especially when such explanations are guesswork. What matters is that we know how and why a canonizing process took place; that canons emerged, and the kind of literature that was canonized, is more important than the individual status of each book, which is of doctrinal rather than of historical interest.

Most emphatically, what cannot be done is to reconstruct with much confidence the growth of the rabbinic-Masoretic scriptural canon, since "growth" is an inappropriate term for this canon. We shall see, rather, evidence of the growth of canonized writings, and the generations from these of a number of canons or collections, which both combine and break up into other canons. The notion that "*the* canon" "grew" into its present shape is perhaps the most pernicious of all our assumptions, unfortunately reinforced by theological approaches to canon that find such a process doctrinally congenial.

Chapter 2

Canons in the
Ancient World

This chapter attempts to provide us with an appreciation of the kinds of ways in which major cultures in the ancient world to which Israel and Judah belonged canonized their literature. The reason, let us remind ourselves, is not so much to look for direct influences on Judaism but to illustrate the fact that canonizing was part of their world and to offer some clues to the connection between that process and social and ideological structures. Broadly, two different social models emerge: one (Mesopotamia, Egypt) demonstrates scribal canonizing, which takes place within a socially well-defined class that enjoys more or less a monopoly of writing, and of literary education. The other model (Greece) has no scribal class, but a more literate body of citizenry. The Hellenistic world provided perhaps a third model, in which elements of the previous two combine, and in which conditions for the definition and study of more prescribed canons are present.

SCRIBE AND SOCIETY

To understand scribes, writing, and thus canonizing, it is first important to rehearse the social structure of agrarian (preindustrial) societies.[1] The states into which such societies formed themselves in the ancient Near East were typically small (Egypt is the exception), with an urban center (or centers) surrounded by an area that the city ruler controlled. The vast majority (well over 90 percent, or a ratio of 15:1[2]) of the population were peasants, who generated most of the wealth in the form of produce. Whether voluntarily or not, the peasants ceded a portion of their produce to the ruler, who in return offered protection. The surplus was used for the administration of the state and for the consumption of the rulers. In Mesopotamia and Egypt temples were economically and politically powerful; in Greece less so. But both the priesthood and the ruling aristocracy—those who assisted the ruler by reason of lineage or wealth or patronage and who comprised perhaps about 5 percent—

constituted a governing class and were sustained by the produce (whether offered or extracted) of the peasants. In addition, rulers and temples usually possessed lands of their own and thus generated their own wealth; the lands would be worked by slaves or free peasants rendering service to the ruler.

The religious structure of such societies is pluriform: a city may have several temples to various gods and goddesses. There may be city gods (official patrons of the state) and dynastic gods (patrons of the ruling lineage). But the peasants, living in rural areas and dependent on harvests for their livelihood, will have their own religion(s), based not on the culture of the city but on the crucial issue of fertility and the gods/deities who sustain and guarantee it. Finally, in both urban and rural domains there are personal deities. These various deities and religious cults are not mutually exclusive. But to speak of "the religion" of the agrarian societies of Babylon, Egypt, Israel, or Judah is inaccurate. However, religious ideology is of immense importance to the functioning of the state, because at one level it is believed to guarantee security to the peasants, and at another level it is used by the ruling class (or the ruler himself) to give divine approval to the state or to his kingship. Typically, temples justify their income as the guardians of the state or of the fertility of the countryside. Thus, depending on the particular form the religion takes, religion(s) will be integrated formally into the political government.

It may be a common modern assumption that writing is a desirable skill and that as many people as possible should acquire it, especially when a cumbersome syllabic script (such as in Mesopotamia) is replaced by an alphabetic one (as in Ugarit or Palestine). But the uses of writing in an oral society are limited, and most people have in fact no need of it: should a legal or economic document be required, a village or town may have its own scribe (or there may have been itinerant scribes; both phenomena are observable in some contemporary societies). The administration of justice was very largely based on traditional practices and communal wishes; the elders or the head(s) of the village administered it according to local customs, without recourse to written instructions, or to records of decisions.

This would not mean, of course, that a strict boundary between "literacy" and "nonliteracy" should be drawn. A limited ability to read and write characters (for example, one's own name) will have existed among the peasantry too—how widely is very difficult to say.[3] The important distinctions are: (1) between societies or groups within society in which literature is a normal or necessary form of communication and recording, and (2) between the ability physically to recognize and write a limited number of characters or combinations of characters and the ability to compose and to understand literary texts. The latter requires considerable learning.

An agrarian society requires no formal educational system. Children are brought up within the household, the extended family, and the village to learn the traditional stories, values, and skills, a task in which women play a major role, at least in the years up to adolescence. And, obviously, to these traditions we have no direct access. The formation of a centralized state, however, creates a nonagrarian elite, concentrated in the capital city (or if the state is extensive, in more than one city), where governmental functions are located. An important instrument of centralized power is the existence of written accounts of payments, instructions, names, and agreements—accessible, of course, to the administration in the form of copies. As writers, the scribal class were in origin servants of ruler or temple. But they became much more than mere clerks.[4]

THE SCRIBAL CLASS

Writing was first used to record economic transactions: receipts, letters, or records, and had little or no use beyond this. The scribes were thus a class employed by the rulers, but not themselves rulers, and they lived mostly in administrative centers (in Egypt, a larger and more bureaucratic state, scribes were more dispersed). They were sustained from the revenues of palace or temple. Priests and rulers themselves were not necessarily able to write, and peasants certainly had not the time, the opportunity, or the need to write; possibly a few could inscribe their own name to identify property. But writing, of course, is capable of recording more than inventories and receipts: it became also the medium of diplomacy. The scribe was at the same time the administrator, the "civil servant." The expertise which the scribes accumulated made them indispensable. Among the diplomatic activities of the scribe, the composing of inscriptions, annals, and treaties ("covenants") related to the main activity of the ruling class, that is, warfare, is not to be overlooked. A reading of either Joshua or Numbers, for example, will show the extent to which military language and ideology have permeated the writing.[5]

But archiving was also an important part of the scribe's duties and helped in the intellectual formation of this class. The terms "archive" and "library" are sometimes used interchangeably, but it is useful to make a distinction (which will be discussed below in chapter 5). An archive is a repository of documentary records, of necessity organized so as to enable the efficient retrieval and comparison of individual records. An archive is an administrative resource, and its contents are preserved for such purposes. Such records are not read except when the information they contain is needed; they are not copied, nor edited. They are not used to inculcate any cultural values. They are in no sense "literature," and their contents are not expected to be internalized as cultural values. They are not read for instruction or pleasure. A library is a cultural resource: its contents are literary works that are typically collected for their intrinsic (as well as for their practical) value: they are often copied and edited. Their preservation and transmission is subject to aesthetic and cultural evaluation. The information they contain is to be internalized. Thus, according to Posner,[6] ancient *archives* typically consist of: the laws of the land; records consciously created as evidence of past administrative action; financial and other accounting records; records of a ruler to assure his income from lands and persons (e.g., land records); records facilitating control over persons for military service, forced labor, etc.; and "notarial" records of state agencies to safeguard private transactions. Wherever there is a reasonably advanced state administration, there will be archives, since literacy is pointless without records. Palaces and temples will typically always have had archives, since both were recipients of taxes, and palaces additionally entered into diplomatic and administrative correspondence. Where archives have been unearthed in the ancient Near East they have been either at temple sites, such as at Ugarit, or Memphis, where there was a medical archive, or at palaces, such as at Ebla or Mari or Akhetaton (Tell el-Amarna). Archives require to be indexed by a systematic manner of storage and by the provision of catalogs.[7]

Scribes thus accumulated and codified knowledge for their masters and perpetuated their own craft through education; but they also wrote on their own account, creating the kinds of texts that would typically comprise the contents of a library. It is hardly surprising that an urban elite should develop its own culture, distinct from the rural culture of the peasants and, importantly, distinct from the ruling class that it served. Its stories, its values, and its skills will have differed from those of village, but also in some respects from temple and court as well, because its economic interests and its intellectual horizons were different. For example, religion for the scribe will have been, professionally, an instrument of political ideology and of intellectual reflection, but not the wellspring of political or social behavior, in which the scribe was guided increasingly by rational and empirical considerations. This culture will have been expressed no doubt partly orally, but also in literary form, in writings created, copied, and cataloged. For this reason it is their culture to which we have a better access than any other.

Scribes, then, were in possession of a resource—writing—unavailable to others and often regarded as magical, divine in origin, occult. A very rough analogy may be found in the modern distinction between a politician and a diplomat. Career diplomats serve governments, but do not belong to the ruling party, and quite clearly this class has an ethic quite distinct from that of party politicians, even though the two have to cooperate closely. Like modern diplomats, scribes are trained to express sentiments not their own as well as those they genuinely feel. What they express as agents of a particular ruler or ruling class and what they express as members of a class (both of which may be found in their surviving literature) are not necessarily identical. This is important to bear in mind when evaluating their literary output. The gift of writing provides scribes with a social identity that is distinct from their political functions, an identity that is both adopted by them and ascribed to them by others. Insofar as the economic transactions between ruler and ruled are expressed in writing, scribes have enormous control. Moreover, in respect of diplomatic activities, the scribe is also in contact with others of the same class who exercise identical functions in other states. Again, because of this, scribes may carry—and recognize that they are carrying—an enormous amount of influence, as well as being members of an international elite.

Hence, though the scribe was an indispensable part of the administration, he was not of the ruling elite itself. Scribes absorbed the culture of the regime that they served, and also, to a much lesser extent, perhaps that of the rural population as well. In that sense, written texts, though overwhelmingly the product of the scribal *hand,* are not necessarily all products of the scribal *mind.* And the necessity of serving rulers to whom they may have regarded themselves as intellectually superior no doubt instilled in the scribes the techniques of satire and ambiguity: the ability to inscribe on the surface of a political text their own traces. This is an important observation, given the considerable evidence we have for ambiguous and satirical features in the contents of the Jewish scriptural canon.

Since their writing ability (and cuneiform in particular was extremely complex, containing many hundreds of characters representing syllables), as well as their professional diplomatic skills, had to be passed on, some of their intellectual and professional effort was directed toward the education of their successors, who were taught not only simply how to write, but how to compose: to be familiar with the dialects and technical vocabulary; to be competent in several languages and be able to translate correctly; and to master the appropriate literary conventions. The earliest schools were thus for scribes.

THE CUNEIFORM TRADITION

With the foregoing character sketch in mind, we can now begin to consider the canonizing activities of the ancient scribes. Leo Oppenheim,[8] in a study of scribal activity in Mesopotamia, distinguished three particular roles for this class: bureaucrat, poet, and scholar. As bureaucrat the scribe would be employed by either the palace or the temple (and these were usually closely associated institutions) to keep archives, write annals, and compose diplomatic correspondence and liturgical pieces. This activity comprises the economic base of scribal culture. But from absorption in the techniques of writing and its ability to convey shades of meaning in ways different from the oral; from training and experience in the methods of classifying records for retrieval and comparison; and from observation of the mechanics of diplomacy, scribes could not but develop also literary and intellectual skills. The study of language and of literature makes scribes, or at least those appropriately gifted, into poets and scholars. This is not to deny that poetry and scholarship exist also in oral culture, of course. But scribal poetry and scholarship are not merely oral poetry and scholarship written down; they emanate from a different kind of person and culture, however much that culture may have been influenced at various points by oral culture.

The "cumbrous writing system restricted literacy to a highly trained corps of professional scribes."[9] These scribes always came from the upper classes of society, were venerated by those above and below them, and accordingly took themselves seriously, undergoing examinations and long training. The majority of them were state administrators, but twenty percent perhaps were privately employed, and some were specialists in one or other arcane branch of lore, such as spells or medicine. Even among the administrators there were specializations, such as priest scribes, medical scribes, and army scribes.

The Mesopotamian scribal class had emerged by at least the beginning of the third millennium B.C.E. to maintain record offices for transactions involving royal courts and temples. But it also created archives, as we can deduce from the extant literature itself and from the excavation of ancient cities. The earliest Mesopotamian texts we possess were composed in Sumerian, and although Sumerian was replaced at the end of the third millennium by the Akkadian language of the immigrant Amorites, these Amorites absorbed a great deal of Sumerian. Indeed, Sumerian continued to be written, and even to develop, until about the end of the second millennium, as a scribal language. Alongside Sumerian, however, the scribes of the Old Babylonian period (2000–1500 B.C.E.) also composed literary texts in an Akkadian which, unlike documentary texts such as letters or administrative records, represented a distinct dialect, with its own grammar, vocabulary, and even spelling. This may have represented, or evolved from, an actual ancient dialect,[10] or it may have constituted a "fabricated antique style deemed appropriate for higher expression."[11] A similar conservatism is evident in the literary dialect known as "Standard Babylonian," used for literary works from the middle of the second millennium. This remained little changed for over a thousand years, and was then succeeded by an archaizing kind of Akkadian, until the use of Akkadian died out at about the turn of the era.

For the whole of the second millennium, and well into the first millennium, before being systematically replaced under the Assyrians by Aramaic, Akkadian was the diplomatic and literary lingua franca of the Near East, and with the language came a body of learning. There must have been an enormous amount of cuneiform literature produced, to judge by even the fraction that has survived.

A necessary feature of Mesopotamian (especially Babylonian) culture is classification and ordering, and the early Sumerian texts include lists of objects and signs, including lists of kings (always only one king ruling at a time). The Babylonians inherited and developed this culture of classification, and extended their recording to the movements of heavenly bodies and other omens (such as the entrails of animals). Since they wrote in Akkadian but also copied Sumerian we find extensive bilingual lists and also primitive dictionaries comprising lists of synonyms and homonyms. Such writings represent the bulk of what has been preserved of Akkadian literature, and they are frequently classified as "scientific" in the sense that they are attempts to describe systematically the natural world.[12] Thus, along with transmission we find codification, which is both an archival and an intellectual activity. The linkage is important. Writing itself permits the transmission of knowledge, but archiving forces the mind to classify it.

Because, as we have seen, writing was further distinguished from ordinary speech by the use of literary dialects, a veneration for real or presumed archaism, and was underpinned by a belief that writing, and indeed sometimes the inspiration for individual texts, was a divine gift, some texts came also to be seen as containing divine knowledge. This was sometimes true of "scientific" ancient texts as well as cultic texts which imparted the secrets of the gods, and as such literature itself was highly venerated. More cynically, we could perhaps say that since writing was the means by which scribes earned their living and gained their power, scribes would inevitably celebrate its power and importance. But presumably among the illiterate a similar view could be instilled if indeed it needed instilling.

The vast bulk of preserved cuneiform literature is documentary. About 60,000 tablets recording temple administration were recovered from an archive in Sippar (ca. 2000–1500), while beyond the boundaries of Mesopotamia proper (i.e., between the Tigris and Euphrates), tens of thousands of cuneiform texts have so far been unearthed at Ebla in northwest Syria, dating from the end of the third millennium onward. Mari, on the Euphrates, has yielded twenty thousand texts to date, from the early second millennium. Both these archives contain almost entirely administrative and documentary texts, and were attached to royal palaces, and in neither case are we speaking of a library: "record office" would be a more appropriate term. However, a number of texts at both these sites betray the existence of scribal schools, in the form of various writing and composition exercises.

Archives contain records that have to be stored and have to be classified for access. A library, on the other hand, is a collection of materials worth keeping for their intrinsic value. Typically a library holds *literary* rather than, or as well as, documentary texts: myths, cultic texts, legends—anything worth reading. It represents an accumulation of what is *desirable* to possess for cultural reasons and not what is administratively *necessary* to possess for economic or political reasons. We have a reasonable amount of evidence to associate libraries, like archives, with temples or with royal palaces. But at Ugarit, where there were several temples, collections of texts were also found in areas of the city occupied by private dwellings. One such dwelling was apparently the high priest's house, and another belonged to a "magician priest"; the house of one called Rapanu included scientific and diplomatic texts. Another "private library" has also been identified, containing a copy of the "Flood" story. But "private" means in this case belonging to an individual who was certainly a state or temple functionary, and such collections (which sometimes contain some literary texts as well as, predominantly, documentary texts) are better seen as official or professional collections, serving largely an archival or reference function.

The development of libraries, as opposed to archives, has been attributed to the Assyrians. The most famous of these libraries is probably that of the Assyrian monarch Ashurbanipal (669–632 B.C.E.), who claimed to be literate (unusual for an Assyrian monarch), and sponsored the development of a large collection of cuneiform texts at Nineveh, containing at least five thousand tablets, including myths but also omen lists, magical, lexical, and ritual compositions.[13] By the time of Ashurbanipal libraries were installed in most Assyrian cities. In Babylonia, at Nippur and Ur, private collections have also been recovered. Another library from the eighth century, at Sultantepe in modern Turkey, produced about two hundred tablets, and another library at Sippar, dating from the Persian period, was found more recently. Other sites in Syria and Mesopotamia may also betray the existence of private or royal cuneiform libraries throughout Mesopotamia and beyond.[14] In all of these sites scribal schools must have existed, and exercise tablets at sites such as Ugarit confirm this.

How were texts stored in archives and libraries? They were consigned for future reference to purpose-built premises, and usually placed in specially made clay containers, fastened by bullae that indicated the contents. These containers were thus used like modern filing drawers. Pigeonholes, shelves, and jars were other devices also used to put texts into categories for access. Ashurbanipal's librarians grouped the documents by subject and cataloged them by lettering them on the outside, often consecutively, and numbering them in the case of longer compositions. The administrative archiving mentality "pigeonholes" texts into different archives, different rooms, and different shelves or cases. In Ugarit and in other sites, different kinds of records were devolved into separate offices.[15] But in the large royal and temple archives, literary texts usually comprise only a small proportion (at Mari there are none at all), while "documentary" texts are by far the bulk.

The scribes of the cuneiform tradition produced and copied cuneiform literature over a long period, from the middle of the third millennium B.C.E. until the end of the first millennium B.C.E.—into the Greco-Roman period. It may therefore seem oversimplistic to treat it as a single culture and its canonizing as a single phenomenon. Yet this can be done, for we are dealing with literature that continued to be copied and canonized, even beyond Mesopotamia, throughout the changing political and social scenery of the Near East and into the Hellenistic period. It was a highly conservative tradition, though not, it seems, as conservative as Egyptian tradition. And both changed with the emergence of Hellenism.

EGYPT

Much of what was said about scribal activity in Mesopotamia can be applied to Egypt. However, a feature of Egyptian literature is that much of it was not written on papyrus but on walls of tombs or public buildings. Such writing, even when "literary," was "archived" in a rather unusual way. Occasionally, however, a papyrus copy was preserved and reused.

Like cuneiform, the Egyptian writing system required considerable learning. There were in fact two writing systems: Hieroglyphic was used for monumental writing, and the cursive hieratic for administrative and other literary texts, being more suitable for papyrus, ostraca and so on). As in Mesopotamia, writing was venerated as an art given by the gods, and a specific literary language was employed at certain periods. The hieroglyphic script remained in use in scribal circles for certain kinds of texts (notably biographies and in funerary texts) long after it had been supplanted for everyday purposes by hieratic and the later demotic. Indeed, trainee scribes had to learn to copy texts in an archaic language they did not entirely understand, as their mistakes show.[16]

But despite these restrictions, the demands of Egyptian bureaucracy seem to have extended further than in Mesopotamia, and to many walks of life, including most of the crafts and professions. Or, perhaps, the relative ease of use of papyrus and a climate more congenial to preservation have enabled more such texts to survive. For, even more than in Mesopotamia, Egypt "used records as a tool of management but also contributed toward making record-consciousness integral and important in the life of the people."[17] Unfortunately, because of their use of papyrus, which is not durable as is clay, we have far fewer of their records. However, as elsewhere in the ancient Near East, pottery shards (ostraca) were used for occasional purposes, while leather was used for some particularly important texts. Only one major royal archive, at Tell el-Amarna, has yielded a number of important texts, because these are on clay and thus in cuneiform—or perhaps the other way round, for of course alphabets and writing materials were designed for each other, cuneiform being suitable for marking soft clay with wedges and hieroglyphs for writing with pens on papyrus. However, from inscriptions and especially paintings, it can be seen that very few transactions at all did not involve the presence of a recording scribe. The most famous scene of all, the weighing of the soul of the dead, was attended by the scribal god Thoth and his scroll. Thus in Egypt, as in Mesopotamia, administration was carried out by scribes and consisted largely of recording and archiving. But this activity extended well beyond the vicinity of the court and temple and into every aspect of rural as well as urban life. This system served a highly centralized administration, in which the pharaoh was legally owner of everything, so that even private transactions were regarded as state matters. Because of the annual inundation by the Nile of the fields, obliterating boundaries, precise records of property dimensions were vital. The entire cultivated and populated land, and all the population, were "on file" at the office of the vizier, who oversaw several archiving departments. And because the legal system was also based on record-keeping, the vizier was also head of the judiciary.

Again as in the cuneiform tradition, we have evidence of the taxonomic mentality, as if the business of archiving extended to the intellectual organizing of phenomena. An illustration of such activity is afforded by *onomastica,* lists of names of such things as professions, animals and plants, and meteorological terms and occurrences (e.g., the onomasticon of Amenemope from the eleventh century).[18]

It would be very advantageous to know how royal archives were classified, but because of the lack of organized excavation at Tell el-Amarna, this cannot be ascertained. Nevertheless, there are examples of papyrus rolls having been stored in chests and identified by a small tab on the edge that described the contents, showing that an appropriate system corresponding to that used in Akkadian libraries and archives was in use, as of course it had to be. Libraries have, however, been found at the Ramesseum (13th Dynasty), from Deir el Medinah (20th Dynasty), from Elephantine (Khnum: the Ptolemaic period) and Tetubnis (Roman), which included catalogs of the works held in the libraries.

Temples in Egypt also played a large part in the maintenance of the scribal class. We know of scribal "houses of life" attached to major sanctuaries and headed by priests. These were centers for the "composition, preservation, study and copying of texts,"[19] mainly of a religious kind, intended for cultic use, but including magical texts. For these institutions, "the term 'academy,'" says Williams, "may be an inaccurate as well as an anachronistic term for it, but it was the resort of the intellectuals of the day." Its members also composed books of instruction and attempted to predict the future. Consisting of schools and libraries, the "houses of life" fulfilled ritual as well as literary purposes, producing magical and medical as well as cultic texts and, as in Mesopotamia, the bulk of literature produced in these institutions was "scientific"—ritual, astronomic, therapeutic, magical—though literary works, such as wisdom texts, were also included. Unlike Mesopotamia, a category of "'sacred" or "holy" texts seems to have emerged in these circles, and the recitation of certain religious texts was restricted to those specially initiated or in a state of purity.

Certain works can actually be identified as schoolbooks, containing standard forms of salutations, maxims, model letters, prayers and exercises of various sorts, exhortations, and even satires. Medical and mathematical manuals exist in great numbers, though there is no evidence of standardization among the various schools. In the Ptolemaic period, the picture changes, and we witness a great deal of codification ("canonization"), especially in the area of geographical texts, perhaps hinting at earlier and no longer extant lists of geographical information. Indeed, a "uniform and canonized tradition of religious geography for all the temples of Egypt" has been suggested.[20]

GREECE

The structure of Greek society was quite different from both Mesopotamia and Egypt, and government in the Greek cities in the classical period was not administered by a professional scribal class, nor were temples major economic and administrative centers. But like Mesopotamia, Greek society (in which we include not only the Greek peninsula, but its colonies) was comprised of city states. A history of Greek society may be divided into the Homeric, the classical, and the Hellenistic epochs. Until a democratic system of rule began to emerge in the fifth century, these states were ruled by persons who surrounded themselves with an aristocracy of warriors through whom the ruler exercised his rule and who comprised his own social circle.

During this period of Greek society (first half of the first millennium B.C.E.) the culture of this warrior-aristocracy combined sport and war with singing and dancing. Marrou has likened such a lifestyle to the "courtly" culture of the European Middle Ages.[21] Unlike the cultures of the Levant, this was not a bureaucratic society: there was no specialized class to administer the economy, and no priestly caste with its esoteric sacred literature; thus it was not a literary culture. Education took the form of apprenticeship at court and, at least in some cases, instruction by a personal tutor.

Nevertheless, most scholars feel able to assert that this culture had a literary canon, though this was at first oral. The influence of Homer (or if you like, the works attributed to Homer) is observable from as early as the sixth century as a canon. This influence was spread through the oral recitation of the Homeric epics by rhapsodists (Hesiod was one such). But the effect was no mere entertainment; the culture and the cultural values which Homer portrays functioned as the ideal for Greek aristocracy. Recitation, of course, also implies memorization, and the indispensability of Homer for any kind of Greek education persisted to the end of the classical age; many children, though not rhapsodists, were to learn Homer by heart. To an extent, the role of Homer (who was credited with a good deal more than he is today) corresponds to the role of instructional literature in Mesopotamia and Egypt, but with important distinctions: it was largely oral, not written (at least for several centuries); it was not a product of scribal schools, and it did not inculcate ethics by means of admonition but by narrative (as did some wisdom narratives from the Levant, like the story of Ahiqar). Surprising as it may seem to one who knows the origins of Greek philosophy, it was also devoid of the kind of scientific literature produced in Mesopotamia and Egypt.

In the classical period (sixth to fourth centuries B.C.E.) many of the features of this aristocratic education persisted, but the transmission of culture, besides Homer, remained the responsibility of tutors. Greek culture remained artistic rather than scientific, and practical rather than intellectual. A modified Phoenician alphabet that included vowels as well as consonants (and could thus be phonetic—a very important innovation) had been created in the eighth century, and literacy was surely becoming more widespread, yet the culture of Greece only slowly evolved into a literary one. Contrary to the impression that many moderns may have, it was Mesopotamian culture that displayed philosophical and intellectual features rather than Greek, which remained wedded to music and athletics (athletics partly replacing warfare). However, the advent of democratic political structures inspired the need for wider political education, and the importance of democratic politics for our interest lies in the emergence of the art of rhetoric. Correct speaking is, of course, a feature of aristocratic societies and of "wisdom"; courtiers must know how to observe the conventions of the royal court, but also courtiers who are able to advocate, to give reasoned advice, will be of importance to the king. However, the emergence of the professional teacher in the form of the Sophist represented a move toward a *rhetorical* education. With the rise of the Sophists in the fifth century Greek literature emerges in written form. Thus, Socrates can acquire written texts of a fellow philosopher, while the comic dramatist Aristophanes includes in one of his plays a plague of bad books.[22] Indeed, it seems likely that Athenian plays were also issued in book form (i.e., in scrolls).

The importance of the Sophists' emphasis on rhetoric, however, is that the *recitation* of Homer (and other lyrical poets) is now partly replaced by the *study* of these poets. The Sophists aimed at correct diction and understanding of grammar, but they also trained the mind by teaching it to discover contradictions, or to work out the precise nuances of words. The goal, however, was analysis of language as an aid to rhetorical debate, not the development of aesthetic sensibility or the science of language.

Plato's contempt for the literary works (in particular Homer and the ancient myths) that were regarded as classic in his time (fifth to fourth centuries) is well known: he opposed philosophy (search for truth) to poetry (artifice, illusion). But although he was unsuccessful in unseating Homer, he initiated a critical tradition with regard to classic texts—and might perhaps deserve the credit he has received for having invented scholarship because of his insistence on truth and reason as the means to knowledge.[23] But the ideal education that he prescribed included reading poetry and prose, and he also approved the use of anthologies—selections of passages—in education.

The scribal penchant for listing and categorizing the natural world also finds a counterpart in Greece. In his remorseless quest for encyclopedic knowledge, Aristotle compiled lists and categories of all manner of things: for example, in works such as his *Politeiai* and *Didaskaliai,* he assembled respectively the constitutions of 158 cities and tribes, and cataloged the performances of Athenian dramatic productions. Perhaps the explanation for this kind of enterprise has nothing to do with the taxonomic proclivities of ancient Near Eastern scribes, yet the value of comparative analysis lies not only in demonstrating historical connections, but with typical features or traits. Aristotle was not an archivist, but he was a polymath who sought to systematize all human knowledge, and in this he is engaged, albeit in a more reflective fashion, in one of the traditional pursuits of his Near Eastern predecessors.

Although a public archives office came to be part of every city's government, and both archives and legal translations (including private ones) were preserved there, Greece did not develop an archiving culture. It did, however, develop a bibliothetic culture. By the end of the fifth century public libraries as well as public archives existed in Greece,[24] but there are also references to collections in the possession of individuals, though probably for professional use: according to Strabo (*Geography* 13.1.54) Aristotle had a large collection. But schools also had libraries; for instance, the Academy, which served as a model for the foundation of the Museum library at Alexandria in the third century B.C.E.[25] Aristotle created the library that subsequently passed to his school at the Lyceum. However, with Aristotle we are already at the point where the Hellenistic world is dawning.

Although this can be overemphasized, the spread of literacy in Greece was not entirely the outcome of political and social structures but also because of the alphabet, for although the Phoenicians had invented an alphabet centuries earlier, it was without vowels. To this must be added the flexibility of the Greek language itself. But whatever the various factors involved, the Greek world, and the Hellenistic world which it came to rule, were worlds in which literacy was no longer the prerogative of an administrative class, nor of an aristocratic class, but of a wider cross-section. Whether or not the typical peasant of the Levantine countryside, for instance, became literate we cannot know, but we can classify Hellenism as a literature culture unlike any of those that preceded it in the eastern Mediterranean and its hinterland.

THE HELLENISTIC WORLD

The advent of the Hellenistic age (late fourth century B.C.E.), is characterized above all by the scroll-book. As Pfeiffer remarks:

> [T]he book is one of the characteristic signs of the new, the Hellenistic world. The whole literary past, the heritage of centuries, was in danger of slipping away in spite of the learned labours of Aristotle's pupils; the imaginative enthusiasm of the generation living towards the end of the fourth and the beginning of the third century did everything to keep it alive.[26]

The spread of books is partly to be explained by technological and socio-economic factors. But it is also a manifestation of a certain self-consciousness among Greeks living outside Greece concerning "Greek culture." Greek culture came to be objectified as a means to capturing and perpetuating it, and in this the book, the school, the library, played an important part. They were agents in the spread and cultivation of an intellectual culture that was more homogeneous than it might otherwise have been. It was also more through literature than through trade or military settlement or political integration that Greek became the major cultural force in Hellenism, though it would be incorrect to say that Hellenism was Greek culture spread outside

Greece; for the political systems it generated were far from Greek, as were much of its philosophy and religion. Indeed, Hellenism, at least in the Eastern Mediterranean, absorbed much of the culture of Mesopotamia and Greece, including their scribal traditions.

Education was the core component of Hellenistic culture: schooling was the means by which the universalizing civilization could be instilled, and the geographical spread of Greek culture throughout the ancient classical world. Reading included the learning of certain pieces of literature, and from fragments of reading books we can see how certain works recur. It would be incorrect to speak of a canon, but certain authors, forms, and passages might have acquired a sort of classical status. Nevertheless, the sense of a "classic" heritage develops strongly in Hellenistic civilization. From Egypt (which is where the vast majority of the extant evidence derives) the appearance from Ptolemaic through to Byzantine times of the same texts shows the extent to which a literary canon encapsulated that culture. Together with that absorption of a Greek canon (however loosely defined) went the study of the Greek language, not merely the ability to speak fluently the common Greek, but also to understand (and even reproduce) various Greek dialects, for example the Attic, the influence of which can be seen in so many authors, including Josephus.

In the Hellenistic world, state and private libraries multiplied. Antiochus III (third century B.C.E.) established a library at Antioch (whose librarian was called Euphorion of Chalcis); Pergamon had one by the mid-second century B.C.E. Libraries were matters of public and personal pride, and were often taken as spoils by Romans, who were responsible for introducing public libraries. By this time, then, the library has ceased to be a royal, imperial, or temple-sponsored collection for the use of the state or cult or their servants, and has come to reflect the spread of literacy and reading, a development which in turn derives from changes in the social structure that brought into existence a new reading and writing class (or perhaps classes).

It is above all the great Museum at Alexandria, however, that exemplifies the book learning of the Hellenistic world and, perhaps, the birth of the scholar as our Western tradition understands it. Instituted by Ptolemy I in the fourth century B.C.E., this "assembly" (it was a collection of persons rather than a building) was headed, in the Egyptian tradition, by a priest, though the physical location was in the precincts of the palace. It did not, as did many Greek schools, comprise philosophers but students of literature and scientists. As well as studying, they apparently taught; but most of all they wrote: they were the heirs of the ancient Near Eastern scribes, but without any administrative responsibilities. For their use a library (or libraries) was accumulated from the literature of the classical world, either by Ptolemy I or by Ptolemy II. But, unlike the ancient Near Eastern tradition, the library was not reserved for the scribes but open to the public.

How were the contents of this library arranged? Did Ptolemy (or his librarian) derive anything from ancient Near Eastern archival practices? Each papyrus roll had its title placed at the end and the catalogs listed this title; the number of lines were also sometimes written and even cataloged. It is unclear, though, whether the system of dividing the whole of Greek literature into categories[27] owes anything to precursors. But once this system was established (and the total number and names of the categories is unknown: "laws" and "rhetoric" are two of them), all authors could be cataloged alphabetically under these headings, and, within the canon of a single author, alphabetically by the opening words.

Alexandrian scholarship is best known for its contribution to the science of textual criticism, of establishing "correct" texts of Homer and other classics from the variety of texts available in the library. The further work of the Alexandrian scholars in detail extends beyond the scope of Jewish canonizing, but several relevant points will be reviewed presently. The incorporation of Judah into the Ptolemaic kingdom from the late fourth century until the end of the third century B.C.E., and the presence of a large Jewish community in Alexandria nevertheless make it unlikely that the Museum and the library were either unknown or entirely uninfluential upon the course of Jewish canonizing.

ANCIENT CANONS

Four specific features of the behavior of scribes in the cuneiform tradition point to the presence, from an early stage in its history, of a "canonizing process": the categorizing and annotating of writings, the preservation of the same compositions in several different times and places, the influence of certain compositions on others, and the standardization of the texts of some writings. In the history of cuneiform literature we can regularly observe the influence of earlier works on later ones, sometimes conservatively, sometimes creatively. Standard phraseology and genres can, of course, be demonstrated throughout, but compositions such as the Atrahasis epic (early second millennium) are the result of the creative combination of traditional materials, as are works from later in the second millennium such as the Creation Epic or Poem of the Righteous Sufferer (to cite works well-known to biblical students). These compositions display, in all their originality, a familiarity with inherited forms of writing, leading in some cases to the quotation of texts within other texts and of allusions to presumably well-known compositions. There are also several instances of the same passage being incorporated in different literary works.

Evidence of a more formal process of canonizing within the Akkadian scribal tradition is the fact that in a literary corpus stretching over a large area and a long timespan, particular texts frequently recur. It is virtually certain that only a mere fraction of Akkadian literature is extant, and so we cannot claim anything like an adequate picture of what might have been regarded in this tradition as the "classic" texts. But a canonizing process is evident enough. Although the majority of the recovered libraries date from the first millennium, many of them contain copies of much older compositions. What is more, in many cases (but not all) the various copies exhibit virtually the same textual form, suggesting that some texts, at some time, and perhaps in some places, were standardized.

These observations surely mean that within Mesopotamian literature factors that lead to the production of canons were present, and that in a very loose sense, at least, we could refer to canons (as do many Assyriologists). But can we go further and identify any actual Akkadian "canons"?

Opinion is not unanimous, and disagreement usually depends on the definition one gives to the term "canon." The best known champion of a "cuneiform canon" is W. W. Hallo, whose views are echoed by N. Sarna.[28] Both in fact suggest that Jewish canonization ultimately derives from a Mesopotamian precedent. In both cases, the two scholars find the emergence of a recognized corpus, tendency toward a standardized text, fixed arrangement of content, and an established sequence. W. G. Lambert, on the other hand, while prepared to acknowledge some features of canonicity in Akkadian literature,[29] denies that "canonical" activity goes much further. He does nevertheless concede that a good deal of Akkadian literature achieved a fixed form, which included a fixed text, though he notes that some works continued to circulate in variant editions (which is also true of Jewish scriptural texts such as Jeremiah, Esther, and Daniel). Due to the limitations of the evidence, it is sometimes difficult to be clear: while Lambert believes that the Gilgamesh epic was an "unfixed" text, Hallo has argued that it did in fact achieve a definitive form, in which it is found in several ancient libraries, although it is also extant in earlier variant forms. If this kind of analysis is possible, and valid, as Hallo maintains, it may be possible to trace the progressive "canonization" of certain Akkadian texts over time.

Yet "canonization" can perhaps be detected not solely by the fixing of textual form, but in the provision of a fixed place in a fixed collection. Hallo has refined his analysis of Akkadian texts to identify four such "canons," stretching from a Sumerian (ca. 1750 B.C.E.) to a bilingual (Sumerian-Akkadian,

ca. 250 B.C.E.). His use of the word "canon" for these collections is founded
on the presence of the following phenomena:

1. The systematic selection of texts, evidenced by their being
   copied and by the creation of model compositions from existing archives, leading to the creation of new texts according
   to the "canonical" paradigms
2. The standardization of texts by arrangement of poetic texts
   into fixed verses, counting of lines, glosses, and marginal variants, collation of variant copies
3. Provision of a fixed order of texts, as evidenced by exercise
   texts in which "canonical" texts recur in the same sequence,
   miniatures of whole collections of texts, and catalogs of correct sequences of tablets and texts.

Whether or not Hallo's line of argument will be widely accepted (which is
unlikely), evidence for a less strictly developed form of canon has already
been exceeded, and we can show evidence not only of the necessary canonizing mentality of culture in the cuneiform tradition, but also of the emergence of specific, if provisional and open, canons.

In the case of Egyptian canonizing, we have less quantity of evidence on
which to reach a verdict. But in some cases it is clear that texts were being
copied over a period of over a millennium, sometimes with evidence of editorial revision. The following passage, from a 14th- or 13th-century B.C.E.
text shows that certain authors, scribes of old, had been canonized:[30]

> Those learned scribes since the time of those who existed after the gods
> . . . they made themselves heirs out of writings, of teaching which they
> had composed. Teachings are their pyramids, the reed pen their child,
> the stone surface a wife. . . . Is there one here like Hardjedef? Is there
> another like Imhotep? No-one has appeared among our kinsmen like
> Neferty or Khety, the foremost of them. . . .

The writings of the "learned scribes" referred to here date from a millennium
earlier than the manuscript.

As for Greece, we have seen that Homer was canonized in Greece from
at least the beginning of the classical period. Later, through the schools that
both Plato and his pupil Aristotle founded (respectively, the Academy and
the Peripatos [or Lyceum]), the works of their founders were preserved as
canonical books. There is some evidence of an official "Academy edition"
of Plato's works. Characteristically, however, a theory of canon was also developed in Athens. It was Aristotle who first addressed the question of why

the classics (especially Homer) *were* classics. He argued for an aesthetic reason: the perfection of such works. This opinion naturally gave grounds for the practice of textual criticism (to recover the perfect text) and the careful study of these works as models that could not be repeated but only imitated as far as one was able. His teacher Plato had already advocated a state education system in which a selection of approved literary works was included and thus, although there already existed the notion of a literary canon, with the development of a school curriculum it takes a step further—though for Plato, the study of literature was only preparatory to philosophical pursuits.

During Aristotle's lifetime, an official copy of the works of Aeschylus, Sophocles, and Euripides was deposited in the Athenian public archives and adherence to this official text was enforced. Whatever the immediate or practical reasons for this move (such as the defacement of the plays by reason of improvisation), the notion of the authenticity of the written word, together with that of a classic corpus, argues that by the onset of the Hellenistic age the notion of canon, together with certain canons themselves, was firmly embedded in Greek culture, to be transmitted throughout the Greco-Roman world alongside the older canons in Egypt and Babylon. Thus, in the Hellenistic schools, lists of great persons (legislators, artists, scientists) came to be codified, and lists of works to be studied. Canons of Greek literature drawn up by the schools (or by individuals) included Homer, and almost always Euripides, Menander, and Demosthenes. Hesiod, Pindar, Sappho, Aeschylus, Sophocles, Aristophanes, Herodotus, Thucydides, and Aesop were also regulars. Sometimes a selection was made of the works of certain authors, and such anthologies made certain *extracts* canonical rather than the authors. The Hellenistic world, then, was without doubt a canonizing world.

ANCIENT SCRIBES
AS CANONIZERS

Having argued that in Mesopotamia, Egypt, and Greece, and in the Hellenistic world that engulfed all these areas, we have evidence of canons, it remains to review the factors and inclinations that induce and accompany such a process. In the manner of these ancient scribes, it might be appropriate to list them, though not in order of significance.

1. The *ethos of classification and cataloging;* labeling cases or appending catalogs of texts to identify contents or index a collection. This mechanical process provides the basis for the intellectual or cultural classification of literary texts.

2. The *use of an artificial archaic language,* which marks off literary texts from other writing and from speech, endowing
   such texts with a property that belongs to (though it does not
   of itself constitute) canonical status.

3. The *conservatism* that, transmitting texts and styles over millennia, cultivates a veneration for what is contained in the very ancient. Antiquity of itself becomes an intrinsic quality quite distinct
   from the aesthetic or functional value of the text, and contributes
   to its canonization. But what criteria would influence this
   collective-cumulative decision? It is, of course, possible that once
   a text has, for whatever reason, been copied for several generations it acquires the aura of antiquity and becomes *de facto*
   canonical.

4. A text may become canonized through its *association with an
   event or festival* so that it remains in practical use. An example
   of this may be the "Creation Epic" (*Enuma Elish*) used in the annual New Year festival in Babylon. This annual occasion may
   have ensured the survival of the poem, though it is not absolutely clear that the text was originally *composed* for this or
   any other festival.

5. The use of a text as a model for learning or copying in
   scribal schools will canonize it. Creating and developing a
   "syllabus" is an important canonizing process in itself. The
   criteria for selection of texts for this purpose can be varied:
   aesthetic excellence, clarity of form, linguistic peculiarities,
   or, of course, canonical status already achieved by some
   other criteria.

6. The *creation of libraries* involves—where the aim is not com-
   prehensiveness—a process of selection and judgment about the
   works that are worthy to be included. Whether or not the legend of the translation of the Hebrew torah canon into Greek is
   true, it illustrates the kind of judgment by a librarian (or a library
   patron) about the texts to be included. The holdings of a library
   are, after all, a kind of very large and very broad "canon."

7. The existence of multiple copies of texts in archives or libraries can give rise to the problem of variation, and *the urge
   to produce a definitive text.* This process is evident in Ashurbanipal's library (among other ancient examples) and most explicitly in the work of the Alexandrian libraries and schools.
   Such activity constitutes the canonizing not of a particular

work, but of the work *in a specific textual form,* both reflecting and accentuating the authority of that canonized work.

8. *A sense of a classical age already past.* This is clearly a major factor in Hellenistic canonizing. A conscious effort to define Greek culture by means of its most excellent exemplars was induced by the physical, but even more, the temporal gap that separated classical Greece from Greek culture of the Hellenistic world.

9. *The authority of school founders.* Particular schools may elevate to a canonical status writings attributed to their founders, and augment them by the writings of other famous members of the school. A related phenomenon is the veneration among Egyptian scribes (mentioned earlier) of certain distinguished predecessors, the Egyptian scribal tradition being understood as a single "school."

10. *The formation of a social identity.* The canons produced by the scribes reflected their values and thus helped to define the scribal class. But a canonizing society does not have to be a class; we have seen that it can be a philosophical school. It can, as in the case of Christianity, also be a religious community or institution. Canons arise, then, typically in and for social groupings.

CONCLUSION

Perhaps the most important point to make overall is that canonizing is a function of the cultural transmission of knowledge. In the first instance knowledge is accumulated as a means of social and economic control. But it has to be accessible. The art (science) of archiving is necessary. If the art of *classifying knowledge* is transferred from the sphere of documentary texts to that of literary texts, and culture, rather than economics, becomes the underlying rationale of archiving, we can see canonizing as one of the mechanisms by which knowledge is evaluated in the process of being transmitted. The institutionalized transmission of a body of necessary knowledge from generation to generation—the school—defines even more sharply the canonizing process, since the choice of texts to be studied there is smaller, and the study more intense.

Without yet having considered Judean-Israelite-Jewish canonizing, we have already accumulated a good deal of theoretical knowledge about it. The Jewish canon contains no extended myths, no omen literature, no incantations, but it does include extended historiographical and other narrative texts, as well as unique compositions of prophetic oracles, to name only the more obvious instances. But is the matter of content entirely relevant? On the other hand, there are certain features of the Jewish canon that might be illuminated by what we know of other canonizing cultures: the standardization of the Masoretic text, the use of a literary dialect, imitation and variation of standard genres (Psalms, Prophets), of the fixing of the order of scrolls (Torah, Prophets), of genealogical lists.

The question of direct influence from Mesopotamia, Egypt, or Greece should of course also be considered. It must not be forgotten that in some of the material in Genesis 1—11 and in the Enochic canon there is concrete evidence for strong literary influence.[31] But this does not necessarily point to a date for the *commencement* of Jewish canonizing, since, as we have seen, the Akkadian and Egyptian canon(s) were still in force well into the Hellenistic period. All the canonizing features that have been mentioned, or at least nearly all, can be considered as contemporary in the period of the Judean Second Temple, and thus with the main epoch of Jewish canonizing. That period was also one in which a great deal of scribal activity was turned toward a past golden age, possibly a reflection of that instinct that drove Hellenistic canonizing to define the classical culture of Greece.

The survey of canonizing points us to look for certain features in the history of Jewish canonizing: to the indispensable role of scribes, be they attached to temples, palaces, or even private individuals, as creators of canon. It indicates the likely importance of scribal schools and libraries but also of libraries and schools whose membership and access went beyond the scribal community. Not least in importance is the need to identify the *social group behind any canon,* which in the case of Judah can be anything—a religious sect or community, a scribal or rabbinic class, or possibly a political dynasty or party.

CHAPTER 3

Canon, Canonizing, and Canonical Criticism

Approaches to Jewish Canonizing

CANONS OF ANCIENT JUDAISM(S)

At the beginning of chapter 1 a number of basic misconceptions about Jewish canonizing were listed, as follows:

1. The concept and the role of canons within the system of rabbinic Judaism
2. The view of pre-rabbinic Judaism as a unitary phenomenon
3. Overreliance on the canon's own history of itself
4. The assumption that the rabbinic-Masoretic canon experienced an organic growth

This chapter offers a brief account of some major approaches to Jewish canons and canonizing, and is intended partly to acknowledge the work that has been previously done on the topic and remind the reader of the variety of approaches possible, but also to illustrate the wide influence of some or all of the above misconceptions. It should also be noted how infrequently any study of Jewish canonizing has proceeded from a review of canonizing generally, perhaps in some cases exhibiting a fifth misconception, that Jewish canonizing is not to be treated as just one more example of a widespread human phenomenon.

To be fair, a number of important recent treatments have brought quite radical new perspectives to the debate. Among them should be mentioned the work of James Sanders (see below), who attempted to marry a theological approach to canon with an improved historical-critical account of canon formation; James Barr's *Holy Scripture: Canon, Authority, Criticism,*[1] which attempted to compensate for an overly theological emphasis in biblical scholarship on the centrality of "canon"; John Barton's *Oracles of God: Perceptions of Ancient Prophecy after the Exile*,[2] which threw doubt on the conventional tripartite approach to the formation of the Jewish scriptural canon and introduced a number of common-sense observations about the non-coherence of books and collections of books; an all too brief methodological essay, and later a book, by J. N. Lightstone;[3] and two very recent publications: an article by David M. Carr,[4] which develops, in Carr's own view, the approach commended by J. A. Sanders; and a very thorough treatment by M. Haran,[5] crowning a series of articles on various aspects of Jewish canonizing (see below).

Any modern historical treatment of canon in early Judaism ought to begin by recognizing that what is being dealt with is a rabbinic-Masoretic text, stabilized textually by the Masoretes over more or less the first millennium of our era, and more or less fixed in sequence by common sense, tradition, and finally by the advent of printing. This canon, however, is just one survivor of a number of canons that Judeans and Jews produced, and while it incorporated some of them into itself, it did leave some writings out. Thus a history of canonizing in Judaism cannot confine itself to the history of one particular canon that survived. Even if the Samaritans are disregarded (and strictly speaking they could be if we insist that "Jewish" means "Judean" as in the ancient languages), we have strong hints that beside the rabbinic Bible and its fixed "Masoretic" text there was also a collection or collections of Jewish books in Greek, containing a larger canon or canons, and, indeed, providing the Christian churches with the material for its "Old Testament."[6]

While it remains likely that the Mosaic canon (the Torah) was widely shared as a canon among different Judaisms, including by Samaritans, the authors of the Qumran scrolls (probably), and the writer of *Aristeas*, it is not clear that all Judaisms were necessarily based on a Mosaic Torah; the Enochic canon, for example, seems to represent a Judaism of a quite different kind. As for other canons, the Samaritans had no scriptural canon other than Torah, neither, probably, did the Sadducees, while Philo's writings on the scriptures scarcely range beyond the books of Moses. We can suggest (though the evidence from the many forms of Judaism in the Diaspora is inadequate) that while most if not all Judaisms possessed a notion of canon, there was no such thing as a single canon or set of canons. Moreover, we are speaking of literate Judaisms; whether the notion of canon played any significant role for the illiterate among the Jews is doubtful.[7]

If this picture resembles the actual state of affairs, we cannot realistically speak of a history of "*the* Jewish scriptural canon," because that canon itself has a history that does not go back earlier than the rabbis. We cannot know in advance what each Judaism had by way of a canon, or what it made of whatever canon(s) it had. In many cases we shall have to guess.

CANON AND CANONIZING: CURRENT ISSUES

The range of scholarly approaches to Jewish canon and canonizing is quite considerable. It was once fairly usual to see the topic (together with "text") placed at the end of an Old Testament Introduction, as a topic that could quite easily be separated from a consideration of the actual books and their composition. Typically, while the composition of these books, including in many cases multiple redactions, was energetically reconstructed, the process by which they were compiled into a canon was understood as a separate one, and involved three stages: first of all law, then prophets, then writings. With the final decision at the end of the first century C.E. at the "council of Jamnia" the canon was completed.

On this view, the process of making the canon could be more or less separated from those which produced the books themselves, composition and redaction. But in recent decades there has been a shift toward an integrative view, in which a "canonical shaping" of the scriptural books constitutes part of the redactional process itself. This (see below) has been very popular because it allows the question of the authority and value of the received canon to play a role in historical research, bringing history once more within the grasp of biblical theology, whence historical criticism was thought to have kidnapped it. But with the aid of literary criticism canonical criticism has made some useful contribution toward the identification of larger structures below the surface of the text. Within Pentateuchal criticism, of course, it had long been suggested that the borders between the five (or six) books were of little significance, since behind them were earlier sources that had extended across the entire material (and on some views had even gone further). Martin Noth's classic work on the composition of the Pentateuchal traditions[8] summed up a century or so of criticism in positing an original historical narrative assembled out of a series of themes and developed by a Yahwist and an Elohist before being combined by a Priestly writer. The theory of F. M. Cross of an "early Israelite epic"[9] offered a broadly similar view: an ancient historical outline lay close to the origins of the Pentateuch, which, with the incorporation of the originally independent Deuteronomy, was treated as a single composition that had undergone a series of "redactions." Much the same is true of Noth's "Deuteronomistic History" theory.[10] The rabbinic-Masoretic scriptural canon was not a collection of independent books, but at least in some cases a collection of larger works that happened to have been broken down into scrolls for the purpose of convenience: Genesis, then, for example, was not a book, only a scroll, as were Joshua and the two Samuels.

The situation with the prophetic books is partly different. While the twelve smaller books of named prophets have been traditionally examined by scholars as separate works, a recent tendency to reconstruct them as a single work is noticeable. The signs of unity between them are rather uncertain, but it is known that they once comprised a single scroll. Yet, if a single scroll can be only part of a multiscroll work, cannot a single scroll also contain more than one separate work? After all, a scroll and a literary work are not necessarily the same thing at all, as the Qumran scrolls have reminded us. By contrast, the larger scrolls of Isaiah and Jeremiah display an evident compositional history of their own, with little (and mostly no) sign of connection to any other of the books attributed to individual prophets. There is a good case (and it will be made) for treating these two books, and indeed Psalms and Proverbs, as canons in themselves, exhibiting as they do clear signs of the kind of activity (classifying, arranging, supplementing, assigning authority) that the building of canons entails. That some scrolls do not exhibit an evident literary unity may indeed mean that they are not literary units, but simply works conveniently assembled on the same scrolls and provided with a certain minimal coherence.

There is in current scholarship undoubtedly a tension between on the one hand a recognition that, at least in the books belonging to Torah and Prophets, a good deal of literary activity can be reconstructed, with a range of different source materials and an often complicated sequence of editing process by means of which these sources reached their final form; and on the other hand a perception of unities of theme, ideology, and language, often extending across several books. To achieve a balance between these two perceptions is not easy, and sometimes it is abandoned, as, for example, when the Pentateuch is presented as a single composition of a single author (as R. N. Whybray[11]), or on the other hand, the book of Jeremiah understood as a product of a process of accretion which in the end did not produce a coherent composition (as by William McKane[12]).

It would be fair to suggest, I think, that many scholars, rather than taking individual cases on their merits, or struggling for a synthesis, have opted in principle for a particular view. The emergence of literary (as distinct from literary-historical) approaches and the advent of "canonical criticism" have created an agenda in which the final form of the text is granted a theological or literary unity as of right. But this right has tended to bring with it a predisposition to a *historical* unity as well. Although many literary critics are uninterested in the production of the canon (as they are entitled to be), there is some "overspill" from literary and theological agendas into historical ones.

But another problem arises when we consider the social context in which the entire process from composition to canonizing takes place. Too little work has been done on the sociology of Jewish canonizing. Practitioners of "canonical criticism," although often claiming to operate also at the level of historical description, are essentially undertaking a theological enterprise, aimed at recovering the value of biblical criticism for the church. (Both Sanders and Childs have indeed made this explicit, as will be explained presently.) One of the features of this theological program is to emphasize the role played in the production of the canon by "communities of faith." At this point, the interest of canonical critics in the historical production of the canon generally ceases. The idea of canons as community productions is a promising insight, but only of interest to canonical critics where these communities can be seen as forerunners of Christian ones.

But the appearance of social-scientific methods—or even social-scientific questions—to biblical studies[13] underlines the highly unsatisfactory nature of such vaguely generalized authorship by reminding us of the nature of the agrarian society in which the biblical literature was produced. It has been realized that the literature in the canon, and the canonization process, must have taken place among an elite, and cannot simply represent the "traditions of Israel." And just as feminism has highlighted the (inevitable) patriarchal bias of this literature, so social-scientific reflection exposes the fact that this rather small elite comprising the governing sector had little in common with the majority of rural peasants. The scriptural canon cannot and does not represent an amorphous "Israel" but a set of elitist portraits. Perhaps because of the theological drawbacks of such a view, canonical criticism has not engaged itself seriously with social-scientific accounts of canon formation, though it offers a promising agenda for liberation theology.

Another change to be considered is the prominence recently being given to "reception theory." While "history of interpretation" has always played a major role in biblical exegesis, reception theory imports a different perspective. For behind the historical-critical approach that dominated biblical scholarship for several centuries until quite recently lay an implication that the text had an unalterable meaning, though one that at various times was understood differently; and, second, it was usual for the changes in interpretation to be expressed in terms of doctrinal developments or of an individual's own philosophy. Reception theory, on the contrary, does not necessarily accept that a text has any intrinsic meaning that can be "detached" from interpretation. Rather, in the view of many practitioners, at any given time a text requires a reader to supply a meaning. What a text intrinsically means (some would say what it *is*) can only be expressed through particular acts of reading. The history of interpretation *is* the text. Reception theory thus tends to regard the history of interpretation of a text as an intrinsic element of the exegesis of the text itself.

In this connection we should exercise care in our use of the terms "canon" and "Bible." When "canonical" is used of ancient Jewish writings, it might mean simply that the work is in the rabbinic-Masoretic canon. This is an ambiguous use of the term and very strictly refers only to its later reception. I shall therefore use "canonical" only in an historical sense to refer to writings that at the relevant time enjoyed a canonical status. "Biblical" is more obviously inappropriate. There is no Jewish Bible until the medieval period, and even so, "canon" and "Bible" are not synonymous. There are, in any case, by definition no "biblical writers," because Bibles are not written by authors; they are copied out by scribes or, nowadays, manufactured by publishers. As for "scriptures": the term is ambiguous, for it means, in the original languages, "writings," and that is the sense it should probably retain, even where (as is frequently the case, one suspects) it means "canonized writings."

The insights of reception theory can usefully be applied to canon. For in an important sense, the "canon" as a meaningful text cannot be divorced from its history and from the communities that subscribe to it. But that history must not be overlapped with the meanings or readings or writings of those texts during their composition or even during their canonizing. That the "Old Testament" is part of the Christian canon does not make its authors or its canonizers Christian—nor, indeed, rabbis.

The solution to the problem of understanding a canonizing process that leads from composition through redaction to fully fixed and canonized texts is amenable, then, to a bewildering range of explanations. Single authorship of some books, or collections of books, offers an attractive simplicity, but even if it is able to explain why an author wrote a book, it does not explain why the composition was subsequently transmitted. Authorship is only a part of the canonizing process. If the degree of cohesion within and among some of the canonized books is not explained by single authorship, then a collective authorship in the form of a continuous shaping of materials into a final coherent form can be suggested. But is some kind of inherent *purpose* to be assigned to this process, a "canonical intent"? Or is coherence achieved by a series of discrete selections, adaptations, and annotations, a kind of Darwinian process of evolution? Or, indeed, a series of "jumps," hardly connected to one another? A comprehensive review of the scholarship on this question is entirely beyond the competence of any single scholar, let alone an adequate account of the canonizing process itself. And indeed, there is no reason to assume that one particular account will serve every case.

CANON OUT OF
CONFLICT/DIVERSITY

Marc Brettler makes the following claim:

> [T]he idea [of a canon] was radically new in the context of the ancient Near East. To the best of our knowledge, no other ancient Semitic civilization attempted to sort through the literature, raise some works to a high status by deeming them canonical and relegate others to a lower status by declaring them unworthy of being admitted to the canon.[14]

Brettler goes on to develop his case that the notion of canon originated specifically in Israel, choosing a narrow definition of "canon" as meaning an explicit judgment about writings that are to be placed inside and outside the canon. A rather rigid definition (indeed, a Christian one) is imposed so as to effect a sharp contrast with other Near Eastern civilizations. But having imposed such a narrow definition and celebrated this as the world's first canon, he encounters the difficulty of its diversity. For having suggested that the Jewish canon began (as Torah) with a selection of texts "from a multiplicity of legal and historical traditions" that, during the early Second Temple period, the "leaders" established as laws that had to be observed, he needs to explain why these leaders did not make a more consistent job of their Torah canon, which he describes as a "diverse and sometimes contradictory work."

He meets the problem by concluding that the Torah canon is the result of a conflict between several competing groups, none of which was able to "foist its texts on the others as the only legal teaching." But this creates a further problem, not addressed, which is why the previous diversity of authoritative texts could not continue. Having lived for some time with literature but not a canon, why make a canon now? In any case, there is no evidence until the rabbinic period for any explicit indications of a conscious process of selection of books. It may seem a rather unfair verdict, but Brettler's solution is to a problem of his own making.

There is nevertheless a respectable history behind the conflict theory. Morton Smith's account[15] of the conflict between the "Yahweh-alone" party and the "syncretizers" attempted, in part, to explain the presence of disparate material in the Masoretic canon, suggesting a distinction between the "nationalistic" literature of the national legends, laws, and prophecies of the former and the "belletristic" writings of the lay, humane, wealthy, leisured, and cultured classes who were more attached to Hellenism. More recently, John W. Miller[16] has constructed in some detail a theory of rival priestly houses (represented by "Levites" and "priests" (Aaronite-Zadokites); after the marginalization of Levites, Ezra and Nehemiah restored them to the center of the Jerusalem cult, after which the Levites, absorbing some Zadokite materials, produced the "law and prophets." The Levites, in charge of the postexilic Jerusalem library, were then charged with developing a national canon, and, with the addition of other writings, did so. Like Brettler, Miller thus combines the idea of canon as a resolution of conflict with a deliberate process of canonization by selection.

David Carr's essay on canon formation[17] also accommodates the notion of rivalry. But he understands that until the end of the Second Temple period, canons remained fluid with no fixed boundaries agreed between the various Judaisms. Only with the destruction of the Temple did the process of consolidating a single Jewish scriptural canon occur.

The value of this perspective is that it does not try to discover some principle of unity within the Masoretic canon by means of which to explain its shape, nor to assume a process of organic growth. But several different explanations have been offered for the process of combining the differing contents: compromise between parties (Brettler), reconciliation leading to a national program of canon-building (Miller), consensus within the rabbinic movement (Carr). Each explanation also settles upon a different time frame for the decisive moment, from the early Second Temple period (Brettler) to the rabbinic period (Carr). (In the theory of Morton Smith the final resolution of the Masoretic canon is postponed to the Maccabean period, with which he does not deal.) The explanations also vary in postulating different kinds of communities or groups as the decision makers: political parties (Smith), "leaders" (Brettler), religious communities (Carr), and priestly/levitical castes (Miller). Of these four, all may contain scribal elements, but only Miller assigns the composition of books and their canonizing to a group that might legitimately be called "scribal."

"TRADITIO" AND "TRADITUM"

No account of canon or canonizing can afford to overlook the evidence of an ongoing process by means of which canonized writings are to some extent brought together by the provision of cross-references, chronological arrangements, superscriptions, and intertextual allusions. It is here, rather than in the process of either writing or list compiling, that the heart of the canonizing process is located. These features show that at the very least individual texts and groups of writings were not transmitted in complete independence of each other, but came to be conceived, during the process of copying and recopying, as something like a corpus, or rather a set of corpora. The process is not uniform or universal, nor indeed is it confined to the Masoretic canon. But it does provide evidence of a process that can legitimately be called "canonizing," to which the constitution of lists of books was, in some Judaisms, a sequel, while in others the less precise notion of a body of classic writings was perhaps sufficient.

Michael Fishbane has brilliantly illuminated these various processes in his classic treatment of "inner-biblical exegesis," *Biblical Interpretation in Ancient Israel*.[18] However, Fishbane also operates within what is perhaps the most widely held theory of the composition of the canon, which embraces the outcome of over a century of source-critical, form-critical, and traditio-historical work on the biblical literature. He sums it up as follows:

> [I]n modern scholarship, it is the method of tradition-history which has focused most extensively on the lively relationship between the traditions and their transmission in ancient Israel. Fully appreciative of the long prehistory of many of the themes, legends and teachings now found in Scripture, and the fact that over time these deposits of tradition were adapted to new situations and combined in new ways, the practitioners of this approach ideally seek to discern the components of a tradition-complex, to trace their origins or attribution to certain locales, and to show the profoundly new meanings which result as these materials were integrated into more comprehensive units. At each stage in the *traditio,* the *traditum* was adapted, transformed, or reinterpreted. . . . Materials were thus detribalized and nationalized; depolytheized and monotheized; reorganized and reconceptualized. The integration and reworking of many types of tradition at many different times and places thus had the result of incorporating non-Israelite and local Israelite materials into a national corpus whose telling and retelling was a new basis for cultural memory. Accordingly, the movement from the small oral traditions (native and foreign) to the final written state of Scripture is not only a process of tradition-building but of *Gemeindebildung* as well.
>
> (6–7)

Whether or not Fishbane would accept that he is dealing here with a "canonical process" (the language suggests it), the evolution he describes is surely one that would have to be called "canonizing." The important features of his version are these: the process took place over a long period of time, from independent oral traditions to larger written compositions. It also took place over a wide area: materials from many different locales were assembled and integrated into a growing corpus. Finally, this corpus, as he sees it, reflects the "national development."

Similar to the "canonical critics," this view regards the canon as a record of
the long growth of Jewish identity, and justifies, to a large degree at least, the
equation of biblical historical theology with an account of the religion of ancient Israel. What is more, it posits a "tradition" (that which is "handed on"; the
traditum) as something that is clearly conceived and can be shaped in a certain direction by a process he calls *traditio*. Fishbane rightly calls this the *background* to his investigation of the way in which biblical texts allude to each
other, because it is a presupposition and not a conclusion. Indeed, this picture
is more of a presupposition of tradition-history than an argument for it. Yet the
exegetical processes that Fishbane so thoroughly documents clearly point to a
learned medium of transmission, and thus to a scribal community or communities. But Fishbane views this scribal community as seeking to compile from
a wide range of materials a national "tradition" in a way that is not paralleled
in the other canonizing cultures we have seen. A systematic absorption of "popular" material is not commensurate with the scribal mentality. There is in Fishbane's perception a tension between the recognition of a learned scribal elite
as producers of canonical literature, and an inherited disposition to view the
canon as "national literature." It is necessary to ask what exactly is meant by
his phrase "telling and retelling"? Here obtrudes a vision of a society in which
scribes write up a national memory for the populace to accept and make their
own by telling and retelling it. If it is implausible that scribes set out to incorporate all kinds of local traditions, it is even more problematic that they do so
in order for this national tradition to be handed back to the populace for recit-
ing. If Judean scribes operated in this anomalous way, then particular reasons
need to be found.

But they are not even sought; and Fishbane's study reinforces the conclusion that in order to treat canonizing historically, one cannot ignore the nature
of the society in which the process took place. At the moment when his precise analysis of the literature needs to be matched by an equally precise investigation of the *sociology* of such literary activity, Fishbane collapses back upon
woolly generalizations of tradition-history, perhaps the least historically vali-
dated of all the traditional historical-critical methods. As things are, it does seem
that in presenting the canon as the national literature of Israel he has offered
the closest Jewish equivalent to canonical criticism yet published. But this criticism must be qualified by the recognition that Fishbane has drawn, if implicitly, a wonderful map of the scribal mentality and its attitude to canonized texts.

CANON AS PRESERVATION

Haran's recent account of canonizing[19] covers a great deal of territory and
offers some radical suggestions. He argues that, although literacy was not

widespread, there were *scribal* schools in the monarchic period, and they were producing works that were *intended to be canonized,* in the sense that they were written for preservation. He also suggests, contrary to Fishbane, that they were not composed over a period of time, but effectively at one stroke. In his view, the Masoretic canon is a collection (Hebrew אסופה) of already canonized works, and not a process of selecting. These works, which were the monuments of a past that was disappearing as newer literary forms and ideas developed, were therefore subjected to a deliberate act of *preservation.* Thus, canonization is not an act of selection from a wider range of literature, nor is it a long process. It is an act, but an act coterminous with final composition. No books that were finally included in the Jewish collection were ever "outside the canon."

This picture is filled out with some interesting details. For example, in the monarchic period papyrus was the normal medium of writing, except for occasional display copies, which were written on skins (such as the Deuteronomic code).[20] Large compositions such as J, E, and P would have required more than one scroll to contain them, whereas Deuteronomy was written specifically to fit onto a single scroll. At the beginning of the Persian period, however, literary works in Judah were written, following the general practice of the Arameans, on skins rather than on papyrus.[21] This, according to Haran, implies a canonization of scriptural works, so that it was more suitable for them to be copied on more durable material, and also it enabled all these canonical compositions to be written on single scrolls, as was (apparently) required.

The notion that the canonized works were written for the *purpose* of being a canon has, of course, some parallel in Greek literature, where we have seen examples of books entitled "Canon." Haran is also quite probably correct to suggest that none of the texts in the Jewish scriptural canon was ever "outside" the canon, for canons do not come into being by a sudden selection of texts not previously established as classics. His suggestion that what we call the "canon" is really a process of collection for the purpose of preserving the classic resource of a vanished culture is also valuable. But his account raises a number of detailed problems: the dating of many of the texts is too early, and the evidence of textual variation (Jeremiah, Psalms) is not really adequately accounted for; the inclusion of Chronicles (alongside Kings) makes little sense, while it is hard to understand works such as Ecclesiastes, Esther, Ruth, and Song of Songs being composed for the purpose of canonization. They are probably not the product of institutional scribal schools, and there is some difficulty in understanding how such authors had the authority to "canonize" their works. Even though Haran does admit exceptions, there seem to be too many for comfort. But he has made a number of valuable and persuasive observations: that the canonized books are (largely) scribal in composition; that the rabbis did not create a "canon," but rather ensured a collection; that a "postclassical" mentality has something to do with the establishment of that collection.

An account similar in some respects was offered by Shaye J. D. Cohen, though unlike Haran he does allow for some process of selection and uses "canonizing" to denote that selection:

> Jewish culture in the latter part of the Second Temple period was hardly unique . . . in selecting the *best and most enduring works of its literary patrimony* and according them "canonical" status. Their contemporaries in the Greek world were engaged in a parallel process.[22]
>
> [italics added]

For Cohen, all literate cultures canonize, and Jewish canonizing was specifically modeled on the Greek process, which sought, in a postclassical age, to retrieve and preserve the heritage of the past. But the italicized words indicate the extent of agreement with Haran: "patrimonial" works have already been preserved by a process of continuous selection (Haran would say by composition). Canonical lists, as he recognizes, presuppose some prior developments by means of which the texts considered for selection, and the criteria by which they are selected, have already been partly formed.

The gap left by Haran (deliberately) and Cohen (because it is not within the scope of his discussion) is the context in which "canon" introduces itself as a concept and succeeds in imposing itself more widely. If we inspect the notion of "patrimony" we shall reason that these texts hardly identified themselves as a national heritage, nor were they likely to have been acclaimed as such by popular decree. They were selected by a process of copying, studying, teaching, or whatever, by the scribal institutions that preserved literary culture, before being accorded the definitive status they finally received from the rabbis. The definition of the canonizing process surely needs to be extended to cover these earlier stages of copying and "improving" texts as they gradually become classical. A study of canonizing cannot, then, dispense with a study of scribal institutions and practices by means of which literature is both formed and becomes classic.

CANON CRITICISM:
JAMES SANDERS

With the term "canonical (or 'canon') criticism" are usually associated the names of James Sanders and Brevard Childs. Both have generated an agenda of biblical criticism that has been seen by many scholars as *theologically* fruitful, though in terms of understanding canon as a historical process they differ. Both the influence of "canonical criticism" in biblical studies and its benefits and shortcomings require a discussion at this point.[23]

A very clear distinction needs to be made between the programs of the two scholars. Unlike Childs, Sanders[24] regards his agenda as a natural extension of the historical-critical disciplines (tradition, form, and redaction criticism), because in his view it continues the study of the Bible from the processes by which the canon was formed to the processes that take place at and after the creation of the canon. This process involves both the various forms that canon took, and the process of interpretation that interacts with these canonical texts. Childs, on the other hand, emphasizes the "final form" of the text as the proper object of study, and argues that the canonical shape imparts a definitive message to the contents. Both find inadequate the earlier forms of historical criticism; Sanders because they are incomplete in dealing only with the precanonical stages and Childs because they are dealing with a precanonical text. Both agree in their reaction against the "biblical theology" movement, which transferred the locus of authority and revelation from a biblical text to the events that it testified—a theological objection to a theological agenda.

An undoubted gain of Sanders's approach is to shift the focus of attention away from precanonical processes toward postcanonical ones: to deal with the time when bibles existed rather than the times before they did. This focus entails a recognition that the significance of canon derives more from its reception than its formation. Yet Sanders also wants to emphasize a continuity between canon formation and canon reception in an ongoing relationship to communities. He suggests that canons receive their authority only from communities, and implies that canons are formed for the purposes they fulfill: the ongoing ratification of the beliefs of those communities. But while this is certainly arguable for the final stages of canonizing, the effecting of a list of books (and, in the case of Judaism, the fixing of a text form), it is far from obvious that the literature ultimately composing a formal canon has arrived at this final point by identical processes. Sanders rightly emphasizes the ideological plurality of these canonized writings, yet insists that at all times there exists a relationship between the texts, singly and in collection, to "*believing* communities" (my italics). Locating such religious groups in the context of canon formation certainly has theological value, since it allows the agenda of historical-critical scholarship to be embraced within a confessional discourse. But both terms invite inspection: what exactly is a "community" and what does it believe?

For the gain of theology is at the expense of sociology. If, as Sanders has suggested, we see monotheizing tendencies at work in the editing of the canonized books (and the evidence is persuasive to a large degree), under what impulses and conditions are these operations conducted? Are we not thinking necessarily of scribal communities? If so, are they simultaneously acting as religious believers? Or is he thinking rather of the final stages of canonizing in which already canonized literature assumes an enhanced, definitive, and religiously authoritative form? In speaking, as he does, of the "editors" of the biblical books who belonged to such communities and of books produced for and by religious groups, one wonders if Sanders is influenced too much by the theological agenda and is imagining an ancient canonizing nation made up of local churches. There is, indeed, evidence of ideological organization within certain books (Isaiah and Jeremiah) but not in others (Psalms, Proverbs), while in the "book of the twelve" the evidence is inconclusive. The suggestion that the canon was formed by affirming "what the communities, scattered in space and drawn out in time in their corporate wisdom . . . found valuable and gave life"[25] is unrealistic: how, historically, does "corporate wisdom" operate? Sanders does not in fact conduct a historical investigation, but remains content to posit the existence of "believing communities" as a sufficient explanation. From the first act of writing to the final act of canonization and (in Sanders's view, though not in Childs's) beyond, to the postcanonical act of interpretation, there is an almost seamless unfolding of the work of the Holy Spirit—and here Sanders makes his theological agenda quite explicit: "Its focus is on the function of the Bible as canon in the believing communities which formed and shaped it and passed it on to their heirs of today. Canon *and* community. They go together."[26]

There is a lack of historical reflection here. Had Sanders focused on the history of biblical interpretation, he could have observed that until recent centuries the interpretation of the biblical writings was not a matter in which believing communities led the way. Rather, theologians and scholars have taken the lead. They still do, for the debate about canon is confined to scholars, and the vast bulk of churchgoers have little concern with it. The Bible becomes, after its canonization, not only confined within the confessional life of the church, but confined (within the Western church) to Latin. Within Judaism, too, study of the sacred books was not a popular pastime, but the work of "sages." Certainly congregations *read* their Bibles (or rather, very small sections of Bibles); the last few centuries of more widespread literacy and Protestant congregations does not provide a more fitting image of ancient "believing communities" than centuries of illiterate feudalism. That religious doctrines must "speak to the people"[27] in order to be canonized is counterintuitive and bespeaks a faith in the universal principles of democracy even where the institutions do not exist!

Enough of "communities": what of "believing"? Given that the writers of the Jewish holy books (as they became) must, like all people, have believed something, how far does it matter *what* they believed? Christians they were not; rabbinic Jews they were not. Monotheists, of a sort, perhaps mostly. The point is to what extent specific religious beliefs really explain the formation of the canon. The answer will not be entirely in the negative. But the scribes of Mesopotamia, as we shall see, also created canons, and no doubt also formed believing communities. They even replaced, in the "Creation Epic," the god Enlil with the god Marduk in keeping with the beliefs of their "community." But from the books of the Masoretic canon, for instance, it can sometimes be difficult to establish what the *authors* believed, let alone those whose beliefs somehow embraced the collection. If we wish to know what was believed about the canon *after* its fixation, then we do not go to the canon itself, but to the commentaries on it.

CANONICAL CRITICISM:
BREVARD CHILDS

Despite similarities implied by the term "canonical criticism," the differences between Sanders and Childs are considerable. Both, however, claim to be conducting a historical as well as a theological method. Thus Childs can assert: "[I]t is a basic misunderstanding of the canonical approach to describe it as a nonhistorical reading of the Bible. Nothing could be further from the truth!"[28]

Indeed, Childs (like Sanders) charges historical criticism with not being *adequately* historical: the "historical-critical" approach *fails to understand* the real historical process in the formation of the Old Testament. But while Sanders's challenge lies in extending the history beyond the canon to its reception, Childs accuses historical criticism of missing the key factor in the *production* of the canon: the "religious dynamic"[29] consisting of the interaction between community and text: "It is constitutive of Israel's history that the literature formed the identity of the religious community which in turn shaped the literature."[30] Yet this fundamental claim about "Israel's history" is nowhere backed up, not even discussed. It is a theological dogma. Childs is interested in canon not as historical product but as literary icon. Where Sanders is at pains to stress the variety of possibilities open in interpretation of canon, and finds the pluriformity of text as helpful to his own recommendation about the use of canon in Christianity, Childs insists on a much more rigid frame, in which the canon as a whole shapes the meaning of its parts, and the "final form of the text" provides the basis for exegesis.

He does not, then, explain how *various* Christian canons came into being or how and why the various "communities" for whom Bibles function as a canon differ from one another—for "canon" is not viewed the same way in every Christian denomination. He has been particularly and repeatedly criticized for taking as his Old Testament canon the most recent of all (if one excludes the Mormon canon)—the sixteenth-century Protestant one, which corresponds in content to the Jewish canon, but not to any canon of the earliest Christian communities. In fact, his *Introduction* classifies according to the threefold *Jewish* division of the scriptural canon; he is not even dealing with the canonical shape of the Old Testament, which derives from the classification of the Greek Bibles of Christianity. The reception of the canon *even in the Christian churches* is evidently a "canonical" *process,* but while it is a fundamental element of Sanders's agenda, it is curiously irrelevant to Childs's "canonical" approach. His insistence on canon as a historical fact conflicts with his de-historicizing of it, idealizing it as a set of texts independent of any particular church at any particular time.[31]

It is very clear that while Childs is apparently discoursing at the level of "history," he is actually uninterested in historical processes, and unconcerned with historical argumentation. Like Sanders, he regards the canonical process as an extension of redaction criticism (a historical-critical method), with its focus on community rather than individual editing ("shaping" is a favorite term of Sanders and Childs). But unlike Sanders he speaks rather of a single "community of faith," corresponding to his single and arbitrary canon. Also, while Sanders regards the production of a fixed canon as a moment in an ongoing process in which interpretation continues, Childs regards canon as a defining moment, an absolute authority in its own right. Whereas Sanders's approach fails to do justice to historical research but remains a plausible historical exercise, Childs's method is antihistorical. It also leaves him open to a charge of idolatry: "Thou shalt have no other canons before me"! That other churches have different (and, as Christian, much older) collections, including different editions of Jeremiah, Esther, and Daniel, shows clearly that canons are a product of history in a way that Childs does not begin to entertain.

Childs certainly makes many perceptive literary and ideological links within the books of the Old Testament, which make an interesting extension of the redaction-critical procedures of the "historical critics." But surely the crucial links for his procedure must be *between* the books. Most of Childs's analysis in fact operates at the level of individual books, and evidence that these were copied and recopied so as to reach a final theological shape (and this shape itself is often hard to verify!) does not explain the canon at all.

The essential mistake here, I think, is not merely to simplify the process by which literature became canon, but to refuse to examine it. The effect that canonization has had on the contents of bibles is to preserve them for us, but also to preserve them as part of a religious whole. Canon is part of the "reception history" of this literature (as Sanders well appreciates). Being included in a bible is something that happened to works of literature composed and copied before bibles and canons were invented. Until fifty years ago, we did not know these writings except as "biblical." However, we now have Hebrew and Greek manuscripts of books from our Bibles that are, in the strict sense "nonbiblical" because they predate any Bibles. There is, indeed, a sense in which a notion of canon operates during the process of canonization. But there is, for example, an important difference between regarding a book as canonical (which is a judgment about its individual quality or value) and regarding it as merely a part of a larger whole (a canonical list). Childs cannot, or does not, see the difference. The "canonical perspective" is not one that can be imposed on a precanonical period. It is perfectly possible to have sacred writings without a canon, as it was once possible to have a Christian faith without a New Testament, a point that Barr makes very clearly.[32] To make canon a theological norm may be fine (though only within the relevant community); to offer it as a historical norm is misguided.[33]

Despite the criticism of "canonical criticism" as being unhistorical, either in practice (Sanders) or in principle (Childs), the use of the term (or concept) "canonical process" has contributed a useful insight to historical studies. For clearly there are signs of editing ("shaping") of the scriptural literature that point to some integration between various works. There is evidence that in the transmission of the scrolls efforts were made to relate them to one another: by chronological ordering, by textual allusion, by cross-referencing. The canonizing process was not confined to the selection of books that had shared no common scribal history. The shortcoming of canonical criticism in the area of history was that this process was too easily glossed in the interests of Protestant Christian biblical hermeneutics, in which the relationship between Bible and confessing congregation is the model. The attempt to superimpose this model on the "producers" of the canon bypassed historical enquiry. An important heritage of canonical criticism is its challenge to historians to deliver an account of the canonizing process that explains what they call "canonical shaping" by means of historical, and not theological, research. Sanders's affirmation that historical criticism should be "scientifically thorough"[34] can be upheld.

CANONIZING: A HISTORICAL
AND CRITICAL APPROACH

Wilfred Cantwell Smith notes two basic recent trends in our understanding of scripture: it is "more varied than our understanding has recognized," and it has been "more integrated in human life than is appreciated by current ideas either of scripture or of the human."[35] Thus a modern perspective, claims Smith, must be both more "human" and more "comprehensive." The point, as I take it, is that both in the production and reception of canons, a wider human community than the groups that write and create canons or venerate them is involved. The other point that Cantwell Smith's book makes firmly is that canons are human products, and that to understand their history involves a study of human (i.e., social) processes.

A historical agenda, however, is complicated in this instance by the fact that we know very little about the history of the societies from which the canon was formed. Virtually every account of Judean/Jewish canonizing relies to a large extent on a canonized history. The consensus of the scholarly literature (with a very few recent exceptions) is that we can speak of the "Josianic reform," the "Babylonian exile," the "restoration" under Ezra and Nehemiah, as historical pegs in the history of canonizing. But these events are, as literary narratives, also canonizing events: the product of a process that generated a "canonized history." The primary question is not "what do they tell us about history," but "what contribution do they make to our understanding of canonizing"? Of course, an understanding of the social history of Judah must be acquired before its canonizing can be evaluated. But before even that can be undertaken (see chapter 4), the question of the canonized history and its function must be considered.

Here I am reproducing, with some embellishment, the argument advanced in *In Search of 'Ancient Israel'*[36] that because the picture of the history and society of "ancient Israel" is a product of (canonizing) literary activity, it tells us about the identity of those who wrote it up—our chief "canonizers."

CANONIZED SOCIETIES

From Genesis to Kings runs a continuous historiographical narrative. We have seen over the last few centuries how elements of that canonized history have been eroded by the growth of the natural and human sciences. But a canonized history is not dismantled by eroding it. Indeed, erosion is entirely the wrong process, because it starts from the assumption that a canonized history is a kind of imperfect critical history that needs correcting. The result is that a canonized history, projected as a kind of critical history, loses some of its status as history, creating an unnecessary and rather silly battle between "maximal" and "minimal" interpretations of that history.

The canonized history presents us with a society that it calls "Israel." This "Israel" is continually reinterpreted, usually so as to denote the chosen people of its god; thus it is now a name of the ancestor Jacob and his descendants; it is an ancient state ruled over by Saul, David, and Solomon, a part of that divided state, then once that state has vanished from history the name persists, in a religious sense, for the society of Judah. (Postcanonically, it persists as a name for the Jewish people conceived as a religious entity and also for a modern state.)

The canonized history in the Jewish canon falls into four phases (the division is somewhat arbitrary, of course). The first phase charts the history of the world and the election of the ancestors of Israel (Genesis). The next phase describes the creation of the nation (from the descendants of Jacob, in Egypt), and the bestowal on this nation of constitution (law) and land—theoretically all of Palestine and some regions of Transjordan. The third phase is a period of decline as theocratic rule, from the ideal leadership of Moses and Joshua to the less ideal judges, then via Saul to the ideal (but not perfect) kings David and Solomon, and then the decline throughout the monarchies of the two kingdoms of Israel and Judah, culminating in the exile of Judah to Babylonia. (This runs from Exodus to Kings, plus Chronicles.)

The fourth phase sees the restoration of Judah and the rebuilding of a temple in Jerusalem under the patronage of the Persian kings, the reintroduction of the law of Moses, and the reconstitution of Judah/Israel as a religious congregation devoted to the covenant with Yahweh and to the worship in his temple (Ezra and Nehemiah). Here canonized history ends—though with the inclusion of the books of Maccabees some Christian canons contain a further phase before the effective history of the Jewish people comes (on the Christian view) theologically to an end with the advent of the Messiah.

If the picture of a single twelve-tribe Israelite nation divided into two states is a canonized one, the picture of a restored nation, in the shape of a post-monarchic Judah, is also canonized. The canonical picture paints the history of "Israel" as moving temporarily from its Palestinian home in Judah to Babylon, and then returning some years later to rebuild the temple to Yahweh in Jerusalem. Two aspects of this story, narrated in Ezra and Nehemiah (and discussed in more detail later in this volume), need highlighting. One is that those who did not go into exile are either ignored or criticized (as "people of the land"), and the whole focus is on the group of returnees who, paradoxically, are presented (though not only nor primarily in Ezra and Nehemiah) as the "preserved" nation, in which alone pure ethnic descent can be guaranteed and whose experiences constitute the genuine history of "Israel." The other is that this reconstituted "nation" is reborn through a set of dramatic moments: the edict of the Persian king Cyrus sets in train a return. Nehemiah and Ezra (some while later) ensure the building of the Temple and the walls of Jerusalem, and, more importantly for our interests, the making of a covenant between Yahweh and the "congregation," marked by a reading of the lawbook. That lawbook looks, and is perhaps intended to look, like a canon!

For the canon gives a prominent place to authoritative books. The Israelites, returning from Egypt, hear a law given by their god through Moses, and make a covenant on Mt. Sinai; Deuteronomy has the king governing through a lawbook; 2 Kings 22—23 has Josiah promulgating a law on the basis of a recovered book, also with a covenant ceremony; Ezra and Nehemiah also preside over a law reading and covenant. Among the prophets, Jeremiah recites all his words from Yahweh and has them written into a book. We have the collection of royal proverbs assigned to Solomon. A writing from Qumran (11QCompDav) makes explicit the notion of David composing a fixed number of psalms. *The rabbinic-Masoretic canon, then, is itself full of allusions to canons* and reflects a mentality in which they are regarded as central to the political and religious government of the Jews.

We may also recognize alongside these *literary* canons a canonized set of institutions: the dynasty of David (whence one form of messianic belief); a canonized priesthood, represented by a tribe (Levi) or, more strictly, descendants of Aaron, or even more strictly descendants of Zadok. Then there is a canonized institution of prophecy, represented by a *series* of figures who are called simply "my servants the prophets" (especially in Jeremiah: 7:25; 25:4; 26:5; 29:19; 35:15; 44:4; 38:17; but cf. Amos 3:7; Zech. 1:6; Dan. 9:6, 10). To an appreciable extent, Jewish literary canons can readily be associated with the canonization of such institutions, linking the canonical books with real or ideal political institutions.

FROM COMPOSITION
TO SCROLL TO CANON

With these observations, we are revealing what canonical critics would call a "canonical process" or "canonical consciousness." The term is not inappropriate to designate a mindset in which literature functions in an authoritative way. But none of the above comments embraces the totality of the Masoretic-rabbinic canon, only canons within it. It is true that only one history has been canonized, but within that we can perhaps see traces of earlier canonized (or potentially canonized) accounts that have been incorporated. Within the canonized texts of scripture, we can also find traces of the existence of other canonical collections. Several collections within the Psalms canon are headed "of David." Whether or not these originally implied Davidic authorship, there are some Psalms whose headings explicitly make such a claim, while other writings from Qumran and the New Testament appear to assign the whole canon of psalms to David. We may argue as to whether this extension is logically speaking a canonical or postcanonical development. Several psalms possess headings that assign a different authorship. Similarly with instructional literature: Proverbs as a whole is assigned to Solomon, yet within the canon of instructional sayings are some collections assigned to others. The book of Ecclesiastes plays with Solomonic authorship—how seriously we cannot know— and may reflect the existence of a canon of "Solomonic wisdom." (The instruction of ben Sira, however, makes no such claim, and yet there is evidence that it was included within some canons of Jewish instructional literature).

Psalms and Proverbs appear to be composed of once separate collections brought together in a single scroll. The process of writing them on one scroll had implications for archiving. In all probability, the contents were given a single name. They would be copied, sooner or later, as a single composition. Hence the Psalms scroll is Davidic and the Proverbs scroll Solomonic. A similar process might be suggested for the scrolls of Isaiah and Jeremiah, both far too long for any serious refashioning as a single coherent "book." Despite recent attempts to argue otherwise, it still looks likely that what we now call chapters 40—66 were at first written on the same scrolls as what we call chapters 1—39 (and archived as "Isaiah"?). The scroll represents the canon of Isaiah: copied and altered, supplemented and cross-referenced as a single entity, it becomes a "book" of Isaiah. A canon of Daniel stories may also be mooted: in this case supplemented by a series of later additions, this work, written on a single scroll, became the "book of Daniel" (in different Aramaic/Hebrew and Greek forms).

This process must not be imposed on every scroll, however. Jeremiah's scroll developed differently. Had Lamentations been written on the same scroll, that scroll would have represented the Jeremiah canon, and these poems would have become part of the "book" of Jeremiah. This did not happen. There was, undoubtedly, a prophetic canon represented by a scroll of twelve different parts. But because of the desire to distinguish the individuality of these prophets, they did not merge into a single "book" in the sense that they were regarded as a single work. Like Psalms and Proverbs, the "Twelve" constituted a single-scroll canon.

At the other end of the scale, we also have multiscroll canons such as the Mosaic books, while scrolls that contain accounts of a period of history will, under the guidance of a process seeking to create a single comprehensive history, become molded into a sequential narrative. Once a single more or less coherent narrative is achieved, it can become canonical. The point I am making here is that canonizing is a process that involves all the stages from composition, editing, archiving (combining on a scroll), and collecting scrolls into larger units. But equally important, there is no *single* canonical mechanism or "trajectory." There are "canonical processes," however, and they operate within the *formation* of scrolls as well as in the *grouping* of scrolls.

Let me take a concrete illustration of the impossibility of dealing with canonizing in the shadow of later lists. If we were to find in some church's library in, say, the second century C.E., some codices of the Mosaic canon alongside a codex of some letters of Paul (let us say excluding Colossians and Ephesians), a scroll of Enoch, and a codex of the letters of Ignatius, how would it be decided which of these were canonical? We would have before us (a) a clearly recognized Mosaic canon; (b) a collection of works that would be canonized in the Western "New Testament" but did not match the final list; (c) a work that was canonized but not in the Western church; and (d) a collection that was not later canonized. An illustration such as this shows not only how difficult it is to decide what "canonical" might mean at any given time or place, and indeed how inappropriate it is to allow the category "canonical" to get out of hand. "Canonical" does not imply only a fixed status in a list but can reflect a number of degrees of "canonization" prior to that. Even where it does make someone's list, it may fall out of another's. This is why the subject of this volume is not "canon" but "canonizing." What is often called the "formation" of the Jewish canon (the end of canonizing "holy books") is a different process, an act performed *on* canonized literature in the interests, usually, of politics, since it is an act of authoritarian imposition.

Canonizing begins and continues as an open-ended process. To canonize a work is not an entirely conscious process at all stages and does not entail that other works have to be barred from being canonized, or definitely excluded from such a status. Only when definitive canonical lists emerge does the canonizing process stop. While canonizing does entail listing, organizing, and labeling, a single definitive list is not, indeed, the *purpose* of the canonizing process, any more than death is the purpose of life: merely its end.

CHAPTER 4

A Sketch of Israelite
and Judean History

The purpose of this sketch is not to engage this complex topic at all fully, but to fill in the general background in the light of which the process of canonizing within Israel and Judah may be considered. In particular, we shall be looking for (1) the economic and political conditions that stimulate literacy; (2) the infrastructure that supports the production of literary works; and (3) the political and religious regimes that promote, exploit, and close canons.

As was explained in chapter 2, writing emerged as an aid to economic bookkeeping, and scribes as instruments of state administration. The possibility of canonizing does not exist without a scribal class of a certain size and complexity, and the creation of this class in turn depends on the evolution of a centralized state.

THE MONARCHIC STATE

Prior to the emergence of the monarchic states of Israel and Judah, we can identify their populations as settlers in the central and southern Palestinian highlands from the early Iron Age (ca. 1200 B.C.E.). These settlers lived in villages for which clearings had to be made in the forests, and it is likely that they were socially organized on a kinship basis. Over time, these village societies coalesced, or were coerced, into larger groups governed by an individual. Whether or not these villagers were originally nomadic or came from the urban population of the Palestinian lowlands, their social organization was not itself urban, and the social system they devolved was not centralized. The possibility of a scribal class in such a society can be ruled out.

These villages at some point formed into states under a paramount chief or "king" (the terminology is irrelevant here). Whether the reasons for integration into a state were economic (cooperation for terracing, harvesting, irrigation) or internal political and social processes (population density leading to specialization, the emergence of dominant lineages), or external pressure, or all three, also does not matter here. In some ways, however, the process represents a modification of the patronage system, in which the head of a major family (a lineage) extends protection (and authority) over family, clan, village, or tribe. This patronage takes the form of a reciprocal arrangement in which in return for protection, favors, justice, or any form of assistance, the head of the society accumulates increasing power and income, since his "subjects" pay through gifts and services. With the formation of a state, this authority becomes institutionalized.

Thus, a state is said to exist where this system of patronage becomes organized to a certain degree,[1] including, typically, a fixed territory, a fixed population, and the exertion of absolute authority within both of these. The chief ceases to function as the pinnacle of a lineage-based system and increasingly becomes a ruler over a group of subjects. Power once exercised through lineage structures becomes exercised through officers loyal to the king himself. Economic transactions between ruler and ruled become formalized in taxes and other payments in kind. Monarchic rule is typically exercised from an urban center which is often expressly built or resettled by the king to emphasize his independence; it becomes *his* city, the royal city, and often quite sparsely populated, since it is occupied largely by officials and contains storehouses, administrative buildings, perhaps a royal temple and, of course, strong fortifications. Various city-kingdoms of such a kind inevitably enter into diplomatic relations, including that common "extension of diplomacy," warfare, by means of which the territory and the population ruled by a king can be extended and his power and influence increased.

Social stratification is a key feature of state formation, and directly relevant to writing. An urban society is parasitic and differentiated. It derives its income from the work of the rural population, and within itself comprises all the specialized functions of state administration. The state increases the need for writing as part of its rationalization of administrative functions; but at the same time its mechanisms concentrate those functions into the hands of a specialized class. The scribal profession is thus created, and grows, specifically as an instrument of state administration, at a certain stage of its development.

A network of cities, each with dependent rural areas, ruled by a king (or "mayor," if you prefer) was the common pattern in Palestine in the Middle and Late Bronze Age (roughly, second millennium), and reasserted itself in the Iron Age. The same pattern is found in neighboring regions of Syria and Transjordan. Such kingdoms, often at war with each other, vied to extend their domains over other cities. Israel (i.e., Samaria) succeeded for a time in extending its territory (or sphere of control) over neighboring cities in central Palestine and over the Jordan; Damascus also occupied areas within the same territory from time to time (and thus, for instance, the city of Dan was occasionally "Israelite" and occasionally "Aramean," as, no doubt, was Hazor). Whether cities such as Megiddo, Hazor, and Gezer were rebuilt by kings of Samaria or even Jerusalem, or were at first independent city-states incorporated for a while into a more extensive state remains to be decided. Similar questions can be asked concerning Lachish, Arad, Hebron, and Beersheba: were they always part of a kingdom of Judah, ruled from Jerusalem, or were they rather for a time incorporated into the Jerusalem sphere of influence before later becoming part of another state called Edom? The geographical extent of a state is determined by the answer to two fundamental questions: for the rural territory, who enjoyed the surplus? (who collected the taxes?) and for fortified cities, which ruler's soldiers comprised the garrison inside? The size of the kingdoms of Israel and Judah, and the length of time these kingdoms persisted as centralized states, is, of course, crucially important in determining the possibility of a large scribal class and the origins of a canonizing process. It is also, however, very hard to evaluate and is not indicated by simply coloring large areas of the map.

For the problem for historians is that without accepting as basic the canonized record of the history of monarchic Israel and Judah, there remain many unanswered questions about the antiquity and extent of both kingdoms, and especially Judah. Whereas once the reign of Solomon was once regarded as a time of unparalleled cultural achievement, of "enlightenment," the very existence, let alone the extent, of a single kingdom uniting Israel and Judah before the ninth century is now uncertain as the weight of evidence shifts from the canonized narrative to archaeological data. The kingdoms of Israel and Judah no doubt *did* need written records, and we need not doubt the existence of state scribes in Samaria or Jerusalem. But Samaria vanished even as a quasi-independent royal city in the eighth century, while Jerusalem, which may have become a significant capital only in the eighth century,[2] was quickly subject to Assyrian vassalage and lasted for only a few generations before its ruling classes were deported. How far do canonizing processes develop in these circumstances?

In the case of Judah there are special difficulties, because the archaeology of Jerusalem is able to tell us very little about the origins of the city as a Judean capital. But it seems to have grown in population gradually during the ninth and eighth centuries, possibly because it was free from Assyrian threats (by paying tribute to the Assyrian king). If it was originally only a royal (temple-garrison-administrative) city, Jerusalem seems to have become a major market center as well. From the time of Hezekiah (late eighth century), there is archaeological evidence of a much enlarged city, perhaps as big as 150 acres.[3] Certainly, the canon has preserved an account of this ruler as a pious, successful, and powerful monarch. But he may in fact have been one of the first, and certainly one of the last, semi-independent Judean monarchs until Hasmonean times. His territory was reduced to little more than the city of Jerusalem itself (and the population growth in the city may be the result of an influx of refugees from other Judean cities). During the seventh century, although the semblance of independence may have been maintained, Jerusalem was effectively under close Assyrian control. The end of Assyria as an empire saw a brief power vacuum. The reign of Josiah, who, it is speculated, may have had imperial designs on other parts of Palestine, was extinguished by the Egyptian king, and his successors were extinguished by the Babylonians when the vassal monarchs of Jerusalem finally rebelled once too often.

What can be deduced from this about the literary activity taking place in Samaria and Jerusalem? We are entitled to assume that documentary texts such as diplomatic and administrative letters, tax records, treaties, cultic texts, and perhaps annals, were filed and preserved in well-kept archives. The records of the kingdoms of Judah and Israel, then, did not vanish without literary trace. Foreign conquerors may destroy a city and even remove most of its population, but they do not necessarily destroy administrative archives. For this there is an obvious reason. If the conquerors intend to govern the conquered territory, or in any event to permit it to deliver the necessary revenue, it will be advantageous to have records of population, property, legal records, even law codes. Royal inscriptions, of course, may be broken up, but archives have little propaganda value and are more useful if retained. We ought to reckon that written materials remained in Samaria and in Jerusalem after the fall of these cities to Assyrians and Babylonians respectively. The question is, however, whether such materials constituted literary works that were potentially or actually canonized. Here there seems less likelihood. If we could identify with reasonable certainty any such works in the extant canons, doubts could be removed. But we cannot. The problem lies, of course, in using the canonized history as a tool for evaluating the antiquity of the canonical writings.

A word may need to be said about temples and sanctuaries. The canonical picture is that Judah had one legitimate sanctuary, the Jerusalem temple built by Solomon. It allows, however, that there were other temples within the territories of these kingdoms, which seems probable. In Mesopotamia and Egypt, as we saw earlier, temples were the homes of scribal communities, who recorded a good deal of economic information as well as copying and composing religious (cultic and theological) texts. While the Jerusalem temple in the monarchic period was almost certainly a royal sanctuary and unlikely to have exercised any independent economic functions, its priests may have been maintained by payments to the temple from the populace rather than (or perhaps, as well as) by royal support. The Jerusalem temple, or its priests, could well have owned land, and thus needed to keep economic records. Whether the sanctuary functioned, as it did in the Second Temple period, as a treasury, is unclear, as is virtually everything about this building. However, with the demise of the Jerusalem sanctuary, and indeed with the demise of other sanctuaries from time to time at the hands of Judean or Assyrian kings, it is possible that records of the cult and liturgy of these sanctuaries were somehow preserved, possibly written for the first time. But even with the Jerusalem temple destroyed, did the local cult(s) and cultic centers continue as they had throughout the monarchic period? Quite possibly, but how far they possessed written records is hard to know. It is clear enough, however, that the subsequent canonization of any literature from such centers, if and when this took place, arises from their rediscovery and incorporation into other works or collections and not because they themselves generated a canonizing process during the monarchic period.

Under the Babylonians Judah itself continued, as far as we can tell, as a political entity with a Babylonian-appointed governor. However the Babylonians administered it, the royal archives of Judah would have remained in or near Jerusalem (the book of Kings suggests Mizpah[4]), and the local governor would have employed scribes. Taxes, records, and correspondence were still needed. These scribes, who were presumably Judean, carried on from the monarchic period and into the Persian period. There was thus in all probability a real scribal continuity in Judah, though it is unlikely that in these circumstances any Judean literary classics would have been officially condoned, even had they existed at that time. The official culture of these scribes is an extremely interesting and important issue. They would have continued to write in the language of Judah (Hebrew) but also in Aramaic, the language adopted by the Assyrians and Babylonians (and then the Persians) for the western parts of their empires. It was the Assyrians who had created the political map of the Levant, and both in Samaria and Judah during the seventh century, their influence upon the scribal activity in both cities must have been considerable. Long after Nineveh was destroyed, Jerusalem scribes will have continued to use words and forms that had entered the diplomatic language of the Assyrian empire centuries earlier, including influences from that other great imperial language, Akkadian. There is certainly no reason to suppose a great linguistic revolution in the sixth century among either peasants or scribes, and, unfortunately, we cannot date any literature to the monarchic period on the basis of Aramaic or Akkadian linguistic or literary conventions. Scribes are, after all, notoriously conservative, especially in the absence of any imposed novelty.

The rupture in Judah's scribal history did not come, then, with the fall of

Jerusalem. Nor was its continuity preserved among the deported Judeans in Babylonia, among which most of the scribes were probably found. It is known that many of these deportees formed close communities-in-exile; it is not known, but unlikely, that these deportees took with them any written records, or composed large-scale literary works. Indeed, it is likely that many with the necessary administrative experience became scribes and officials in Babylon, serving other kings and, indeed, other deities. The fact that the Jewish canon nevertheless draws the line of continuity from monarchy through exile to hierocracy in the Persian period shows either that the Judean scribal tradition that persisted throughout the sixth century was rudimentary or that it was overwhelmed by an immigrant scribal culture under the Persians. Perhaps both; at all events, the new scribal elite saw its origin in exile, but claimed their exilic culture as the continuation of the old monarchic culture, or rather an idealized form of it, these exiles bearing the mantle of the real "Israel." Exilic experience was, of course, no part of the indigenous Judean scribal tradition. But the extent to which the scriptural canon reflects an experience of coming into Judah from elsewhere as a pure race, under threat of contamination from the indigenous population, and yet representing it as the experience of "all Israel" shows that the real rupture in the Judean scribal culture occurred not with the deportation to Babylon but with the immigration back into Judah of a new population that ideologically (as well as economically) supplanted the remnants of the "old" Israel. If we may generalize, the canonized history is a colonial, immigrant one, not an indigenous one. In terms of English history, we would call it Norman rather than Saxon; just as American (canonized) history used to begin with Columbus.

In conclusion, then, the state of the evidence is too incomplete for the monarchic period for us to be able to declare how far literary canonizing had reached, if indeed it had reached anywhere. There is, I would suggest, enough ground for doubt that any substantial literary (as opposed to documentary) writing had been accomplished, let alone any process of canonizing. The emergence of a substantial corpus of classical literary works is unlikely in this epoch, because of the monarchic states' lack of a tradition (they no doubt assumed the tradition of the lowland cities), its brevity (less than two centuries for Israel, less than three for Judah), and the imperial surveillance by the Assyrians, to which scribal activity was no doubt subject for most of the time. Even had such an improbable canonizing process begun, it has been interrupted and reformed entirely by the activity of the new immigrant administration that ran the province of Judah under the Persians. If there were a history of canonizing in monarchic Israel and Judah, it cannot be written.

THE PERSIAN PERIOD

From the last third of the sixth century Judah was a Persian colony, created, populated, and regulated by imperial policies.[5] The goals of the Persian kings were to develop their territories, not in order to benefit their populations, but to increase the revenue necessary for the upkeep of the empire which was at first expanding, and to create complaisant local populations, especially in border areas, to strengthen the frontiers. Accordingly, Cyrus announced that several groups should be allowed (encouraged? compelled?) to return to the areas from which they had been taken, and temples were to be rebuilt at imperial expense. The transfer of population from Babylonia to Judah did not happen immediately or suddenly, but seems to have occurred over at least a century and probably longer. There is archaeological evidence of the building of new settlements to increase agricultural production in Judah, many on new sites.[6] During this time the balance between immigrants and native populations must have steadily moved in favor of the former, though the exact proportions cannot be known. However, the immigrants clearly had the explicit support of the Empire and would have assumed the governing roles.

A degree of conflict between the two population elements must have been inevitable. The canonical accounts in Ezra and Nehemiah make no direct reference to any such conflict; but these same accounts identify "Israel" with the immigrants and do not even seem to acknowledge the existence of any other group. Conflict in these accounts is with "outsiders" (Samarians). The theory of J. Weinberg suggests that the immigrants formed into a society within a society, a coalition of temple authorities and local aristocrats; this he calls a "citizen-Temple community."[7] His thesis is that over time this community grew so as to embrace the entire population, so that the values and privileges of the elite slowly became the values of more of the society. The importance of Weinberg's thesis is that he sees the community as embracing both priestly and lay interests, an alliance between the authorized priestly caste and the entrepreneurial classes. Whether or not Weinberg is correct, it is surely important to recognize that prominent in the province were a number of wealthy individuals who were sent, or who agreed, to go from Babylonia (or elsewhere) to Judah for the purpose of developing and exploiting its economic potential. These persons, not necessarily part of the governing class, and certainly not of the priestly class, constitute an increasingly important third element—not only in the economic makeup, as landowners, traders, and investors, but, more importantly for our purposes, in the literate society of the province.[8] During most of the Persian period, their interests probably remained broadly similar to those of the priesthood. But with the increase in trade and the advent of the Hellenistic kingdoms and of *poleis* into the region, a tension between their interests and those of the priesthood can be detected (the "Maccabean revolt" seems to have been partly a symptom of this conflict). But it would be wrong to oversimplify what may have been a more complex set of social negotiations between different priestly and lay groups. For immigration into Judah was not a single nor a homogeneous process. Over centuries, and in fact throughout the Second Temple period, both migration into and out of Judah was considerable, and within Judah there came to be people of many different geographical origins.

The building of a temple in Jerusalem was not commenced under Cyrus. Exactly when it was completed is uncertain; the canonical accounts say that it was commenced under Darius and completed a century or so later (depending on the date of Ezra). The delay may have been due to Persian procrastination or to local opposition, or both. For who was to run this temple? The local Judean priesthood(s) or immigrant priests? Also, perhaps, there was the question, which deity or deities? Yahweh had been one of the local deities, and he was duly installed, though as a different kind of god. Another initiative of Darius was the promulgation of the "king's law," which in effect meant not a single law for the entire empire but a basic law that incorporated local variations. We know of the case of one Udjahorresnet, an Egyptian priest, who was sent to Egypt to restore the "houses of life" which were scribal schools.[9] This may have been in connection with the codification of cultic regulations; in any event it is known that Darius had the traditional Egyptian law codified and written up in Aramaic and Demotic Egyptian.[10]

Was there, then, a Judean law codified at this time? According to the account in Nehemiah 8:1, Ezra the scribe brought a scroll of the "law of Moses" from the Temple and had it read out. Scholars are undecided whether this lawbook may have been Deuteronomy, or the "priestly code," or even the Pentateuch in some earlier form. In chapter 6 this episode will be discussed in more detail, but it can be said already that none of these candidates plausibly fits, *in its canonical form,* a realistic basis for such a law. But this is not to deny that Darius's initiative was carried out in Judah, nor that a set of laws was provided. If it was, and if the Temple was successfully completed and in operation, then two important unifying mechanisms were at last in place. Over the following centuries, this temple, and its priesthood, assumed the political and symbolic power that paralleled that of the king at an earlier period, while a common law provided a basis for ethnic identity within an imperial context.

Perhaps we can go further. How far did Judean "law" extend? Ezra 7:25 has Artaxerxes commissioning Ezra to "judge all the people in the satrapy of Beyond the River who know the laws of your god; and you shall teach those who do not know them." Without being required to accept the historicity of an instruction from Artaxerxes to Ezra, or indeed the mission of Ezra himself, the narrative implies that the law of Judah was recognized beyond the province itself. The evidence of the Samaritan Pentateuch is strong support for the suggestion that Samarians[11] embraced this law, while even the Judean colony in Elephantine, writing for instructions to both Samaria and Judah, seem to have acknowledged that in claiming Judean ethnicity they were subject to the legislation of their homeland.

The territory mentioned in the commission to Ezra, comprising the satrapy in which Judah was located, corresponds with the origin of the canonical definition of Israel's ideal geographical extent, namely the maximal territory promised to Abraham (Gen. 15:18) and the territory ruled by Solomon (1 Kings 4:21). Did the Persians acknowledge the validity of Jewish laws over those who wished to acknowledge Judean ethnicity west of the Euphrates? Would it include Babylonia, which, prior to Xerxes, had been part of that satrapy, and which continued to contain many claiming that ethnicity? Despite the absence of strong evidence for such a Jewish law, there is some circumstantial evidence to commend it, including the extent and size of the Jewish diaspora.

The construction of a temple in Jerusalem by the Persians had economic reasons as well.[12] It is likely that the Jerusalem temple was used as the means of raising imperial taxes. For it was the custom under the Babylonian rulers (and in this respect, as in almost everything else, the Persians followed the custom) for temples to be used to collect taxes. A tax to the temple was compulsory, and from this revenue, the ruler extracted income. The Persians required taxes in the form of precious metal (mostly silver), of which the payments made were then melted down; as coinage was introduced, the metal could then be minted. The process was under the supervision of a royal official, but where there were temples, there was no separate imperial tax raising system. The temple became a storehouse not only for religious taxes, but for imperial taxes.

The relevance of this to canonizing is that taxation (poll taxes, property taxes, levies on trade) is one of the major preoccupations of scribal activity. The weighing, recording, and accounting of such monies, and the basis on which it was accumulated, was the main instrument of imperial government of the provinces. Accordingly, temple officials (probably Levites) acted not merely as religious functionaries but as guards of the temple treasury and custodians of imperial revenue. A fairly large scribal class worked with or at the temple.

The successful conquest of Egypt by Darius and the increasing attention given to Asia Minor and Greece by Xerxes and his successors were also opening up trade across Judah, and this was increasingly dominated by Phoenicians and Greeks. Attention should be drawn to the causes and effects of this trade.

First, it was Persian policy to stimulate wealth creation in the satrapies to fund the empire. Second, the introduction of coinage (whether or not coinage was the compulsory form of tax payments) facilitated speculation and investment; wealth was increasingly vested in coinage, and was thus more mobile. As a result, the temple, as a repository of well-guarded wealth, could function as not only a bank but also as an investor alongside the private wealth that trade and investment were accumulating. One of the ways, incidentally, in which wealth could be invested was in the running of large estates producing cash crops, a development that is reflected in a good deal of "prophetic" literature. Such estates could be run by debt-bonded peasants or even slaves: new kind of wealth, independent of imperial or temple patronage, developed through trading and investment.[13] As a result of these developments the class of wealthy, relatively leisured people grew—literate, cosmopolitan and demanding education. The scribal class had no more monopoly of learning. They did, however, have a source of income among these people, and the kind of education that they acquired is likely to have been based on scribal principles. The encroachment of Greek forms of education, of course, provided an alternative. But more of that presently. We should nevertheless expect to see alongside scribal literature and canonizing the emergence of new forms of writing. How, or whether, the educated lay classes canonized *their* literature can only be through the provision of libraries or, indirectly, by affecting the numbers of copies of books that scribes (who might increasingly be privately employed) were called upon to produce.

But what of the intellectual culture of this period? Judean society during the Persian period was colonial, and this characterization can be spelled out in a number of ways. It meant political loyalty on the part of the local rulers, who owed their high position to imperial appointment; but also it provoked a desire to discover some symbols of national identity consistent with the status of a province. Colonial regimes also develop loyalties to their adopted land, especially if they come to believe (as may have been to a large extent true) that their ancestors belonged here. For the Persian kings, temples were not only tax-raising institutions but also symbols of ethnic identity, and no doubt the Jerusalem temple functioned in this way. The law and language of Judah were other symbols of this kind. The high priest could serve as a national figurehead, without compromising political loyalty. The wealth and importance of the Jerusalem temple, which can be seen very clearly reflected in the canonical literature, enhanced its cultural-political function. The size and influence of the temple scribal community, as already observed, surely exceeded that serving the governor, who was a Persian appointee, though usually a Judean.[14] It will be among the scribes of the Jerusalem temple, then, that the impetus for a literature of national ideology is likely to have developed. The temple of Yahweh, and the Judean/Jewish law which supposedly emanated from him, identified the Jewish *ethnos,* in Judah and beyond.

The beginning of the canonizing process that finally created the Jewish scriptural canon can largely be attributed, then, to the temple scribes; and here is an additional reason for placing the process in the Persian period; it is temple and law, not monarch, that symbolizes the leadership and identity of Israel. Kings exist in the past, to be mostly condemned, and replaced by the great King worshiped in the temple. There is also a close association between cultic and social law, brought together (in the case of Leviticus especially) under the theory of a divinely owned land leased to the chosen *ethnos* and kept pure by the proper payment of temple taxes as well as the observance of what we would call "social" regulations.

It is, incidentally, likely that the favor with which the cult of this deity (known as Yahweh but also as Elyon, El, Elohim) was obviously viewed by the Persians is due to their recognition of many common elements with the Achaemenid religion of Zoroaster, and that they viewed (and did the priests of Jerusalem?) Yahweh as the Judean manifestation of the one great high god Ahura Mazda. This is also not irrelevant to the question of canon, because the deity functioned as an important symbol of the identity of Judean society also, and a good deal of the literature to be canonized will focus on the relationship between him and the *ethnos* (Judaism) to whom he gives an identity.

The one missing element so far in this historical reconstruction is commonly overlooked: the contribution of Samaria. Because the canonical account dismisses the kingdom of Israel and brands the post-722 population as non-Israelite in religion and at the very least racially mixed, biblical scholarship is tempted to do the same, and, when identifying "northern" or non-Judean features in what is clearly the Judean canon, assigns such material to pre-722. The book of Nehemiah also identifies Samarians as opponents of his work. But the connections between Samaria and Jerusalem in the Persian period must have been closer and more harmonious than the common scholarly interpretation allows. First, there is the fact of the Samari[t]an Pentateuch. On the reasonable assumption that the Pentateuch in its Samaritan form does not predate 722, an explanation for this is needed. Possibly (but improbably), the Samaritans are a Judean sect having no pedigree from Samaria, and only in the Greco-Roman period distinguishing themselves from Judaism ever more distinctly. But that supposition still leaves the question of Samarian religion in the Persian period unanswered. The Elephantine letter addressed to Jerusalem and Samaria[15] betrays no awareness of a rift between the two cities, and we cannot think that the Persian authorities would have easily tolerated such a rift. How did the Persians treat Samaria? We have no extant literary sources relevant to this question.

In the absence of evidence, we must make some assumptions. The usual assumption is that Samaria was cool if not hostile to Jerusalem. But it has also become generally recognized that a formal rift between the two did not occur much before the Seleucid period at the earliest. We know that a Samaritan temple was built later at Shechem. Before that, either an earlier Samarian temple was also built, or the Jerusalem temple served Samaria also. The "all-Israelite" claims made in the Judean canon suggest a Persian context for the inclusion of Samaria with Judah in a single religious community,[16] while the anti-Samarian polemic in the books of Kings points to a *growing* rift between the two societies/communities, and Nehemiah indicates a more serious rift. In Kings loyalty to the Jerusalem temple is the issue, in Nehemiah opposition to the status of Jerusalem. Since in this book we are dealing with canonizing in Judah, we are not obliged to consider Samari[t]an scriptures at all. But clearly the relationship between Samaria and Jerusalem cannot be overlooked, nor the Judean canon's account of Samaria be taken as reliable.

The view taken here is that Judah and Samaria were closely linked during the Persian period and that the canonizing of the Torah, and possibly some early stages in the canonizing of the prophetic canon, betray that relationship. The line of argumentation here is rather crucial, for it underpins the contention that the non- or anti-Samari[t]an character of many of the Jewish (Judean) canons *postdates* a rivalry, if not a rift, between the two cities, and places the weight of the canonizing process firmly in the mid-Second Temple period.

As far as the canonizing process is concerned, then, the Persian period requires the existence of a scribal class engaged in duties related to the temple in Jerusalem as well as to the political government (and the two appear to converge); the introduction of an immigrant elite and the problems of self-identity which both it and also the indigenous population probably felt; and the existence of an *ethnos* (Hebrew עם) organized by law. During this time the communities in Judah and Samaria were closely connected. What the Persians regarded as "Judean" religion and law were possibly recognized by them throughout the satrapy of "Beyond the River" (from the Euphrates to the borders of Egypt and probably including Babylon) and, if so, not only is the existence of "Judean" communities throughout this area in succeeding centuries explained, but also the canon's geographical description of "Israel" as stretching from the Nile to the Euphrates. How else would a historian account for the distribution of those whose ethnic identity was linked to the Jerusalem (and/or Samarian?) cult? Finally, although it is widely doubted that the economic prosperity of the province was very great, growing trade gradually saw the rise of a wealthy lay class. But these developments came to fruition only in the Ptolemaic period.

THE HELLENISTIC PERIOD

The advent of Alexander the Great came after a period in which Greek influence had been increasing in Judah. It brought Judah under the control of the Ptolemies in Egypt, and with that increasing bureaucracy, increased contact with Judeans in Egypt, and a broader use of Greek as a lingua franca alongside Aramaic. In the economy of Judah, bureaucracy extended to the lowest levels, with governmental officers operating even within the villages, while the introduction of Greek-speaking officials increased. Judah was no longer a small province in a large empire but had become again part of what Egypt had always regarded as its own backyard, while at the same time, a new wave of colonization brought Judah face to face directly with the political forms of Hellenization rather than with Greek culture: the Greek language, trade, and of course, education.[17]

The Ptolemaic rule in Judah is, unfortunately, obscurely lit by the sources. The succeeding Seleucid period, by contrast, is well documented. The continuing struggle between the two kingdoms probably had its effect in Judah, with different groups taking different sides. The war that broke out in 167 B.C.E., which led to a century of so of (varying degrees of) independence, was induced directly by the measures of the Seleucid king Antiochus IV, but his actions were prompted by rivalry for the high priesthood, and with it control over the temple finances. A similar struggle (or perhaps the same struggle in another form) was between those who wanted to create Hellenistic political structures in Jerusalem, making it a self-governing *polis* with its own citizen body, its schools and temple, and those who regarded such a move as destructive of the traditional political structures. The argument is not about "Judaism" or "Hellenism" here but about different definitions of Judaism. In fact, although politically the battle was won by those opposing Antiochus, the ensuing Hasmonean dynasty hardly rejected Hellenistic political structures at all, while Judaism in the diaspora accommodated a good deal of Hellenistic culture without such upheavals. But the political struggle itself led to a renewed crisis of definition: with a formally independent Jewish state, what *Jewish* structures were appropriate to a now independent nation? And given the extent of disagreement among various Judean groups, compromise was not always possible.[18] The Hasmoneans supported one group after another. But they also adopted the high priesthood themselves, and promoted the idea of Judean nationhood though reviving the use of Hebrew (and in an ancient script), and, in all

probability, promoting a Judean library and educational system that was intended to control the Graecization of Judeans and create an *individual* Judean
identity. Here we can see important implications for canonizing: a political
regime that has a need and a motive for *political canonizing*, which means the
promotion of certain texts in the life of Judah. The liturgical calendar and the
regulation of the cult were standardized, and to accompany this went a policy
of extending the boundaries of Judah into the "canonical" territories of Galilee,
the coastal plain, Edom (Idumea), and some parts of Transjordan, ideologically
to recreate the "golden age" and politically to keep the physical encroachment
of Hellenism in check, to ensure the integrity of "Judaism" throughout the
Levant and, of course, to build an empire (this is what all dynasties wish to do).
Under the Hasmoneans, then, emerges a "Judaism" that needs a "canon."

But while it seems that in this period conditions were optimal for the
more widespread promotion of a canon, it cannot be simply said that Judaism became the religion of a book. Almost all these terms contain error.
There was no single "Judaism," although there was a political Judaism represented by the rulers; Judaism was not necessarily or in every case understood as a religion; and there were forms of Judaism for whom canon meant
little, or for whom other canons were in force.

Jewish/Judean nationalism was only one of a number of nationalisms
among the nations and territories now transformed into Hellenistic kingdoms.
In Egypt, Syria, and Babylon as well, ancient mythologies and histories were
being written up, but in Greek (Berossus for Babylonia, Philo Byblus for
Phoenicia, Manetho for Egypt). Universal historiography was, indeed, a genre
probably inspired by the already canonical Herodotus.[19] The concerns of
Greek colonies and Hellenistic kingdoms—to nurture the Greek canon and to
introduce education as a means of inculcating Greek culture among the populace (not only among scribes)—had a similar paradoxical effect, being both
copied and challenged. The explicit *idea* of a literary canon and the foundation of libraries and schools of study, such as in Alexandria (see chapter 2),
stimulated the importance of canon among the many cultures and societies absorbing Greek culture, prompting in reaction a wider education based on non-
Greek classics, either in place of, or alongside, Greek classics. Among these,
of course, were the national histories. To the Greek notion of its own superi-
ority the Levantine and Oriental cultures opposed their own greater longevity
and, indeed, the Greeks came to respect the ancient cultures of the Orient. In
Judah this process had no doubt begun before the Hasmoneans, and, interestingly, its authors used not Greek but Hebrew (and in a few cases, Aramaic).
There are two reasons that can be given for this. One is that Judah was relatively more isolated from the Greek language than these other regions (which

is true); the other is that while Babylonia and Egypt (and Syria?) had considerable ancient bodies of literature in non-Greek languages (Akkadian, accessible no doubt through Aramaic translation), Judah, a rather small and not very ancient society, did not. But such writings as it had were made to compete, and of their great antiquity no doubt every educated Judean was both convinced and proud.

THE ROMAN PERIOD

Herod's policy seems to have been to unite the Jews throughout the empire under his kingship, to promote the status of Judaism everywhere, to create a temple worthy of Judaism, and to increase revenue by further encouraging temple pilgrimage. But the politically sharpened sense of Jewish identity could not tolerate a Roman regime, even in the form of a client king, though antagonism toward Herod and the Romans must also be understood as a function of inner-Jewish dissent and rivalry for power. Among both those supporting the Romans and also those opposing, there were differences. The destruction of the temple, hardly after its renovations were complete, and later the loss of Judah itself, led to the emergence and the ultimate victory of a form of Judaism that accommodated the loss of both. Rabbinic Judaism is based on the idea of personal holiness, in which temple and land are both transformed into symbols. The role of literature in this transformation is considerable, and rabbinic Judaism is a religion of books. With its installation, a new and open process of canonizing starts, beyond the scope of this book.

CHAPTER 5

Judean Scribes, Schools, Archives, and Libraries

Having examined scribes in relevant ancient cultures,[1] and surveyed the social history of Judah, the one remaining preparatory exercise is to consider the place and the extent of canonizing institutions in Judean society: scribal and other schools, archives, and libraries. There is no doubt that during the history of Judah, all these institutions came into existence. A history of canonizing, however, has to consider the crucial question of when we can adequately document them. We must, of course, be careful to avoid here the danger of circularity. Decisions about the date of emergence of all these institutions will obviously have a bearing on the dating of the literature itself, which obliges us to exercise caution in using canonical data that cannot be independently dated. For that reason, direct statements in the canonical writings are of little use, indirect evidence of slightly more use.

SCRIBAL SCHOOLS

Scribes were in large measure insulated from the majority of the population: physically (they lived in cities), economically (they were supported by the taxpayer), and culturally. At a royal court, perhaps even a provincial governor's court, traditional storytelling (the cabaret of the ancient world) may furnish a bridge between the two parts of the society; meeting-places such as the city gate or the market also afford social contact and cultural exchange, and in general we must not rule out all meaningful contact between popular culture and the world of the scribe. The emergence of a significant artisan and merchant class during the Second Temple period afforded the opportunity for social class mobility (in both directions) and a medium for the negotiation of cultural values between peasants, "middle classes," and the governing classes. But these contacts played little part in the forming of the scribal identity.

The scribal duties, as has been seen, traditionally embraced a range of activities, amounting to a good deal of ideological control: archiving (possession and control of the present), historiography (possession and control of the past), didactic writing (maintenance of social values among the elite), predictive writing (possession and control of the future).[2] The traditional ethos of the scribal class itself generated works of instruction, speculation on the meaning of life, social ethics, cosmology, and manticism.

Hence in Judah, as elsewhere in the ancient Near East, the scribes can be identified as "intellectuals," or as "sages,"[3] or as "the wise," and especially responsible for "wisdom literature." A succinct profile of the Judean scribe has been drawn by M. Weinfeld:

> persons who had at their command a vast reservoir of literary material, who had developed and were capable of developing a literary technique of their own, those experienced in literary composition, and skilled with the pen and the book: these authors must consequently have been the *soferim-hakamim*.[4]

But Weinfeld is talking about the Deuteronomic school, which he places in seventh-century Judah. Yet is it possible, given the foregoing historical sketch, to take for granted as Weinfeld does that at this time the scribal class had reached the point of sophistication achieved in Mesopotamia and Egypt, and had developed its own distinctive tradition? Such an accomplishment implies the existence of scribal schools, or at least an extensive educational system, in which not just the writing of Hebrew, but the reading of other languages and mastery of diplomatic forms, principles of archiving, and so on would be passed on. At some point the number of scribes and variety of their functions makes the provision of a rationalized educational system inevitable. We have seen that the Mesopotamian and Egyptian civilizations possessed scribal schools. But whether in monarchic Judah such schools existed—or, if they existed, reached more than a rudimentary state—is hard to tell. What evidence do we actually have of literacy, of administrative complexity, and of scribal education in monarchic Israel and Judah, whose cities, compared with those of Egypt and Babylon, and even with those of Late Bronze Age Palestine, were minute?[5]

There is sharp disagreement on this question. Part of this debate, of course, hangs on the value placed on the canonical texts' own accounts. How far do their accounts of state functionaries, for instance, reflect monarchic practice or the later practice of their time? It is indeed widely assumed that a scribal class did at some stage function within Judean society, and an important piece of evidence given for that is the existence of "wisdom literature," which purportedly represents their ethos. But Norman Whybray[6] has argued strongly against the notion of a professional class of scribe (*hakam, sofer*) in Judah, and thus against the existence of any scribal schools, until the time of ben Sira in the second century B.C.E.. (It is important to point out that "school" is being used in this chapter for an educational institution and not a group of like-minded scribes; the term is ambiguously used in biblical scholarship). Instead, Whybray opted for the term "intellectual tradition." With Blenkinsopp,[7] however, we ought to doubt whether an "intellectual tradition" can exist without some social mechanisms to support it.[8] Would we have a modern intellectual tradition without schools, colleges, universities, established theaters, or publishing houses? Moreover, intellectual traditions without institutional support (recording, copying, editing, archiving) are unable to canonize. Traditions do not float in the air. Resisting Whybray's notion does not, however, mean accepting the establishment of scribal schools in the monarchic period.

At the other extreme, E. W. Heaton's recent discussion of Jewish schools comes to the conclusion that the canon is the product of the scribal school system. But he approaches the matter by a quite different route. He takes as his starting point ben Sira and Qoheleth and works backward to Solomon.[9] He notes that ben Sira invites his readers to attend his school (*bet midrash*, 51:23), possibly even without payment (51:25). The range of topics in ben Sira's book, however, makes it clear that he is not now training scribes, but offering an education to any who would acquire the Judean form of worldly wisdom, including the national literature, practical etiquette, sound ethics, piety, and so on. As Heaton says, the conservative scribal values "came to color the whole ethos of educated society," the "mobile middle class."[10]

This is an important insight: where education extends beyond the scribal school, it is still likely to be the scribes who educate. And so while it is pretty obvious that ben Sira is acquainted with Greek culture, his curriculum owes a great deal to the traditional scribal school, and he himself had almost certainly enjoyed a career as a professional administrator. But surely the existence of schools for non-scribes implies a school education for scribes as well. Accordingly Heaton infers a scribal school education in Judah. It seems a reasonable step to move then to a description of scribal education in Egyptian and Mesopotamian cultures, and posit the existence of libraries, including a "Temple Seminary,"[11] preserving the literary tradition of monarchic Judah beyond the demise of the state. But this entails quite a leap in time, and a considerable leap in social context. Moreover, the appeal to Egypt and Mesopotamia is rather too superficial. First of all, the most obvious and direct parallel to ben Sira's schooling is Hellenistic, and before automatically turning elsewhere this needs to be considered. Second, the scribal school system of Egypt and Mesopotamia at the time of ben Sira ought to be considered. In fact, it seems that in these cultures the old canonized texts were still being taught and copied, though the administration of Seleucid Babylon and Ptolemaic Egypt was being conducted in Greek (and Aramaic in Babylon). But both these civilizations had accumulated a vast canon of very ancient works. At the time of the Judean monarchy, both had been more advanced and more populous states and in existence over a very much longer time span than Judah. It is entirely misleading to jump from second-century B.C.E. Seleucid Judah over half a millennium via "Egypt and Babylon"!

Heaton is probably right to assume that canons emerge from the interests of an intellectual elite, and, indeed, to assume that in a small monarchic state this elite consists of the scribal class. This recognition is an important gain against vague formulations about "Israel" and "communities of faith," or "traditions" or "schools" in the sense of "schools of thought" or "groups of disciples," which float on the surface of academic discourse without any anchor in a political, economic, and social system. But it is also curious that in assigning the contents of the Jewish scriptural canon to scribal schools, he is not exploiting the distinction he has recognized between scribal and non-scribal schools, or perhaps we should say education for scribes and education for non-scribes. For some of the writings in the canon look more plausibly to be the products of a non-scribal schooling. This was already recognized by Morton Smith, who assigned some works to the educated lay aristocracy, the "gentry."[12] The reason for this may be a bias about dating: the possibility that some canonized works could be so late is perhaps too easily dismissed, despite the case of Daniel. The fact is, however, that scribal and non-scribal schools clearly existed in Judah in the Hellenistic period, and scribal schools probably grew up in the Persian period. But for an earlier period even a scribal school is a hypothesis. What evidence is there for this hypothesis?

One of the indices of scribal activity is the complexity of state administration. David Jamieson-Drake[13] has offered an anthropological approach to scribes and schools, based precisely on such considerations: a wide range of nonliterary data and some sociological modeling; population size and concentration; luxury goods and monumental architecture; in an attempt to discover at what point in its development a state needs, and can sustain, an administrative class. He concludes that from the eighth century on Judah became a fully developed monarchic state, but that literacy did not spread very far. Of the seven sites in Judah from which we have evidence of writing, Lachish, Arad, and Meṣad Hashavyahu were forts built by the Jerusalem regime; while Gibeon, Tell Beit Mirsim, and En-gedi were industrial sites and part of the economic system centering, he suggests, on Jerusalem; while Ramat Rahel was a royal palace. All the writing is associated with government and thus with a specialized administrative class. We do have scribes in several places. But on Jamieson-Drake's analysis, there is no likelihood of literacy much beyond this not very large class.

What literature did the monarchic scribal class produce? There is certainly evidence of administrative texts from Israel and Judah.[14] We have some ostraca from Samaria, totaling some 66 sherds, probably dating from eighth century B.C.E. and recording deliveries of wine and oil. Although they were not found *in situ,* but had been used as a foundation layer for subsequent building, they probably represent originally part of an accounting system, and presumably an archive. But the area the transactions cover is rather small (a radius of a few miles), which does not suggest a large archive or administrative staff. There are precious few royal inscriptions from the area, and none from Judah, unless we count the Siloam inscription (if genuinely from the time of Hezekiah[15]). The newly discovered Tel Dan inscription(s)[16] are not Israelite, nor is the Mesha inscription. We can assume that Israelite and Judean monarchs had scribes who could erect such inscriptions. Official correspondence has been preserved: the Arad ostraca (if Arad ever belonged to Judah) and the Lachish letters are probably written down by officials (both cities were sufficiently large to contain royal scribes).

An illustration of the difficulty posed by the canonical texts is given by a comparison of the accounts of Samuel, Kings, and Chronicles. 2 Sam. 8:16–18 gives the following list of David's officials:

> Joab ben Zeruiah was in charge of the army; Jehoshaphat ben Ahilud was the recorder (מזכיר); Zadok ben Ahitub, and Ahimelech ben Abiathar were the priests and Seraiah was the scribe (סופר); Benaiah ben Jehoiada ran the Cherethites and the Pelethites; and David's sons were priests.

2 Samuel 20:23–26 adds to these Adoram in charge of forced labor, Sheva as scribe, and Ira the Jairite as a priest. For Solomon, 1 Kings 4:1–6 lists these officials: Azariah ben Zadok the priest; Elihoreph and Ahiah sons of Shisha, scribes; Jehoshaphat ben Ahilud, recorder; Benaiah ben Jehoiada in charge of the army; Zadok and Abiathar, priests; Azariah ben Nathan in charge of the *nitzabim;* Zabud ben Nathan the king's personal priest; Ahishar in charge of the palace, and Adoniram ben Abda in charge of forced labor. The list may be ancient, but if so it lists a very small administration. These may, of course, have been in charge of other officials, but if so, their names were not kept.

The elaborate administrative system ascribed to the end of David's reign in 1 Chronicles 23—27 is quite different. Chapter 23 reckons 38,000 Levites of over thirty (v. 3; v. 24 says "twenty") years old, of whom 24,000 are in charge of running the temple; 6,000 are "officers and judges"; and 4,000 musicians, all divided into the three levitical clans. In chapter 24 the priests are divided into twenty-four shifts, and chapter 25 details the three clans of musicians, trained in "prophesying," singing, and playing. Chapter 26 deals with gatekeepers (also divided into clans, or guilds), treasurers, and judges, and chapter 27 with lay officers. These were divided into twelve teams, each serving a month, whereas the priestly courses served a week each, each course twice a year. We are also introduced (27:25ff.) to officials over the treasuries throughout the land and those supervising the various crops (olive oil, vines) and herds (including camels). The picture strikes the reader as highly impractical in some respect, and pretty clearly a fictional account of the ancient monarchic administration. But underlying the theory is perhaps some realism: the importance of the temple in the entire administration, and especially the assignment of financial and legal matters to temple staff (Levites) fits the way in which the Persian province of Judah would probably have been run. And while the number of staff and the amount of wealth donated to the temple (chap. 29) are surely exaggerated, this portrait is what the Chronicler offers as a vision of how the temple is ideally run. The division of Levites and priests into ancestral houses, clans, or guilds is reflected in the psalms headings: the collection of revenues throughout the province and the subsequent necessity of guarding the temple entrances are all plausible administrative functions. We can glimpse behind this idealistic account some notion of how the temple administration may have been organized in the fourth century B.C.E.; indeed it fits just as well, if not better, the Ptolemaic period.

Regardless of these hints and clues, however, we know, simply from the existence of the canonized literature—all of which reached its canonical shape in the Second Temple period, much of which was revised and edited substantially at that time, and some of which was composed then—that a good deal of scribal literary activity was taking place and that canonizing processes were now underway. The view of Judah in the Persian period as a cultural backwater and as economically poor perhaps needs to be reconsidered.[17] Obviously in the Ptolemaic and Seleucid periods Judah's wealth increased considerably, and the later we move in date, the easier it is to conclude that the temple could sustain a number of scribal schools with a vigorous literary activity. But we do not know how well funded the temple was in the Persian period.

NON-SCRIBAL SCHOOLS

The existence of an extensive school system in monarchic Judah is maintained by a number of scholars, among whom the most enthusiastic is André Lemaire.[18] He goes well beyond the consideration of merely scribal schools and posits a widespread educational system in monarchic Judah. He considers that the major Canaanite cities had scribal schools, and that under David and

Solomon royal schools were also set up in various cities. The system was then expanded, he suggests, to include local schools at Arad, Qadesh-Barnea, and Kuntillet 'Ajrud with larger schools also at places like Lachish. Other kinds of schools (prophetic and priestly) also existed, and young male children were regularly taught to read and write on the basis of an elaborate curriculum. From this curriculum, he argues, the biblical canon developed.

The evidence adduced by Lemaire for this is of three kinds: epigraphic, scriptural, and comparative. The epigraphic evidence consists of bits of writing on ostraca (pieces of pottery commonly used as writing material), which he interprets as abecedaries (exercises in writing out the alphabet) and other school writing exercises from seven sites: 'Izbet Ṣarṭah, Gezer, Lachish, Khirbet el-Qom, Aroer, Qadesh-Barnea, and Kuntillet 'Ajrud. The evidence thus interpreted is then supported by allusions in the canonical literature to books and writing. Finally, the evidence of school education in Egypt and Mesopotamia is adduced as an analogy to Israel and Judah, in further support of the existence of a very early and very extensive school system in these kingdoms.

A number of other scholars have used some of the same evidence to argue for the existence of scribal schools in the early monarchic period, though none has reconstructed such an advanced system as Lemaire.[19] He appears to be describing not a specialized scribal educational system, but a wider curriculum by means of which literacy was widely spread throughout Israel and Judah. But there are difficulties with all the pieces of evidence presented. First, a complete set of letters inscribed on an ostracon does not necessarily betray a school exercise. Nor is the famous "Gezer calendar," one of Lemaire's proofs, necessarily the product of a scribal pupil; it is inscribed on stone. The ostracon from Kuntillet 'Ajrud, where the same word is written twice, is also far from being an obvious school exercise. All these cases show only that people who could write to some extent (and not necessarily to a very advanced level) were present at these sites, living or visiting. Positing a *school* of any sort in each of these places is precarious.

The problem with Lemaire's use of the canonized texts has already been hinted at, though it is also compounded by an overevaluation of the evidence, for clear scriptural allusion to widespread literacy is actually sparse. Yet even if it were plentiful, it could tell us little. We do not know the date of the relevant Hebrew texts, though we can be sure that in their present form they are all later than the monarchic period. They are, in any case, the product of scribes who were trained in schools, and it is not unrealistic to imagine that in writing about the past the authors would introduce scribal schools where deemed appropriate. But as it happens, there *are* no references to schools in the monarchic period.

Objections to such an early date for Judean schools and such a widespread literacy in the monarchic period have thus understandably come from several quarters. Crenshaw refers to "extravagant claims about an elaborate system of schools throughout Palestine,"[20] pointing out the wide scope that the term "school" often enjoys in such discussion. Crenshaw defines a "school" to mean "professional education, which involved both reading and writing, at a specified location to which young people came and to which fees were paid to a teacher."[21] If we are thinking of *scribal* schools, the payment to a teacher should perhaps be left out of the criteria, since scribal education was not necessarily paid for and could have been provided by the state or by scribes themselves. Very probably, individual scribes took on their own sons as pupils. However, as soon as one envisages education being given beyond the professional circle, then certainly the question of payment for education arises.

Crenshaw also considers the three strongest pieces of evidence for schools within the canon. The first, Isa. 28:9–13 ("whom will he teach knowledge, to whom will he explain the message—those weaned from milk, taken from the breast? It is precept by precept, precept by precept, and line by line, line by line"), is not only a corrupt passage, but says nothing about the teaching of writing, and only very optimistically could be interpreted as pointing to school lessons.[22] Isa. 50:4, which reads "the lord Yahweh has given me the tongue of a teacher," takes us no further, since it does not say any more about what is taught or where or to whom. Proverbs 22:17–21, probably borrowed from an Egyptian *Vorlage*,[23] might point to oral and written instruction in a Judean scribal school, but so does much of Proverbs in fact: but what is the date of a written text of Proverbs? As for literacy, there are texts that refer to writing (Judg. 8:13–17; Job 31:35), and, while Crenshaw is incautious to declare that "the evidence clearly points to the existence of literate persons at an early period in Israel," since that involves making a judgment on the date of the texts, it is unnecessary to dispute, since the existence of people who could write in monarchic Israel and Judah is certainly not in doubt. What is at issue is how many, how much they wrote, and how they learned. And here the canonical texts give us no help. There is no valid evidence of any kind of formal schooling in the monarchic period.

Similar criticisms have come from M. Haran,[24] who concludes that even with the increased simplicity of the alphabet, literacy never succeeded in passing beyond the possession of specialized groups. He also points out the wide range of accomplishments that the term "literacy" can denote, citing the difference between an ability to read the signs and an ability to compose literature. Abecedaries written on rocks, and in places far from human habitation, constitute a further objection to the claim that they are necessarily school exercises.

He suggests that artisans whose craft was to inscribe letters on manufactured vessels or jewelry may have been responsible for many of the "writing exercises," without necessarily being able to read scrolls, let alone write them.

In addition to these specific objections, there are two general arguments against Lemaire's case for widespread literacy. First, in an ancient agrarian society literacy hardly spreads automatically without the need for it. But the social and economic structure of monarchic Israel and Judah did not have any use for widespread literacy; neither the agrarian nor the urban population would learn to write unless they could profit from it. There is no likelihood of any demand for the art of writing until we have a class of person who can use it. Second, there is unlikely to be any ready supply, for in a small monarchic state the king (almost certainly illiterate himself) would not promote it, since keeping writing within their control is one of the means by which rulers govern. Nor would scribes willingly relinquish their monopoly on writing. For these general reasons, it seems very unlikely that literacy was widespread in monarchic Judah.[25]

Finally, mere literacy does not account for canon. As Haran points out, writing canonized literature is not quite the same as having your own seal or being able to scratch your name or even read a simple letter.[26] Even in modern societies with 90 percent literacy, fewer than 1 percent write books.[27] At issue is not simply the ability to write, but the capacity, motivation, and opportunity to write scrolls and to write *literature,* not to write business transactions, or letters, or lists of names even, or to scratch abecedaries. Literacy does not automatically lead to canonizing.

When we turn to a later period, the situation becomes much clearer. There is, as has been seen, evidence of non-scribal education in Judah in the Hellenistic period. Education was sought by a wider circle: a new "middle class" of well-off merchants, artisans, and landowners who were able to capitalize their assets and invest them, and, having the resources to pay for it, they indulged their desire and their need for education (see chapter 4). It is also possible that priests and Levites, who do not in general appear to have been overworked or poor, had the opportunity to acquire a broader education themselves and, indeed, to make their contribution to the "intellectual tradition" of Judah beyond the narrower cultic concerns of their professions. For if the Chronicler is reflecting any kind of reality, the Levites regarded their duties as extending beyond temple maintenance to judicial functions as well.

Accordingly, the entrenched educational system of the scribal school broadened, spreading its values to non-scribal classes; literacy spread, the scribes themselves found a wider circle for their services, and, concomitantly, expanded their own intellectual interests to accommodate those of their widened intellectual circle. Changes in the school system in Judah were influenced by the introduction of the Greek *ephebeion,* which we looked at in chapter 3, but this was a specifically religious education, and its curriculum probably does not reflect the system of an earlier period. Josephus and Philo both stress the education of children in the laws, but do not clarify whether or not this was carried out in school. Philo refers to "parents, teachers and educators," but the teachers and educators might be private tutors and confined to the households of the wealthier classes.[28] We cannot learn much about this curriculum from the later rabbinic school system, however, for this focused at first (in the *bet sefer*) exclusively on Hebrew and the learning of the scriptures and not on general education: literacy itself was not part of the curriculum. As Alexander comments,[29] "the function of the *Bet Sefer* was to turn out pious Jews." In the *bet talmud,* this religious education continued with the study of rabbinic texts.[30] But according to 2 Macc. 4:9–14 (cf. 1 Macc. 1:14), a *gymnasium* and an *ephebeion* were introduced into Jerusalem in 175 B.C.E. No doubt they were already present in the many Greek-style cities (*poleis*) already established (and many still to be built), especially on the Palestinian coast and in Transjordan, but including Samaria and Bethshean.[31] According to 2 Maccabees, these were eagerly frequented by the priests especially. If the Hasmoneans officially disapproved of these institutions, they were either unable or unwilling (or both) to halt the spread of Greek education. But they were able to foster the Hebrew language, create a Hebrew library, and, perhaps, encourage the development of a Jewish version of the Greek style of education. Between the scribal school and the later rabbinic school lie important developments of which we have too little evidence, but the existence of schools for Jewish education can be assumed, however extensive or little their influence. It seems likely, however, that a specific emphasis on teaching *Judaism* (in its various forms) emerged, while some of the basic elements of Greek education (music, gymnastics) were discouraged. Given the indispensability of the Greek language and the presence of so many Greek-speaking Jews both resident in and visiting Jerusalem, it is impossible to imagine that education for the priestly, administrative, and ruling classes in Judah did not include many Greek elements.

SCHOOLS AND CANONS

The distinction between a professional education and a nonprofessional education entails a distinction between kinds of writing, too, which is visible in the canonized literature. We can identity (or hope to identify) literary activity undertaken by the scribes in furtherance of their professional interests: writings that display the scribal ethos itself—historiographic, didactic, liturgical, and legal. Such writings, since they belong in spirit as well as in letter to the scribal class, lend themselves naturally to being canonized by copying, studying, and teaching in the schools. Given the likelihood of specialization among the scribes, where different branches dealt with the temple cult, the temple liturgy, fiscal administration, diplomatic correspondence with Persian officials, and perhaps much else, we may be able to identify particular schools as the main agents of canonizing.

One problem we face is that we know little of the provincial governor's administration. In all likelihood, the temple and the provincial center remained separate physically, perhaps ideologically, though there is no extensive evidence of ideological *opposition*. During the Ptolemaic period, the temple may have been integrated even more into the economic and administrative structure of Judah, and the high priest have taken over most of the political functions that were not reserved for the Egyptian bureaucracy. On the assumption, however, that the provincial administration was locally recruited, and perhaps that the governor was Judean, it is possible to argue that these scribes served not exclusively the interests of the Persian king or the satrap, but also of the local ruling elite whom the Persians had installed to administer the province. Indeed, the interest may have overlapped, the Persians being anxious to achieve stability by encouraging the consolidation of local elites.

If so, it is within the orbit of the provincial government (the "palace") as well as the temple that we might look for official sponsorship of the literature that was to be canonized in Judah; and indeed, official sponsorship perhaps implies that canonicity was implicit from the outset. Despite the removal of the Judean monarchy, the royal archives (or some of them) in Jerusalem, together with some administrators, survived, and on the reorganization of Judah under the Persians were no doubt available. Administrative continuity seems a reasonable surmise, and some monarchic archives lie behind the books of Kings, as perhaps (this is guesswork) written oracles from prophets. Literature that makes use of such archived material is most likely the product of the scribe attached to the governor. Whether or not temple archives from the monarchic period survived is harder to establish; some texts may well have, for the idea that the temple was entirely physically destroyed by the Babylonians is probably an exaggeration. In the interests of creating a past in such a way as to prove continuity with the present any surviving materials would be utilized in the official service of these institutions: the governor would be the heir of the monarchs, but better, and the temple as magnificent as Solomon's (though the writer of Ezra disagreed). Accordingly, Cyrus would succeed David as anointed of Yahweh and builder of the second temple (Isa. 44:28; 45:1). The earliest canonized writings, then, should perhaps be attributed to scribes working under official institutional patronage: historiography, legal codes, cultic and liturgical texts. In particular, if we accept that the Persians encouraged (or demanded) the production of a Judean version of the "King's Law" (as many scholars are coming to accept, but which should not be assumed too readily on the basis of the story of Ezra), we might see Deuteronomy (as will be argued) as the earliest official writing in the extant Judean canon.

ARCHIVES AND LIBRARIES

Schools, however, are not by themselves an adequate explanation for the range of topics and genres in the rabbinic-Masoretic canon. The contents go well beyond the needs of a professional *scribal* education, even for the very wide range of administrative and diplomatic services. The scrolls are in many cases much too long and repetitive for any school curriculum. One hardly needs so many examples of an oracle against foreigners, or a psalm of lament. If a scribal school serves to *teach* scribes, it needs much less than all this. The canonization of these books must involve archives and libraries as well.

By "archive" is meant a set of administrative records preserved for administrative necessity; a "library" is a collection of literary works providing for their preservation and consultation. The contents of an archive are determined by administrative requirements; the contents of a library to a greater extent are chosen. But this rather crude distinction may imply an unwarranted assumption that nondocumentary texts were "read" as we moderns understand reading—"as literature." The modern fashion for literary reading, entirely valid as it is, can lend itself to the notion that ancient authors wrote at length to be read at length. This is unlikely—or at least until the habit of reading for leisure grew. It is unlikely that scribes read their own product for leisure rather than for education, for consulting, or for copying. On the other hand, there *are* works clearly intended to be read and enjoyed (and they are brief!): Esther, Ruth, Jonah—these are literature, for reading. Thus, where there are genuine indications of a work having a form that requires or encourages continuous reading, we may well be looking at a text designed not for scribes but for a wider public. This is not an invariable rule, but the adaptation of scribal education to a wider nonprofessional education in the Hellenistic period may have been attended by changes in the canon of scribal literature to suit a new readership.

The spread of literacy in the Hellenistic world, together with the spread of Jews over a wider area, prompted the dissemination in written (and translated: Greek or Aramaic) form of liturgical and other texts for use in the practice of Jewish culture and worship. The same factors stimulated the production of new Jewish texts in Aramaic and Greek. A study of canonizing processes outside Judah lies beyond the scope of this book, because Greek texts did not find their way into the Jewish scriptural canon—underlining again how political, social, and geographic factors determine the extent of canons. The present Jewish canon is a Judean one. There were no doubt at one time several Greek Jewish canons, read alongside Greek canons. For Philo's own canon embraced both Moses and Plato.

We should therefore resist concluding that the Masoretic-rabbinic canon represents solely a school curriculum, whether actually used or intended to be used in this way; and we should also consider that the canonizing of some "literary" works follows an "archiving" logic rather than a "reading" logic. Obvious examples are Psalms and Proverbs, but perhaps the cumulation of stories about origins into a single chronological sequential narrative (Genesis-Exodus) is another, for chronology is a way of archiving and indexing originally independent stories. We can partly explain the presence of such obviously literary works in a predominantly scribal canon by assuming they were popular among the new literate classes (perhaps even part of the school curriculum), but we have also to assume that they found their way into libraries. What do we know of archives and libraries during the history of Judah?

In the monarchic period there were certain to have been royal archives in Jerusalem and the successive capital cities of the kingdom of Israel. The books of Kings and Chronicles make regular references to earlier sources ("the book of the deeds of PN"), which, even if they do not necessarily point to real documents, show that such sources were expected to have existed, and that if so were supposed to be used. If records survived the Babylonian destruction, as suggested above, they were available for consultation in the Persian period, and may have been copied onto skin or papyrus, in which case they would not have survived to our own time (as they might have done in Egypt or even by the Dead Sea). No doubt details of the names of Israelite and Judean monarchs, and perhaps even brief details of their deeds, however preserved, *have* been utilized by the composers of Kings and Chronicles (or their source, if they were using one).

The case for temple archives is not so convincing. Certainly, the biblical literature itself frequently associates literature with the temple. The "tablets of the law" are described as being stored in the Ark (Deut. 10:2), which implies the sanctuary where this box was later said to be housed; Joshua's covenant was deposited at Shechem (Josh. 24:26); Samuel's "constitution" of the state (1 Sam. 10:25) is deposited at Mizpah; Josiah's law-book is found in the temple.[32] The canonical literature itself points us firmly enough to its *own* place of origin. But do we not have here again a case of literature from a later context retrojecting its own practices into the past? Probably these references are better evidence for temple archives at the time of their writing. We possess no hard evidence that the canonical literature in any way draws on temple texts from the monarchic period. Nor can we simply assume that archives existed, because we do not know whether the Temple was anything other than a royal sanctuary, exercising independent economic functions and possessing a substantial scribal corps.

There is no evidence of libraries in the monarchic period; though if the existence of indigenous literary texts from the monarchic period could be proved, the existence of libraries should be presumed. It is not impossible, all the same, that collections of Egyptian and Assyrian texts existed.

In the Persian period, the letters from the colony of Elephantine to the governor of Samaria and the high priest of Jerusalem would have been stored in the relevant archives. In the Hellenistic period, ben Sira may have possessed a limited number of scrolls of his own; certainly he is well read. But the most important evidence for our purposes is in 2 Macc. 2:13, which states that "just as Nehemiah collected the chronicles of the kings, the writings of prophets, the works of David and royal letters about sacred offerings, to found his library, so Judas also has collected all the books that had been scattered . . . ," apparently after Antiochus (according to 1 Macc. 1:56–7) had tried to destroy them. This statement probably means that in the author's day there existed in Jerusalem a library of books which was thought to have been there since the time of Nehemiah, the contents of which correspond very well with what might have been the "canon" of the day. The act of setting up such an archive (whether by Judas or one of his successors) is crucial in the establishment of an "official" canon that had overt political and nationalistic and not merely scribal or school motives behind it. For a fuller examination of this Hasmonean library, see chapter 11.

REFLECTIONS

The preceding evaluation may strike some readers as programmatically negative toward the monarchic period. But several lines of argument have been tested, and it remains the inescapable truth that while scribal activity on a "canonizing" scale *must* (on any account) have taken place within Persian-Hellenistic Judah, we cannot say whether or not it began earlier. We can assume there were scribes and archives, but little more. To assume that the canonized writings originate in the monarchic period, other than in the form of dimly recognized archived source material, is no more than a hunch. In any event, if the canonizing process had begun earlier, these stages will have to be disregarded for reason of our virtually total ignorance.

Yet there is more to the issue than a mere recognition of ignorance! It is necessary to ask always *why* certain works were composed and canonized, and to do this in terms of what we know of social structures. The conclusion that canonizing starts in the sixth, or more probably fifth, century B.C.E. is based on a theory about the purpose of the canonized works and the ideology of their authors. And this dating will continue to be argued for in the chapters that follow.

CHAPTER 6

The Mosaic Canon

INTRODUCTION

It is conventional to consider the formation of Jewish canons from the perspective of the rabbinic canon, comprising Torah, Prophets, and Writings. But as has been suggested earlier, this may not be the ideal vantage point. It will, for example, exclude canons that did not find a place among the rabbinic "books that defile the hands" (for the meaning of this term and a discussion of the rabbinic scriptural canon, see chapter 11). It is also not to be assumed that the threefold division necessarily corresponds to the structure by which various canons evolved. The best course of action is to consider groups of scrolls, or even individual scrolls, that seem to have comprised canons within Judaism. The same is true of chronological sequence. It is not at all clear that the rabbinic-Masoretic canon was built in three distinct stages, starting with only one canon that was then supplemented by other canons. Since canonizing is a continuous process, we may as well assume that the various canons existed simultaneously, perhaps encroaching on each other from time to time, but not merging into a single canonical collection.

It is important, then, to avoid using the categories "law," "prophets," and "writings," the divisions of the rabbinic scriptural canon, as an infrastructure for the history of canonizing. In any case, the terms are misleading: most of the contents of Torah are not actually law, while the first part of the "Prophets" section is not really prophetic. "Writings" also looks like a catch-all name. These names do not help very much to explain the beginning of the formation of canons, though they tell us something about the later canons.

Divisions between canons are also problematic. We are dealing, after all, with individual scrolls, archived in a certain order and cataloged. Cataloging is part of the process by which scrolls form a group, and copying may well have embraced groups of scrolls as well as individual ones. Equally, separate texts may be combined onto a single scroll as a convenient cataloging device, with the result that the contents may acquire, in the copying process, more coherence than they had, and come to form a "book" with a single heading.

To read the evolutionary history from the final shape, then, is not the correct procedure. However, since we do have clear evidence of a "Mosaic law" well before the end of the Second Temple period, and since that collection forms the first part of the present Jewish scriptural canon, we may as well start with it.

"TORAH" AS "LAW"

Legal texts constitute a category of all the canonized cultures we have surveyed. It is true that law provides a potentially helpful model of canonizing, since it seems to be by its very nature written, authoritative, and only minimally changeable. A view thus prevails in some circles that the Judean laws were originally descriptive in intent and prescriptive in effect: that "Israelite law" and "biblical law" were interchangeable terms. But a more nuanced view recognizes that the biblical laws are the result of editing and generated by wider ideological interests, but do nevertheless basically reflect actual social practice; while the literary law compositions may not be entirely descriptive (or even prescriptive) in *intent,* the individual laws are in fact a reflection of actual social practices or norms. A third view attaches the greatest weight to the evidence of scribal composition, intellectual and theoretical motivation, and literary contextualizing, and holds that these literary "laws" reflect essentially their scribal authors' thinking, so that a direct relationship between individual prescriptions and actual practice is improbable. On this view, their authors were concerned not to "describe what was happening," but rather to theorize on what *ought to happen,* or *ought to have happened,* in an ideal Israelite society. Accordingly, law is a mode of social philosophy, or of theocratic idealizing.

Parallels with ancient Mesopotamian law codes are often invoked in favor of the first or second view. Some scholars[1] accept what Westbrook terms the "diffusionist" view of ancient Near Eastern law, whereby a common legislative culture or tradition, facilitated by a range of common economic features, permeated the Fertile Crescent during the second millennium. Such "diffusion" could have occurred through the medium of written sources, migration, and general social and political interaction. Thus the biblical laws represent a broad social-legal tradition stretching from the Tigris to the borders of Egypt. If this approach is correct, then a simple answer appears to the question of canonization: the torah is an authoritative legal document, or at least parts of it are. Moreover, legal canonizing in Israel and Judah could have commenced with an existing legal practice.

The great Mesopotamian law codes, however, are not prescriptive legal documents intended to regulate legal praxis directly. They are rather "prototypical collections of cases"[2] whose function is didactic.[3] Legal practice in Mesopotamia was largely unaffected by them. It follows, then, that if there is a "diffusion;" it is a *literary* tradition that is being spread, not practice. In this event, legal canonizing in Israel and Judah could well have sprung directly from this literary tradition. This process, however, requires no ancient date, for the Code of Hammurabi, though an ancient source, was canonical in the Akkadian tradition and still being copied well into the first millennium. The presentation of laws as divine revelation is, of course, also a convention that points to a literary tradition rather than legal *practice,* which was based on convention and custom (Hammurabi, as is well known, is depicted receiving laws from Shamash.)

But the specific cases encountered in the Jewish canon are not always "prototypical" at all. An obvious example is the single scriptural law about divorce, in Deut. 24:1–4; this provides for the entirely unlikely case that a husband divorces his wife, she marries another and is divorced by him, then the first husband wishes to remarry her. Why should this one law be included, with nothing else on the whole subject of divorce? Is it that the metaphor of Yahweh and Israel as husband and wife has inspired not only its conclusion but its composition? A nation that has deserted (or been deserted by) its marital deity, follows another spouse-god, and then wishes to abandon that god and return to its original spouse-deity cannot do so: the deity will not (*may* not!) receive the wife-nation back. It is not impossible that the same kind of explanation can be given of the absurd law of the rebellious son (Deut. 21:18–21). Did parents of a rebellious son bring him to the elders, and would the villagers stone him? If not, what is the theoretical basis behind this law? It is conceivable that we are dealing with an elaboration of the command to honor parents, but it may also be allegorical: the god's rebellious children will also suffer destruction at the hands of their neighbors. And what of the law (Deut. 23:15) that if a slave runs away from his master, he should not be given back? Again, in the mind of the framer of this law, the runaway slaves rescued by their deity from Egyptian ownership did not think they should have been returned. Each of these laws might, then, reasonably be considered as the product of reflection on wider issues, such as the disobedience of the nation to its father-god or husband-god, and its right to be punished; or of its right not to go back to Egypt for enslavement.

The apparent selectivity of biblical laws owes a good deal to literary context and to ideological programs. Studies of the literary structures of biblical law codes have shown quite sophisticated and developed designs:[4] chiasmus, thematic reiteration, internal integration, and allusions to both the immediate narrative context and the Pentateuch. The law collections are also generated by theory rather than practice. They may be intended to express the logic of a social theory (such as the extermination of Canaanites, since Deuteronomy's utopia has no Canaanites), but may be intended to teach a moral (thus, we might say, are haggadic rather than halakhic in character). Many other laws can be explained as a *logical* outcome of certain basic premises. Thus, the Deuteronomic laws about holy war are derivable from theories about authorized ownership of land (Yahweh owns it and gives it as a dowry or a bequest to Israel) and conditions of the "covenant" that the writers use as a model for their social philosophy. For Deuteronomy is based on a legal theory that between the deity and the society is a contract, the terms of which include land possession. That basic theory determines how one treats non-Israelites, justifies the extermination of idolatrous temptations, defines and protects the *ethnos,* and so on. Likewise, Leviticus exhibits a clear ideology of purity based on proximity to the presence of the deity, the world within and without the "camp," and a universe and lifestyle divided into degrees and states of cleanliness. The fact that one cannot identify a Canaanite in one's own society nor one's eye always detect "holiness" (nor the memory always recall what state of it one is in) makes holiness unenforceable except in some evident cases, and what is the good of that? But of course universal holiness follows very logically from the premise that a holy god is encamped in the middle of his people.

The point of these comments is to show how that the canonization of this legal material has little to do with legal practice, or, perhaps, that if it did, the canonizing process has molded these "law codes" into ideologically coherent theological-social philosophy. In fact, the very opposite of the oft-assumed process actually occurred: one of the *effects* of the canonizing of this literature was to make it the basis for a normative set of regulations. But the problem here is to discover the origin of this kind of material, the basis of its canonization. What is unique about the laws, at least of Deuteronomy and of Leviticus, is that they are drafted in service of a *social theory.* They aspire to a constitution, in which a society (nation) and its deity and its relations to other societies are all carefully defined, and in which ritual and civil regulations equally play a part. The originator of this constitution is Moses, and it is around this figure that the canon now represented by the books of "torah" probably grew.

MOSES

If there is any topic or point of reference that explains the growth of the five scrolls of Torah, that must be Moses. The beginning of Exodus to the end of Deuteronomy tells of the life and achievements of Moses as military leader, prophet, lawgiver: as founder of the nation. Genesis, of course, does not deal with Moses, but combines stories that took place before him, and its narrative has been shaped so as to explain who were the "descendants of Israel" and why they were in Egypt. It is very probably a late "prequel" to the Moses story, though its contents may have grown independently for a while (see later). Hence the term "Mosaic canon" for this collection, in which the laws—both civil and cultic—that go back to him are integrated into an account of his deeds as nation builder.

We are not concerned in this book, of course, with the processes of composition or with tradition-history of the individual scrolls, on which there is anyway a bewildering variety of theories, from the classic documentary source-analyses to the identification of "tradition complexes." What we can attempt, however, is, to explain the driving force behind the collection and organization of the materials. This seems to have been a desire to give a complete account of the deeds and the words of the man who created the nation, not from any disinterested historical or even biographical motive, but from an etiological one: to give an identity to an *ethnos,* the Judeans (and it should be noted that the Mosaic canon does not exclude Samarians). An enormous amount of scribal activity was expended on compiling an account of the work of the nation's founder. When and where did this happen? Why should a founder for the nation need to be discovered and so extensively written up? These questions are, of course, all interrelated. But it is important to discover the chronological framework in order to be able to answer them. The outline of an answer to both questions can be achieved by looking at Deuteronomy.

DEUTERONOMY

The book of Deuteronomy is an appropriate point of departure for three reasons: first, it is the only book to call itself a "torah book" and hence it may provide a clue to the final naming of this canon;[5] second, it affords sufficient clues to enable it to be dated; and third, its ideology points us toward a motivation for the creation of a Mosaic canon.[6] However, as will be argued, it is not the kernel of the Mosaic canon, but a scroll that retained an independent status for a considerable time and was included with the rest of the Mosaic canon at a relatively late stage, forcing some adjustments to the original end of the Mosaic biography in Numbers.

The laws of Deuteronomy are clearly referred to as "this *torah*" in its introductory and concluding material. Indeed, Deuteronomy is the only place in the Pentateuch where the term "scroll of *torah*" occurs. Elsewhere, chiefly in

Leviticus, we find a *torah* for specific practices such as offerings (Lev. 6:2, 7, 18), or leprosy (e.g., Lev. 14:2). But Deut. 28:58 reads: "the words of this *torah* written in this book." Moses is said to have written it down (31:9, 24) and had it placed beside the ark. This identification as *the* scroll of torah carries over into Josh. 1:7–8, where Joshua is instructed not to depart from the "scroll of the *torah*" which "my servant Moses commanded," and reads out this "scroll of the *torah* of Moses" at a covenant ceremony in 8:30–35.[7] In 2 Kings 22—23 a "scroll of the *torah*" (22:8) or "scroll of the covenant" (23:2) is said to have been found in the temple and made the basis of another covenant ceremony and a religious reform.

Deuteronomy retains a separate identity as *torah* even until the time of ben Sira (end of third century B.C.E.). In 24:23 this writer mentions "the scroll of the covenant of Elyon, the law that Moses commanded us." The reference to "covenant" makes one think of Deuteronomy.[8] Indeed, ben Sira seems to regard this book as exclusively the *Mosaic* law, while his reference elsewhere to "law of the Most High" (39:1) refers either to other scrolls or perhaps to something not in a fixed textual form at all. 1 Maccabees, whose composition is to be dated to about 100 B.C.E., confirms such a distinction:

> The books of the law (τὰ βιβλία τοῦ νόμου) that they found they burnt in the fire, tearing them to pieces[9] and where they found a book of the covenant (βιβλίον διαθήκης) with anyone, and if anyone adhered to the law (συνευδόκει τῷ νόμῳ) they put them to death (1:56–7).

The "book of the covenant" is distinguished from "books of the law," though it clearly belongs with them as constituting the law to which pious Judeans would adhere. Slightly later, 2 Macc. 8:23 describes how Eleazar read aloud from "the holy book" (singular) before a battle: probably Deuteronomy, which in chapter 20 contains rules about war, including the priestly speech of encouragement before battle.

Now, by the time of 1 and 2 Maccabees (ca. 100 B.C.E.), a definitive schism with the Samari[t]an[10] community had probably taken place: John Hyrcanus had destroyed the Gerizim temple a generation earlier. That schism (which unfortunately cannot be dated and may have been a process taking some time) marks the *terminus ad quem* for the creation of a Mosaic canon including Deuteronomy, since the Samaritan Pentateuch does not differ in any structural way from the Judean one.[11] This does not have to mean that Deuteronomy could not, however, enjoy a special status within that canon, as it seems to have at Qumran.

Deuteronomy, however, may have enjoyed a promiscuous life during its canonical career. According to the theory of Martin Noth,[12] which has remained a virtual consensus in its broad outlines,[13] its core became the basis for a history written on Deuteronomic principles, comprising the present books of Joshua, Judges, Samuel, and Kings. These formed a single "Deuteronomistic" composition, written during the sixth century, in which the book of Deuteronomy formed the opening. Noth's view was that Deuteronomy 1—3, which is a historical review of events subsequent to Sinai, was intended as an introduction to this larger work.

According to Noth, Deuteronomy was attached to the other books of Moses (Genesis–Numbers) at a relatively late stage, rather than having been composed and edited along with them. Hence the account of the death of Moses, he argued, originally stood at the end of Numbers. Numbers 36:13 was composed to introduce Deuteronomy, which was detached from Joshua to Kings by means of the additional final chapters, leaving the rest of the "Deuteronomistic History" to move into the orbit of a different canon. At any rate, once attached to other Mosaic books, this "torah scroll" may have prompted the name Torah to be employed for the entire collection.

Noth's reconstruction is seriously wrong in its dating of the process but may well be correct in determining that Deuteronomy is not the core of the Mosaic canon's evolution. For while some traces of Deuteronomic language are found here and there in Exodus, there is little evidence of Exodus–Numbers having been influenced by Deuteronomy—or by each other. The organization of all these scrolls into a "life of Moses" is a canonical procedure, evident in links between the books rather than in their internal composition. Deuteronomy's ascription to Moses may be a canonical rather than a compositional feature, if we see some of the introductory material in chapters 1—11 as part of a process of integrating Deuteronomy with other Mosaic books.

Deuteronomy is of central importance in the history of the forming of the Moses canon as a *torah* and in determining the relationship of this canon to the historiographical canon of Joshua, Judges, Samuel, and Kings. But it is also pivotal in another respect as well: dating. The dating of Deuteronomy has, in fact, been a linchpin of biblical studies ever since the lawbook in the narrative of 2 Kings 22—23 was identified with Deuteronomy (or a core of it) by De Wette in 1805. That identification was perhaps not quite the brilliant deduction that it is sometimes held to be, since the narrative offers strong enough clues. Thus, if 2 Kings 22—23 relates a historical event, as nearly all scholars have assumed, we must take the history of canonizing back to the monarchic period, at least to the reign of Josiah and more specifically the year 621 when the lawbook is calculated to have been discovered. But are there strong reasons why the report should be taken as historical? The Deuteronomistic History (including Deuteronomy itself) offers a clear account of this lawbook: written by Moses (revised by Joshua?) and put beside the ark of the covenant (as it is known in Deuteronomic language); then this ark is brought to Jerusalem by David (2 Samuel 6) and installed by Solomon in his temple (1 Kings 8). Having been neglected for some time, the lawbook is then rediscovered and becomes the basis for a religious reform by the last Judean king whom the writers regard as good. Those scholars who accept a pre-621 date for Deuteronomy assume that it was placed in the Temple in the hope of instigating a reform. If so, its discovery under Josiah is the only historical truth about it contained in the canon. But is even that to be relied upon? Given the weight attached to the story, its credibility calls for a severe testing.

Let us first consider how Deuteronomy should be understood. Weinfeld remarks that it appears to have "the character of an ideal national constitution representing all the official institutions of the state: the monarchy, the judiciary, the priesthood, and prophecy."[14] He places this "constitution" generically closer to wisdom literature, which also exhorts in the second person and mixes general with particular directives. Its didactic character is important to bear in mind, for it reinforces the *ideal* nature of the work. The story of 2 Kings 22—23 (and not a few scholars beside!) would have us believe that it was a practical document that was put into immediate effect. Weinfeld's definition actually throws into doubt such an intention, making it strange that he should so unquestioningly accept a seventh-century date for it.

What Deuteronomy represents is the construction of an ideal society, attributed to the founder of the nation (as divine spokesman). But even ideals should reflect present realities in some way. Does even an idealized constitution suggest a real historical period of composition?

The society addressed, and to be governed, by this "constitution" is a twelve-tribe nation defined by a "covenant" between them as client people and their patron deity. Deuteronomy assumes this society/nation to be living amid other nations ("Canaanites") whom the deity has dispossessed and who are therefore to be annihilated before they bring disaster. Now, even granted that external enemies underpin internal cohesion, the brooding presence of an inimical population and a recommendation to remove them make little sense in a monarchic state. Such states do not create a civil war among the king's taxpaying subjects. The kind of ethnic identity being addressed by such rhetoric points toward the creation, or the existence, of a society within a society. The categories "Israelite" and "Canaanite" are symbols of a dichotomy that is at the same time religious and ethnic. Moreover, the Canaanites represent those *indigenous* peoples who do not conform to the norms and regulations of the idealized Israel and its god and thus lose their indigenous rights. This is not a plausible program for a monarchic state. Rather, the kind of society envisioned by the writer(s) of Deuteronomy hints at the reality of an *immigrant* group wedded to a central sanctuary (which Deuteronomy advocates) and its monotheistic cult, surrounded by an indigenous population that is socially distinct. Deuteronomy authorizes the supplanting of these people, their rejection by the national god, and the institution of a single religious system. That is an implausible picture of seventh-century Judah and a very plausible picture of fifth-century Judah under the Persians.

More detailed exegesis will support this verdict. First, how does Deuteronomy treat the monarch?

> When you have reached the land which Yahweh your God is giving you, taken possession of it, lived in it, and decided "I will set a king over me, like all the nations around me," you must at all costs appoint as king over you someone that Yahweh your God chooses, one from among your own kin you must appoint, and not a foreigner who is not of your kin. But he shall not accumulate horses for himself, nor cause the people to return to Egypt, for the purpose of multiplying horses, for Yahweh has said to you, 'You will not return that way any more.'
>
> Nor shall he take many wives for himself, lest his heart turn away; nor accumulate large amounts of silver and gold. And when he occupies the throne of his kingdom, he shall have written out on a scroll, in the presence of the levitical priests, a copy of this law, and it will remain with him, and he shall consult it all the days of his life, so that he may learn to fear Yahweh his God and keep all the words of this law and these statutes. (Deut. 17:14–19)

This passage has a strangely anachronistic air: it seems to imagine a society in which kings are appointed by the people, and have no responsibilities other than not to get too rich, nor marry too many wives, nor lead the population to Egypt (whatever that means); and live according to the *torah*. If we consult the recommendations of Deuteronomy on the administration of justice, or the collection of revenues, or the conduct of war—matters to which kings in such societies attached priority—we find a complete absence of royal function. Justice is carried out not by royal officers administering a written code but according to city, administered by the elders (see, e.g., chap. 21). War is conducted by the priests (see chap. 20). Of the people's dues to the monarch nothing at all is said. This is no realistic constitution for a monarchy and scarcely even a credible ideal for a small monarchic state. All of this monarchic impotence, however, can be contrasted with the importance attached to Levites and to the sanctuary.

For the final arbitrator of legal matters is not the king but a priest:

> If a matter arises which is too difficult for you to settle in judgment, be-
> tween the conflicting families and claims, between injuries on both
> sides, matters of dispute within your own jurisdiction, then you will
> leave and come to the place which Yahweh your God will choose, and
> consult the levitical priests, and the judge that will exist in those days,
> and seek guidance; and they will give you the decision.
>
> (Deut. 17:8–9)

So the highest court of appeal is a "national judge" (whose place in a monarchic system is hard to assign) and the levitical priests. It is also a priest who allows anyone fainthearted to depart before battle begins. Does this suggest a
monarchic society? The above factors rather suggest a time in which imperial
troops guard the security of a nation, while that nation is urged to recognize
its native rulers in the *priesthood. This* is not a regime to be proposed to, let
alone entertained by, any monarch. But it fits the situation in the fifth century.

Monarchy, then, remains *theoretically* the political structure of Deuteronomy, but the reality is *colonial.* The king, says Deut. 17:15, must be Judean.
But was there ever a non-Judean monarch during the period of the Judean
monarchy? No; but behind the figure of a foreign king lurks the Persian em-
peror, and his provincial governor may be meant. The allocation of powers
in Deuteronomy lies between city elders and priests. The throne constitutes
a power vacuum, for the king spends his time reading scrolls and avoiding
wealth. The power vacuum in Deuteronomy's ideal society is occupied by
Persian imperial rule. The Deuteronomic king is a displaced but also considerably weakened colonial governor, subject to the authority of the priesthood and servant of their temple and their god.

Since the identification of the Josianic scroll with Deuteronomy is transpar-
ent, the writers of this account seem to be trying to give their "constitution" the
authority of the last legitimate native ruler they recognized, and afford their
"constitution" some antiquity into the bargain. By endorsing the lawbook with
a prophetic oracle which foretells the coming disaster (2 Kings 22:14–20), the
writers of that story also underlined the divine nature of the law, and explained
the reasons for the exile, which for them is the main motivation for writing the
history. For Josiah's "reform" did not succeed and consequently avert the Babylonian deportation. But his reign thus lies sufficiently far from the deportation
that no hint of blame for it attaches to him. His attempted reform, followed by
the disasters that his successors invited, teach the classic lesson that only adherence to this written body of laws will guarantee security for Israel in the
land promised to them. Here we might recognize a further stage: adherence to
the Mosaic "constitution" as the only guarantee of national security.

The story of the finding of the law scroll under Josiah, then, is a complete fiction, and the idea of a monarch seeking to impose religious orthodoxy over the whole society is highly unusual. Monarchs were occasionally concerned about particular cults, but meddling with popular religion makes no sense. The Mosaic lawbook *par excellence,* then, on the basis of several lines of argument, is a colonial program that moves power toward Levites and enjoins the creation of a temple-centered society in the midst of the "people of the land." It is the work of a society, or on behalf of a society, that *needs* to define itself: to justify its rights, though immigrant, to take over the land, to enforce the temple as the sole site of sacrificial worship. Its colonial mentality is nowhere better expressed than in its choice of the notion of a political treaty. For political treaties were the texts of suzerainty, of political subordination. But Deuteronomy's society is contracted to its own deity who will guarantee its land and its security. And it is made directly between deity and people. The *torah* as a public constitution was read out in a liturgical ceremony and followed by a ceremony of covenant making (or renewal). All Judeans in theory were to hear this *torah* recited and understand themselves to be subject to it.

THE LAWBOOK TOPOS

We can trace the idea of a Mosaic constitution through other canons. If the writers of Joshua and 2 Kings retrojected the idea of a written Mosaic constitution into their narratives, the Chronicler did so even more zealously. He has the "law of Moses" invoked during the reign of Jehoiada (2 Chron. 23:18), while in the reign of Amaziah (25:4) he refers to "the book of Moses, whom Yahweh commanded . . . " while Hezekiah acts according to "Moses the holy man" (30:16). Even Manasseh (33:8) invokes "the whole *torah* and the statutes and the ordinances by the agency of Moses." Thus in the Chronicler's version of events, Josiah, enforcing the "book of the *torah* of Yahweh given by Moses" merely repeats the acts of his pious predecessors. From this presentation emerges the portrait of the ideal king as a follower, or even an enforcer, of a national Mosaic law. And what neater way to underpin the continuity of this process from monarchic to postmonarchic times than to have Jehoshaphat appointing Levites and priests as administers of the law of the land (2 Chron. 19:4–7)? Here, of course, Chronicles is only making more explicit what the laws of Deuteronomy implied: ultimate authority to the priests. But according to the Chronicler this authority is no occasional matter, but an ongoing responsibility. The Levites are indeed the guardians of the law as well as of the temple (and of course its hymnbooks).

But it is the stories of Ezra and Nehemiah that contribute more crucially to the "lawbook" topos. Here again, of course, we encounter problems of historicity, and while the historicity of Ezra remains stoutly defended, it is rather more readily questioned than was once the case. The present form of these books points, at any rate, to the original independence of the Ezra and Nehemiah materials, and the connection of the two figures is rather slim. One ought not to speak so readily of "Ezra-Nehemiah."[15] The two characters come together, after all, only in one episode (Nehemiah 9). Otherwise, the two careers run quite independently. Both ben Sira and the author of 2 Maccabees know of Nehemiah, but neither mentions Ezra; so the connection is no earlier than the second century B.C.E. Had Ezra and Nehemiah actually been historically associated, the fact that their stories remained separate until so late would be hard to explain. This does not mean that Ezra is unhistorical, but it does make the narrative highly questionable as a reliable source.

How reliable historically is the figure of Nehemiah, who *is* known of in the second century B.C.E.? Here the problem is the enmity expressed toward the Samarians. This sentiment suggests that the book has a secondary theme in denying any legitimacy to these would-be temple builders, and may be evidence that the narrative postdates the separation of the Judean and Samarian Yahwistic communities and the building of a Samari[t]an temple. Its suggestion that Samarians were excluded from and antagonistic to Jerusalem has colored our scholarly reconstruction of that period, forcing into the background the question of why there is a Samaritan Pentateuch and excluding from our historical probing the question of what Samaria might have contributed positively to the history of Judaism during the Persian period, and perhaps to the Mosaic canon. Although a firm date for Nehemiah's decidedly anti-Samari[t]an sentiments cannot be set, recent trends in scholarship suggest that a late fourth century date is the earliest probable time for them.

To be fair, some recent trends in Ezra and Nehemiah studies have paid proper attention to their literary and ideological aspects,[16] which lead us rather to the historical circumstances that might account for the production of such narratives rather than vain efforts to reconcile the obvious contradictions between the two. We should start by noting that the books of Nehemiah and Ezra both claim to describe, independently, *the origin of Judaism;* but they have been minimally entwined by an editor no earlier than the second century B.C.E. Hence, it appears that *competing* claims about the origin or the true founder of "Judaism" (and in each case the "Judaism" is differently conceived) have been reconciled editorially. If we want to extract any information relevant to the history of a *torah* canon from these books, we must therefore focus on a time later than the Persian period of which they tell. Now, only the Ezra story bestows much importance on the law of Moses; Nehemiah is more interested in political matters. It would be easy (and possibly not too wrong) to see some rivalry between priestly and non-priestly interests in these two stories, a rivalry overcome literarily by having both participate in the great covenant ceremony of Nehemiah 9. Ezra seems ultimately to have been the more popular figure from the first century C.E. onward, as the "Ezraite" definition of Judaism prevailed, whereas the builder of the walls of Jerusalem under imperial patronage perhaps looked suspiciously like a predecessor of Herod the Great!

This historical context for studying the "lawbook topos" in Ezra (and only incidentally in Nehemiah) can be clarified by involving another account of the origins of "Judaism," which has not found its way into the rabbinic canonical literature (though it may well have been in some group's canon). The *Damascus Document* (CD), whose date of composition is probably not too far removed from that of the Ezra story,[17] describes how the exilic punishment on Israel led to the restoration of a remnant, to whom the true divine will about sabbaths, feasts, and laws was given.[18] The revelation of the true law and the foundation of this "true Israel" is credited to an "Interpreter of the Law" (*doresh ha-torah*). The account is different in some ways from both Ezra and Nehemiah, but the similarities are even more striking and significant; they presuppose the same story of Israel's "preexilic" past (though the historical narrations of that period have quite different emphases)[19] and the exile as punishment for that past. Thanks to the editorial intertwining of Ezra and Nehemiah, all characters are involved in a covenant with the members of the elect group, based on a lawgiving and involving a process of interpretation of that law. They also deal with issues of holiness and separation from "outsiders" (and indeed from other Judeans, the "people of the land" or "builders of the wall").

Here is the proper historical context for Ezra and Nehemiah: evidence not of a unified Judaism under a *torah,* but betraying competing versions of the origin of Judaism. But what is important is that all accounts accept the existence of a Mosaic torah, and understand it as a covenant text. Since the five-volume Mosaic canon must have been in existence before the Samaritan schism, and thus before either Nehemiah or Ezra, Ezra's "lawbook" is probably meant to be understood as the Pentateuch. But the point is not very important.

In the figure of Ezra we can see, then, not a Persian appointee of the fifth (or fourth) century, but a ben Sira, who already in the second century B.C.E. can describe the life of a scribe as the study of, among other things, "the law of the Most High" (39:1), just as Ezra is "a scribe fluent in the law of Moses (or 'law of heaven')" who "had set his heart upon studying the law of Yahweh, and to observe it, and to teach the statutes and ordinances. . . . " The Ezra story is a case of inventing an appropriate origin, and ben Sira, or rather someone like him, knew that his Judaism had to have been introduced by someone like

himself. The Nehemiah story, however, appears to understand Judaism as being based on the security of Jerusalem and its economic activity.

THE MOSES CANON

Relocating the stories of Ezra and Nehemiah in a later historical context
leaves us with a gap in our history of the *torah* canon. If Deuteronomy itself, and thus the origins of the torah canon, cannot be earlier than the Persian period, what is the *terminus a quo?*

From about the beginning of the Hellenistic period (ca. 300 B.C.E.), comes
an extraordinarily interesting source, which permits us a snapshot not only of
the Mosaic *torah,* but of the wider Mosaic canon. Hecataeus of Abdera[20] has
left us an account of Judean history and constitution, summarized by the first-
century B.C.E. writer Diodorus Siculus (40.3),[21] (a further excerpt from a book
"written entirely about the Jews," also ascribed to Hecataeus, appears in Josephus[22]). According to the account in Diodorus, a pestilence in Egypt at some
time (Hecataeus gives no chronological clues) prompted the inhabitants to ex-
pel certain strangers who practiced alien rites; of these, some landed in Greece
but the majority in Judah, which was then uninhabited. They settled under the
leadership of Moses, who founded several cities, including Jerusalem, where
he established a temple. Moses also set up "forms of worship and ritual," laws,
and political institutions. He divided the people into twelve tribes, forbade im-
ages to be made of their sole deity, and appointed priests who were to be not
only in charge of the cult but also political leaders and judges. Thus, says
Hecataeus, "the Jews have never had a king" but are ruled by a high priest,
who enjoys great power and prestige. Moses, Hecataeus continues, also instituted a military education and led the people to many conquests against neighboring tribes, after which he apportioned the land equally, but reserving larger
portions for the priests. The sale of land was forbidden, specifically so as to
avoid oppression of the poor by the rich through accumulation of land. The
people were also enjoined to reproduce. In marriage and burial their customs
differed from those of others, though their traditional practices were disturbed
under the Persians and Macedonians. The Judeans claim that their laws are
words heard by Moses from God.

It is obvious that at least superficially this account demonstrates some Hel-
lenistic features. For instance, Moses appears as a typical colony founder.
There is also an Egyptian legend underlying the account of the origin of the
Judeans in Egypt; in another passage, which he may also have taken from
Hecataeus (1.28.1–3), Diodorus reproduces an Egyptian legend or myth that
most of the civilized world came about through colonization from Egypt:

thus Belus led colonists to Babylon, Danaus to Greece, and others to Colchis and Judea.[23] This type of legend, which aims to demonstrate the originality of one's own culture by showing how others derived from it, can also be found among Babylonians and Greeks, while the Judean version, slightly differently, has Israel descended from an ancient chosen lineage. A few elements of Hecataeus's account are also traceable in Manetho's stories preserved in Josephus, notably the name Moses and the immediate connection between the departure from Egypt and the foundation of Jerusalem.

How accurately might this account reflect Judean culture at the end of the fourth century and, indeed, the account of their history that the Judeans themselves offered at the time? Hecataeus probably acquired his information from Judeans, whether living in Egypt or in Judea itself. Doron Mendels has proposed that Hecataeus's account is fairly accurately preserved and reflects Judean ideas emanating from priestly circles from his own time.[24] This conclusion is based on agreements between the account and the situation described in Ezra and Nehemiah, which he takes to be a reliable portrait of Judah in the Persian period. But whether or not Ezra and Nehemiah can be dated so early, many of Mendels's observations and arguments do suggest that Hecataeus was fairly closely reflecting the state of affairs in Judah during his own time. Thus the Judeans are said to have occupied a land that was "utterly uninhabited" after leaving Egypt. This conflicts with the canonized torah tradition, and with the account of Joshua, but is in accordance with a widely represented Judean ideology that maintains that the returnees from exile had come to an empty land. Mendels cites only Nehemiah 2—4 and Judith 5:19, but the ideology of the "empty land" appears even more emphatically in Jeremiah 32 and Leviticus 25—27.[25] Joshua, as well as Nehemiah and Ezra, has an *ideologically* empty land, in which the indigenous population exists in order to be ignored, removed, or displaced, while the Abraham stories have a slightly less hostile attitude, even though they affirm that Abraham's descendants are to displace the Canaanites.

As for Moses having founded Jerusalem and other cities, Mendels suggests that Hecataeus understood Moses, wrongly, but in true Greek fashion, also to have been a city founder. Moses is credited with conquest of the land, with the creation of twelve tribes, and with the division of the land. These achievements are credited in the canonized torah to Joshua. The statement that the Judeans had always been ruled by priests and never by a king is contradicted in Samuel and Kings, as well as in Ezra and Nehemiah, where references are made to David (Ezra 3:10), a king of Israel who built the temple (Ezra 5:11), Solomon (by name, Neh. 13:26), and Israelite "kings" generally (Ezra 4:20—in a letter from the Persian king that many scholars consider authentic; 9:7 and Neh. 9:32). But the observation that priests act as judges, rulers, and administrators is exactly as Chronicles describes.

Hecataeus's information tells us a little about the role of Moses as lawgiver. But what is more interesting still is what he suggests about the rest of the canonized literature. It seems that Hecataeus's source was unaware of the contents of Joshua, Judges, Samuel, and Kings, as well as Chronicles, and thus knew only a Mosaic canon. Hecataeus ascribes the laws governing the monotheistic and aniconic cult and ritual to Moses, who claimed to have heard them from God. This suggests the contents of Leviticus. In calling this cult monotheistic and aniconic he is presumably also observing correctly. He says that Moses appointed judges (see Numbers 11). He thinks that the high priest is the ruler of the Judeans, and that there are unusual traditions about land tenure. Perhaps these reflect contemporary knowledge of Judean society, or perhaps are inferred from the Mosaic canon, or both.[26]

Then there is the matter of military education. The widespread use of Jews as mercenaries is well known from the Assyrian period (when the Elephantine colony was set up) to the Hellenistic period. The likelihood that Judeans were trained in the military arts is quite high, in view of this and of their initial success during the Maccabean wars, when a quite effective militia seems to have been organized. But does Hecataeus know of this from observation of contemporary Judaism, or from the Mosaic canon? The "holy war" ideology of Deuteronomy and the depiction in Numbers of the Israelites in the wilderness as a nation-army come to mind. Whether in fact Judeans were renowned as mercenaries, whether *Yhwh Sebaoth,* means "Yahweh of armies," is an interesting question, but perhaps not directly relevant. Hecataeus *could* have acquired all his information from the developing Mosaic canon. If his description of Judean society in his time is accurate enough—as far as we know from other sources, a temple cult, the administrative role of the priesthood, and a distinctive land tenure system were characteristic of the time—then we might speculate as to the realistic basis for the profiles of Israel in the Mosaic canon. But was Hecataeus also correct about the state of the narrative that was later to be canonized in Torah? If so, he shows us that only a rudimentary historiographical account had been canonized by the end of the fourth century to explain who "Judeans" were, where they came from, and how they got their constitution: no Abraham, no Joshua, no monarchy. We can recognize elements from Exodus, Numbers, Leviticus, and Deuteronomy, which offer a *complete* account of the origins of Judaism to Hecataeus's own time. Perhaps this also offers us a rare glimpse into the development of Judean canonizing, too?

GENESIS

Hecataeus raises a question mark about the antiquity of Genesis in the Mosaic canon. Among the wildly varying contemporary approaches to the structure of the Pentateuch, one phenomenon is widely (though not universally) agreed; the stories about the bringing of Abraham to Canaan and promising him the land for his descendants is not well integrated with the Moses story. There are, of course, allusions to Abraham, Isaac, and Jacob in Exodus–Numbers, and they can easily be attributed to the later stages of evolution; they are nearly all formulaic. The brief preview of slavery in Egypt in Gen. 15:13–14 is also easy to explain as an attempt to bind the story line more firmly. But the contents of Genesis do not as a whole prepare us for those of Exodus (does Abraham's family need a covenant law, need to rediscover and *conquer* the land promised?). Similarly, the Moses story nowhere states or even implies that the land to which the Israelites are being led is one that their ancestors had lived in for three generations. Nor is the transition from the patriarchal story to the Moses story well conceived. The only narrative link between the family history of Abraham and the escape from Egypt is the Joseph story, a relatively long and self-contained narrative that contrasts with the form and content of the preceding stories in Genesis: in Martin Noth's words, "This Joseph story, a masterpiece of narrative art, is traditio-historically a latecomer in the sphere of the Pentateuchal narrative."[27] Perhaps an earlier connection between the patriarchal narrative and the Moses story is hinted at in Josh. 24:4, which merely notes that "Jacob and his sons went down to Egypt," maybe as Abraham had, at a time of famine, without recourse to Joseph's activities.

The Abraham-Jacob stories represent an originally *alternative* account of how the "Israelites" acquired their land: by settlement from the East. They are a non-Mosaic explanation of the origins of the nation, in which several temples are instituted, and the land is promised, without condition. That this process of land occupation commences with the fall of Babylon (Genesis 11) is highly suggestive, of course.[28] But the addition of the narratives linking the creation of the world to the (genealogical) founder of the nation is probably an even later stage, and this historiographical movement has been convincingly analyzed by Van Seters.[29] But why this addition to the Moses canon of non-Moses stories? Genesis answers questions raised by the Moses canon, and traces the origins of the Judeans to the creation of the world. It also has a strong colonial theme: Abraham's family migrates to a land assigned to it, where it grows wealthy. No doubt these stories existed alongside the Mosaic one, as an alternative account of immigration. But their attachment to the Mosaic canon is entirely understandable.

CONCLUSIONS

The development of the Mosaic canon cannot be reconstructed in detail. But a silhouette can be drawn, and some of the theories about it can be deconstructed. This canon was produced between the beginning of the Persian period and the schism between the communities of Judea and Samaria: a period of three centuries. It was developed from a search for identity on the part of an immigrant elite in a colonial society where they governed but did not feel totally at home. The idea of a national constitution is probably in some way related to Darius's initiative of local laws to govern different ethnic groups in the empire, though nothing in the canon can easily be identified with any specific code. Deuteronomy may have provided such a code, or may have been developed from one. Or perhaps it is represented only (and only in part) by the laws in Exodus 21:1–23:19, which have been reworked during the evolution of the Mosaic canon to fit their narrative context.

The stories about Moses, as about Abraham, meet the needs of the colonial immigrants: he liberates them from foreign oppression and delivers them to a land. In fact, according to Hecataeus he takes them all the way to Jerusalem! The Joshua story, however, has been accommodated in the Mosaic canon very economically. Moses' commission to his deputy and his final speech on the Moab plain enter only at the end of Numbers (27:12 and other passages from Num. 33:50 onward). We can propose, then, an outline of how the Moses canon has been created from an original account of his founding of the nation, supplemented by the attachment of a once independent Deuteronomy and an also once independent account of another founder (or founders), Abraham, Isaac, and Jacob. The organizing principle of this canon, then, was historiographical, for the work of Moses came to be set in the context of a history of the origins of "Israel" from creation onward, and also, through Deuteronomy, to a succeeding history of that people.

It is not necessary to decide that Deuteronomy "moved" from one canon to another in being detached from Joshua–Kings and attached to Genesis—Numbers. Canons do not have to be so rigid, and Deuteronomy might have been attached to either or both, depending on the proclivities of the archiver or the general consensus of the scribal community. But because the idea of a Mosaic canon was so firmly established, writings dealing with events or persons after Moses' death were grouped elsewhere, and the Mosaic canon consolidated into five scrolls. The addition of Deuteronomy appears to have been decisive in giving its own name "torah" to the entire canon. The perception of this Mosaic canon as the constitution of the Jewish people understandably not only led to its preeminence among Judeans, but in some cases (Samaritans, Jews of Alexandria, possibly Sadducees) to a status as the only books of divine origin that Judaism possessed.

Chapter 7

The Canonizing
of Prophets

Both James Barr and John Barton have argued (the latter in detail) that "law and prophets" continued to define a two-part canon rather than "law, prophets, and writings."[1] Barton in particular has stressed that the term "prophets" was often used to embrace all canonized books not included in the Mosaic canon or Torah; while the term "writings" could also be used for such books, this was not a formal name for a canon or a division of a canon before the rabbis' own classification.[2] This assertion is half correct: it is likely that no formal canon called "writings" was acknowledged before the rabbis. But there is evidence that a distinction could be, and sometimes was, made between "books of prophets" and other canonized works by earlier writers than the rabbis.

While there is, as Barton demonstrates, some evidence that the term "prophets" could be used to include writings beyond those later included among the prophets, it is possible to show that a distinct notion of a succession or a group of prophets was in existence, even within the canon itself, even if, as it becomes clear, not every witness to this canon agrees on what prophets were for! Rather than work forward, as with the Mosaic canon, let us this time move backward.

"PROPHETS" AS A
DISTINCT CANON?

Our latest pre-rabbinic witness to a canon of prophets is Josephus (*Against Apion* 1.37–42):

> It therefore naturally, or rather necessarily follows (seeing that with us it is not open to everybody to write the records, and that there is no discrepancy in what is written; seeing that, on the contrary, the prophets alone had this privilege, obtaining their knowledge of the most remote and ancient history through the inspiration which they owed to God, and committing to writing a clear account of the events of their own time just as they occurred)—it follows, I say, that we do not possess myriads

of inconsistent books conflicting with one another. Our books, those which are justly accredited (*ta dikaiōs pepisteumena*) are but twenty-two and contain the record of all time. Of these, five are the books of Moses, comprising the laws and the traditional history down to the death of the lawgiver. . . . From the death of Moses until Artaxerxes who succeeded Xerxes as king of Persia, the prophets subsequent to Moses wrote the history of the events of their own times in thirteen books. The remaining four books contain hymns to God and precepts. From Artaxerxes to our own time the complete history has been written, but has not been deemed worth of equal credit with the earlier records because of the failure of the exact succession of the prophets.

Josephus, then, anticipating the rabbinic classification, presumably puts together the books of Joshua–Kings and those of named prophets under a single rubric, and deems the prophets to have been historians. We must, indeed, bear in mind that Josephus is himself a historian and that he is writing for a particular purpose and audience. We ought not to conclude dogmatically that Josephus regarded prophets only as historians, without further ado. But he does exclude "hymns and precepts" (Psalms and Proverbs, at least) from "prophets," though he recognizes these scrolls also as canonical.

Philo of Alexandria's description of the *Therapeutae*[3] describes how this religious commune, who lived on the shores of Lake Mareotis just outside Alexandria, had a sacred room to which they would go, taking no food or drink but "laws, and oracles delivered through the mouths of prophets, and psalms and anything else that promotes and perfects knowledge and piety." Here again psalms are separated from prophets, though prophets are not presented as historians but as givers of oracles, whose words are conducive to piety.

In 2 Maccabees 2:13 the comment about Nehemiah's library refers to "scrolls about the kings and the prophets, and the writings of David, and letters of kings about votive offerings" (13 ἐξηγοῦντο δὲ καὶ ἐν ταῖς ἀναγραφαῖς καὶ ἐν τοῖς ὑπομνηματισμοῖς τοῖς κατὰ τὸν Νεεμιαν τὰ αὐτὰ καὶ ὡς καταβαλλόμενος βιβλιοθήκην ἐπισυνήγαγεν τὰ περὶ τῶν βασιλέων βιβλία καὶ προφητῶν καὶ τὰ τοῦ Δαυιδ καὶ ἐπιστολὰς βασιλέων περὶ ἀναθεμάτων). Although 15:9 speaks of "law and prophets," and it may be that "prophets" is loosely applicable to non-Mosaic writings, it is interesting that books about kings and about (or by) prophets seem to be distinguished.[4] It is perhaps significant that since this writer (first century B.C.E.) composed in Greek and lived outside Palestine, the distinction between "stories of kings" and "prophets" was recognized among Egyptian Jews (as with Philo) rather than those living in Judah.

Yet in Judah, the Qumran scrolls refer to "law" and "prophets"; the clearest evidence is in 1QS 1.3, "as he [God] commanded by the hand of Moses and all his servants the prophets." A similar conjunction of Moses and the prophets occurs in 1QS 8.15–16 and in CD 5.21–6.1, while the phrase "law of Moses" occurs in 1QS 5.8 and 8.22; CD 15.2, 9.12, etc. In CD 7.17 occurs "the books of the prophets." Slightly earlier, perhaps, ben Sira's grandson, in his prologue to the Greek translation of his father's work (132 B.C.E.), three times mentions "law," "prophets," and other writers/books. But ben Sira himself does not classify the books he knows in this way. Here are his comments (38:34–39:3):

> [H]e who devotes himself
> to the study of the torah of the Most High
> will seek out the wisdom of all the ancients
> and will be concerned with prophecies;
> he will preserve the discourse of notable men
> and penetrate the subtleties of parables;
> he will seek out the hidden meanings of proverbs
> and be at home with the obscurities of parables.

Here is a clear enough distinction between various kinds of ancient writings, though it looks rather as if ben Sira might have regarded them *all* as "the torah of the Most High." This is interesting because in the New Testament we find *nomos* also being used of writings outside the Mosaic five: in John 10:34 and Rom. 3:19 the Psalms are thus called, while Isaiah is *nomos* according to 1 Cor. 14:21. Within rabbinic Judaism, of course, *torah* can mean the entire scriptural canon as well as just its first section. The lesson to learn is that references to holy books should not be taken too precisely; terminology is inclined to be vague. Even vaguer, from a little later than ben Sira, is Daniel 9, which has the hero looking "among the scrolls" and finding a passage from Jeremiah.

We can perhaps go back a little further, to Zech. 1:4–6:

> Be not like your ancestors, to whom the former prophets (הנביאים הראשנים) have cried, saying, "Thus says Yahweh of armies; 'Turn now from your evil ways, and your evil practices'": but they did not hear, nor obey me, says Yahweh. Your ancestors, where are they? and the prophets, do they live for ever? But my words and my regulations, which I commanded my servants the prophets, did they not take hold of your ancestors? and they returned and said, "As Yahweh of armies intended to do unto us, according to our behavior, and according to our practices, so he has dealt with us."

This idea of a succession of prophets is also found quite extensively in Jeremiah: "my servants the prophets" have been ceaselessly sent by Yahweh from the time that the nation left Egypt (i.e., starting with Moses) and the people have never listened (7:25; 25:4; 26:5; 29:19; 35:15; 44:4). The phrase "my servants the prophets" has spilled over into Ezekiel (38:17) and Amos

(3:7)—once each! It can also be found five times in 2 Kings (9:7; 17:13, 23; 21:10; 24:2). The most explicit passage of all is 2 Kings 17:13:

> Still, Yahweh solemnly charged Israel and Judah by every prophet and seer, saying "Turn from your evil ways; keep my commandments and statutes, in accordance with all the law that I commanded your ancestors and that I sent to you by my servants the prophets."

Part of the notion of a succession of prophets is a warning against "false" prophets:

> I will raise up for them a prophet like you from among their own people; I will put my words into the mouth of the prophet who shall speak to them everything I command. Anyone who does not heed the words that the prophet shall speak in my name, I will myself hold accountable. But any prophet who speaks in the name of other gods or who presumes to speak in my name a word that I have not commanded the prophet to say, that prophet shall die. If you ask yourself, "How can we recognize a word that Yahweh has spoken?"—if a prophet speaks in the name of Yahweh but the thing does not take place or prove to be true, it is a word that Yahweh has not spoken. The prophet has spoken it presumptuously. Do not be frightened by him/it.
>
> (Deut. 18:18–22)

> If prophets or dream-interpreters appear among you and promise you omens or signs, and the omens or signs declared by them occur, and they say, "Let us follow other gods (whom you have not known) and let us serve them," you must not heed the words of these prophets or dream-interpreters; for Yahweh your god is testing you, to see whether indeed you love Yahweh your god with all your heart and soul. . . . those prophets or dream-interpreters shall be put to death.
>
> (Deut. 13:1–3, 5)

According to Deuteronomy, Yahweh raises up true prophets, though he may also raise up false ones to test people. However, false prophets can be shown up because their prophecies do not turn out. Even if they do, however, if they then invite the worship of other gods, they are false. Deuteronomy creates the categories of false prophet and true prophet, the latter being sent to reinforce what the Law already says.

The topic can become quite tricky, as when in 1 Kings 22, Micaiah gets his true message by eavesdropping, and the story implies that true prophets can be misled by lying spirits sent from the deity, while the highly complicated story in 1 Kings 13 has a true prophet being given a true prophecy, then a false prophecy by a false prophet, then a true prophecy by a false prophet. But these sophistical examples do not overturn the notion that there are, objectively, true and false prophets, even if false prophets exceptionally get a true message (and vice versa).

The idea of true versus false prophecy is certainly one of the themes of the book of Jeremiah, for example: chapter 28 relates a conflict between Jeremiah and Hananiah, one "true" prophet and one "false" one, while Jer. 14:14 (see 23:32) complains that *all* prophets are false (is he the only true one, or is he not one at all, like Amos [Amos 7:14]?).

The way in which the institution of prophecy has been *inserted* into Jeremiah and other texts has been analyzed by A. G. Auld.[5] Auld's argument, focused on Jeremiah, may be summarized as follows: in the poetry of Jeremiah, prophets are criticized; in the prose common to the Hebrew and Greek, the verb *nb'* is used more neutrally and indeed of Jeremiah himself. In the material peculiar to the received Masoretic Hebrew text, Jeremiah is called a "prophet" (*nabi*) several times. While in Kings there are plenty of persons called *nabi,* only one of these is called a *nabi* in Chronicles as well (Huldah: strictly she is a *nebi'ah*). The argument Auld makes is that the noun *nabi* is a feature *added* (and added differently) to both Kings and Chronicles, just as it develops during the formation of the Jeremiah scroll. In this process we can see *within canonical texts* the emergence of the notion of "prophecy" (represented by the root *nb'*).

The judgment about who are prophets, and which prophets are "true" and which "false" is, of course a judgment about *canon*. For we are dealing not with the question of individuals shouting in the marketplace but with written texts. The words of the "false" prophets are preserved, of course, only in the texts of the "true" ones. Whether or not some written prophetic texts were rejected as "false" we cannot know. But the notion of "prophecy" as a distinct institution, a part of the history of the nation, an agency in the legal relationship established between the god and his chosen people, points toward the existence, or the creation, of a canon of prophetic writings, those writings that represent the enduring message of "true" prophecy.

But the idea of such a "prophetic" institution is not a starting point for the collecting of scrolls of prophetic material; it can be seen to emerge in the canonizing of these books. However, this process does suggest that a distinction between "prophets" and other writings might have come about before the rabbis formally divided "prophets" from "writings." As we have seen, there is some evidence from the second century for this.

However, it seems that "prophets" could be interpreted in two ways: as historians, and as teachers of the law. As historians we have Josephus for evidence, but also the linking of "former" and "latter prophets." Prophets as teachers of the law is the usual rabbinic interpretation—but not for that reason only a latecomer, for the passages cited from Deuteronomy (and elsewhere) show that true prophecy was to be judged precisely on this criterion. Indeed, according to Deuteronomy, the perfect example of the prophet was Moses the lawgiver.

THE "DEUTERONOMIC HISTORY"

Noth's theory about the "Deuteronomistic History" held that Deuteronomy was attached to a "Deuteronomistic History" before being added to the Mosaic canon. If this theory were correct, then the scrolls from Joshua to Kings would have been known from their creation as a distinct collection, indeed as a single "work" spread over a number of scrolls. But even if they were not composed as a single creation, their content is such that they would have been archived sequentially. In fact, the very different character of the source materials and of the themes in each of these scrolls suggests rather that each of them *did* grow independently, and came together to form a historical sequence rather *as a canonizing process*. In other words, they were combined into a sequential history and edited (to varying extents) so as to provide a reasonably coherent interpretation based on a number of themes, some derived from Deuteronomy. Among these themes are avoidance of Canaanite practices, adherence to the covenant, provision of a single sanctuary, and provision of prophets as upholders of the covenant. But these themes are introduced in varying degrees of intensity, while the divine election of the dynasty of David is not a Deuteronomic theme. For instance, the books of Joshua and Judges deal with quite distinct themes though covering the same post-Mosaic epoch. We can even see this quite clearly in the transition between Joshua and Judges:

> Josh. 24:29: And after this Joshua ben Nun, the servant of the Yahweh, died, being a hundred and ten years old.

> Josh. 24:31: And the people served Yahweh all the days of Joshua, and all the days of the elders that survived him, who had seen all the great deeds of Yahweh that he did for Israel.

> Judg. 1:1: Now after the death of Joshua the Israelites asked Yahweh, "Who shall go up for us against the Canaanites first, to fight against them?"

> Judg. 2:6: And when Joshua had let the people go, the Israelites went each one to their inheritance, to possess the land.

> Judg. 2:7: And the people served Yahweh all the days of Joshua, and all the days of the elders that survived him, who had seen all the great deeds of Yahweh that he did for Israel.

Judg. 2:8: And Joshua ben Nun, the servant of Yahweh, died, being a hundred and ten years old.

We can see clearly how the scribes indicated at the beginning of the Judges scroll that it took up from where the Joshua scroll left off. (The same device is evident at the end of Chronicles and beginning of Ezra.) But even this editing cannot conceal the basic contradiction between the complete conquest claimed in Joshua[6] and the partial conquest in Judges. The definition of "judge" in 1 Samuel is quite different from that in Judges; there is no hint of a national institution of "judgeship" (see 1 Sam. 2:10, 25; 3:13; 8:5, 6, 20; 24:12, 15). As for Samuel and Kings, some recent work has begun to show that these have undergone a good deal of editorial and textual development, including the insertion of the Elijah and Elisha material, and perhaps even all the stories about the kingdom of Israel.[7] This is not the place to argue a case for the history of these books, and there is no consensus at present. But the processes seem to have continued after the composition of Chronicles, however early they started. The way is open to consider that Noth is as wrong over the Pentateuch as he is over the "Deuteronomistic History," and the relatively coherent shape of both narratives is due not to some original unity of conception but to a process of copying and recopying, all the whole shaping individual scrolls into a rational sequence with a certain degree of homogeneity—but only as much as a process of editing can achieve. The essential difference between the two models is that in canonizing texts, scribes are concerned to fit the material into some kind of rational sequence (in this case, chronological) but not to dispel every contradiction or remove every piece of unevenness. Another important difference is that canonizing does not mean a respect for the fixed text of a scroll, but quite the opposite: to reinforce the canonicity of texts by making them fit better the use for which they are being preserved.

But why did this historiographical narrative come to be known as "prophecy"? The narrative contains stories about the place of prophecy in the (narrated) history of ancient Israel. From Samuel onward, the confrontation between king and prophets is a familiar theme: Nathan rebukes David and also promises him a dynasty; Abijah pronounces the division of the kingdom under Solomon; Elijah and Elisha dictate to kings when or whether to fight; Elisha anoints kings; Isaiah confronts Ahaz and Hezekiah, as does Jeremiah. The portrait overall reflects a political philosophy centering on the conflict between a direct divine commission and an institutionalized, secular, and rational government. The narrative is clearly overall on the side of the former. This seems strange if the narrative was canonized by scribes! But it is worth remembering that in the Persian and early Hellenistic periods the argument cannot be about prophets and kings, but about something else. Insofar as the narratives oppose

Judean kings, they are not necessarily anti-Persian. These kings (and the population of monarchic Israel and Judah) are ideological targets, not real ones. Good kings observe the law, like Persian rulers.

The historical narrative ends with the exile, because *that is all that needed explaining.* The society that generated this history knew what had happened since. The problem addressed is this: if we are the true Israel, why were we exiled? And who were we before we came back? The answer is, of course: we were seduced by the indigenous population (which will not happen again); we were betrayed by kings (which will not happen again); and we were misled by false prophets (which will not happen again). As for prophecy: the lesson is that false prophecy is dead, and so are the canonized prophets. What remains of legitimate prophecy is within the orbit of the Temple, where its orthodoxy can be guaranteed.

But the importance of prophecy in the Joshua–Kings scrolls can be over-estimated, and is actually not very strong overall. Joshua, Moses' direct successor, is nowhere called a prophet; the only prophets in Judges are an anonymous voice in 6:8 and Deborah. In 1 Samuel the eleven references to prophets comprise one mention of Samuel himself and one of Gad, while the rest are peripheral as well as neutral in tone (and include Saul). In 2 Samuel there are three occurrences, two to Nathan and one to Gad. But 1 Kings has 46 references to prophets and 2 Kings has 29 of them. However, as we have seen, there are reasons to think these are not all part of the narrative as first conceived, but have been inserted. So the narrative of Joshua–Kings, we might say, *becomes* increasingly "prophetic" as the narrative proceeds, *but also as time goes on.* Why?

There are two possible explanations. One is that the narrative (more strictly, the various scrolls that are comprising the narrative), in being influenced to varying degrees by the ideology of Deuteronomy, have also borrowed the Deuteronomic picture of Moses as a prophet, and in making prophecy rather than kingship the ideal instrument of divine governance have accommodated the narrative to the Mosaic constitution. What happened after Moses, then, needed to be narrated with reference to the figure of Moses the prophet as ancestor of the line of true mediators of the divine word. This suggestion works better if we abandon the notion of an original "Deuteronomistic History" in favor of a Deuteronomistic influence on the canonizing of the scrolls.

The second explanation is that the scrolls of Samuel and especially Kings (for it is these we are talking about) have been canonized in connection with other scrolls containing collections of oracles (and perhaps narratives) attached to individual prophets, and that the canonization of these other scrolls into a collection of "prophets" led to the idea of an institution of "prophecy" which was then worked into the historiographical narrative. Neither of these solutions can be demonstrated. We ought, in fact, to resist imposing neat and uniform solutions, and recognize that canonizing is a complex process, not reducible to discrete "editings" but to a more complex process of transmission. We can instead examine the relationships between Deuteronomy, the historiographical narrative of Joshua–Kings, and what we shall have to call the "prophetic" books to learn what little we can about the process by which the last two were canonized.

SCROLLS OF
PROPHETIC SAYINGS

It was argued in the previous chapter that the formation of the Mosaic canon began during the Persian period and not earlier. That conclusion leads us to suppose that the canonization of Mosaic torah and of other scrolls of historiography and prophecy was developing at the same time, and probably in the same place (Jerusalem—where else?). It remains possible that a "prophecy" canon originated as a counterweight to the Mosaic canon and that Deuteronomy's presentation of Moses as a prophet like no other and its concern to control prophecy is influenced by the existence of a prophetic canon.[8] But the wide range of interest reflected in the prophetic scrolls themselves and the differences in their composition (i.e., their canonizing history) make it necessary to think in terms of more than one canonizing process, or perhaps more than one stage in a single but complicated canonizing process. The first produced Isaiah, Jeremiah, and Ezekiel and a collection of twelve individual scrolls. Another grouped these together as a large "prophets" canon. A third (it seems) linked these prophets to the historiographical narrative that told of the historical circumstances in which the contents of the (named) prophetic scrolls made sense.

Let us briefly review these phases. Although there is some dispute about the matter, the scroll of Isaiah probably came into existence by processes of commentary and supplementation. Let us concentrate on the supplementation: a series of poems from chapters 40 onward reflect an originally independent collection. Whether this collection was appended by their author(s) or by a scribe who thought they may belong with Isaiah does not matter here. Nor does it matter whether chapters 56—66 represent a separate collection again or arise from continuous supplementation. The structure of the book represents a perfect example of canonizing in miniature, and the canon in question is the "words" (or the "vision") of Isaiah. Whatever was added to this scroll was deemed by the scribal librarian (and perhaps even intended by their author) to belong in the Isaianic "canon." The grounds for allocating material to Isaiah may have been because of its content: the theme of Jerusalem ("Zion") and its "salvation" (befitting the name of the prophet, which means "Yahweh saves") are characteristic of the original collection. The creation of the scroll(s) of Jeremiah (there are at least two distinct editions) is more complicated (and just as disputed!): an original kernel of poetry has been expanded by prose additions, in a Deuteronomic vein; a good deal of biography (or hagiography) has been inserted as well. The canon of Jeremiah focuses much more on the individual as a typical Deuteronomic prophet, and seems to have grown from within rather than, as with Isaiah, chiefly by supplementation. In both these respects it is entirely different from Isaiah. The one focuses on Jerusalem's deliverance, the other on its destruction. Ezekiel seems to have come into existence as more of a homogeneous composition, and its interests are quite different from either Isaiah or Jeremiah, though there are some slight thematic links with Isaiah in the "holiness" of Yahweh: there is a much greater emphasis on priestly matters; the claims of the Zadokite lineage are pressed.

What unites these three large scrolls, however, is their focus on the fate of Jerusalem. This might also be seen as the basic theme of the narrative of Kings, which commences with the building of the temple and ends with its destruction. They are argumentative scrolls, all of them, making a case for a particular view of the city and its leadership. For this reason they can justifiably be taken as reflecting conflicting or at least differing points of view regarding the politics of the city and its territory. Therein perhaps lies the answer to why such literature was started. *Whether* these actual scrolls grew from a kernel of sayings by the prophets concerned is hard to say. But if so, and to whatever extent, it is not implausible to suggest that the basis for a canon of such writings may lie in the Jerusalem(?) archives, where letters from named or even unnamed prophets, sent to the king or temple, had, as always, been filed away neatly. This we know happened at Mari. If it happened also in Jerusalem, these letters may in due course have been copied onto papyrus or leather and grouped according to authorship or theme. At some crucial point, however, the collections would have ceased to become *archives* of merely historical interest, and have developed into literary texts as the scribes embellished them, engaging in the political dialogue that the original collections had initiated. It is also possible that such literary "prophecies" continued to arrive during the Persian period and onward, and that these texts inspired a great deal of literary "prophesying" on the part of the scribal establishment. Were prophetic oracles part of the scribal curriculum? That would explain the unnecessarily large number of tirades against foreign nations in these scrolls!

Ezekiel was in fact probably composed as an extended literary work from the outset, and not by an active intermediary but by a writer creating a prophetic character. The same is true of some at least of the writings combined into the canon of twelve prophets. This collection of twelve on one scroll is a perfect illustration of a canon. One does not imagine that a thirteenth would ever have been added, though a twelfth was created by separating some text from Zechariah and making of it a "Malachi," and perhaps by constituting an "Obadiah" from a fragment of poetry. Despite some recent arguments to the contrary, it does not seem that the scroll of twelve prophets was intended to be read as a *single document;* there are some hints of scribal links between the contents, but they are neither conclusive nor surprising.

We should, then, think of the first stages of canonizing as comprising four scrolls, each independent of the others. But the notion that each of these (and indeed each of the individual units of the Twelve) represents the product of disciples of prophets will not work. This is clear as we consider the connection between the contents and their eponymous authors. The paucity of historical cross-referencing *within* these prophetic scrolls is significant. Amos and Hosea are presented as contemporaries but have nothing to say about each other; likewise with Micah and Isaiah; while Jeremiah, in condemning all other prophets, presumably included Ezekiel! Each of these prophetic figures is unaware, it seems, of his contemporaries. Or, as we should rather put it, the individually named prophetic books seem unaware of each other to a great extent. The one exception is Jeremiah 26, which invokes Micah. We do, of course, now and then find identical texts occurring in more than one prophetic book, but this is just as probably evidence of free-floating sayings as of cross-referencing.

Also noteworthy is how slender are the links in many cases between the material and the named "minor prophets." Hosea, Amos, Micah, Zephaniah, Haggai, and Zechariah are given dates by regnal years, as in Kings, but of these only Amos and Haggai are mentioned by name outside the superscription, though Zechariah's name occurs in three superscriptions. Joel, Obadiah, Nahum, Habakkuk, and (possibly) Malachi contain only the name in the opening verse. Leaving Jonah aside, only Amos and Haggai have narratives about them. Taken as a whole, we have to conclude that the historical context, the life, and the deeds of the "minor prophets" were of no great interest—only the poetry. This tells against the idea that these collections were attached by disciples of prophets. What is most distinctive of disciples is that they tell stories about their masters. And since the datings are (where they exist) confined to minimal regnal formulae, the little concern for historical contextualizing seems to belong to those scribes interested in linking the minor prophets with the rest of the prophetic canon. It is very likely that these superscriptions are guesswork and that material was either composed and transmitted anonymously or attached to a name and no more.

The view that the prophets had disciples who preserved and updated the sayings of their masters has never been supported by anthropological or literary evidence; it merely supplies a convenient mechanism whereby these edited compositions can be traced back to an individual prophet. One text that has been claimed to support the idea is Isa. 8:16: "Bind up testimony, seal teaching, by/in/with my disciples." This is an enigmatic phrase, without context and without a clear meaning. It could be interpreted as saying that the words of the prophet are somehow preserved in his disciples as in a bound and sealed scroll, but the vocabulary is strange: "testimony" (*te'udah*) and "teaching" (*torah*) are unusual terms for prophetic oracles, and *limmud* ("disciple"?) is a very rare word. A more concrete interpretation of the phrase is that Isaiah wishes something he has had written down (a testimony) to be bound up and sealed (so that it cannot be tampered with), and in the presence of those known to him, or who know him, namely trustworthy witnesses; the idea here will perhaps have been that when his warnings (his testimony) turn out to be well-founded, he will be vindicated. Whether these are in any case original words of a prophet is yet another question: the word *limmud* occurs elsewhere in the book of Isaiah in 50:4 (twice) and 54:13, suggesting it may belong with a late phase in the development of the contents of the Isaiah scroll. In these passages it does refer to teaching, in contrast to its only other appearances in Jer. 2:24 and 13:23, where it means "accustomed to." We shall see presently that Jeremiah was not regarded as having transmitted anything to disciples, but to have written a scroll. None of the fifteen eponymous prophets of the Hebrew scriptures is described as having a band of disciples. This does not mean these characters did not work this way: simply that there is no evidence at all for it and a lot of counter-evidence.

The canonizing process did, of course, produce some linkage between the historiography and the prophets collections. 2 Kings 18:13–20:19 was transferred to the end of the Isaiah collection (36—39), though differences in the extant texts show subsequent changes to the narrative within one or other of the books, and Isaiah was of course lengthened. 2 Kings 25 was copied into Jeremiah at chapter 39 (in the MT edition) and the plot interwoven with the fate of Jeremiah. But Isaiah and Jonah remain the only prophets from the canonized collection to be mentioned in the Joshua–Kings narrative. Jonah is almost certainly a story inspired by the allusion in 2 Kings 14:25. If it could be argued that Isaiah 36—39 was taken from the book of Isaiah and put into Kings,[9] we could even argue that the History betrays awareness of none of the prophetic scrolls. It is in any case still possible to suggest that the Isaiah scroll was prompted by the Isaiah narrative in 2 Kings. It is certainly very curious that while the History has been adapted so as to give more prominence to prophets, it has not made any allusion to literary prophets other than Isaiah and Jonah.

But not only the Isaiah and Jeremiah scrolls have been edited to cross-reference with the History. A number of them have been dated by the scheme of 2 Kings (and, as just observed, the book of Jonah is probably based on a character in 2 Kings). But again, these specific overlaps really highlight the absence of any wider congruence. They are not intrinsic to the structural growth of any of the scrolls. The most dramatic instance of linkage, however, occurs at the end of Malachi (the end of the Twelve), where the coming of Elijah constitutes not only a reference to the History but also, perhaps, to Deuteronomy's promise of a prophet like Moses, understood as a promise of eschatological return (for more discussion of this, see below).

The theory (for such it is) that Deuteronomy furnished a basis not only for the Mosaic Torah but for what was to be called a Prophets collection explains the connections between the two emerging canons. However, as observed, it does not imply that all the books of "prophecy" were composed under the influence of Deuteronomy. The fact that Ezekiel and Isaiah look to have been compiled independently suggests that the process of creating a "prophets" collection involved the incorporation of other works.

JEREMIAH
AND DEUTERONOMY

Detailed, as opposed to general, connections in the collection of prophetic scrolls with Deuteronomy's prophetic Moses are as rare as they are with the Joshua to Kings series. But it is obvious that the Jeremiah scroll has a particularly close relationship to Deuteronomy, which no one who reads the prose "sermons" can fail to recognize. But one dramatic example of a link between Moses and Jeremiah is the famous story of Jeremiah's scroll (Jeremiah 36). The most common misreading of this story is to take it as an account of how prophetic books came into being. But according to this story, the scroll was originally written only so that it could be read aloud by someone else—because Jeremiah himself was indisposed. The scroll is in fact read by someone who was not intended to read it (the king) and another scroll is written, presumably to replace the first, and for the purposes of being read publicly. The story does not explain why prophetic scrolls were written![10]

But it does make, to any attentive reader, important points about the status of these scrolls. The mechanism of dictating is all-important:

Then Jeremiah called Baruch ben Neraiah and Baruch wrote on a scroll from the mouth of Jeremiah all the words of Yahweh that he had spoken to him.

(v. 4)

Then they questioned Baruch, "Tell us now, how did you write all these words? Was it from his mouth?" Baruch answered them, "He dictated all these words to me and I wrote them with ink on the scroll."

(v. 17)

Then Jeremiah took another scroll and gave it to the scribe Baruch ben Neraiah, who wrote on it from Jeremiah's mouth all the words of the scroll that king Jehoiakim of Judah had burnt. . . .

(v. 32)

The importance of these passages is that they emphasize the contents of the scroll as being divine words.[11] While the book contains many statements from Jeremiah, including poetry presumably assigned to him, the contents of the scroll are entirely from the deity. They have come by word of mouth to the prophet. They have equally come by word of mouth from the prophet to the scribe. Ergo: these are the words of God. This puts the prophetic scroll on a par with the contents of the Torah. The story may be meant merely to canonize Jeremiah as a prophetic supplement to Torah (and Jeremiah as the "prophet like Moses"?). If so, Ezekiel's flying scroll (Ezekiel 2) might be influenced by it. At any rate, such a story shows us that one prophetic scroll at least was intended to be understood in light of "torah." That line of interpretation, as we have seen, continues through Ezra 9:10–12, which has prophets "commanding laws" like torah (unless this is an allusion here to Haggai).

PROPHETS AND SAMARIA

One important difference between both the History and the prophets canons and the Moses canon is the attitude toward Samaria. These are *Judean* canons, and contain throughout quite distinct anti-Samari(t)an sentiments. Joshua, it is true, does not evince any discernible bias, much as Deuteronomy, and that may explain why the Samaritan canon includes him. Indeed, the covenant ceremonies in chaps. 8 and 24 at Shechem might even suggest that this book has a Samarian origin.[12] But with the opening of Judges, the pro-Judean bias of the remainder of the books begins. While none of the tribes is said to have succeeded in driving out all the Canaanites, Judah alone escapes censure: with Simeon and Caleb it takes its allotted territory except for the plain, because of the enemy's iron chariots. But note (1:19) "Yahweh was with Judah." By contrast, the formula "they did not drive out" characterizes every other tribe (Dan is even worse). In effect, the "Northern" tribes (including Benjamin) failed to take their land as ordered. The implication is that, never having taken it properly, they were never destined to hold it. Their kingdom was doomed at the outset.

Thereafter, the Benjaminite king is a failure, and only the Judahite David turns out to be the ideal ruler. The story that the kingdom of Israel was in fact a splinter from Judah is a chauvinistic fiction; but the point is made consistently that the one Israel is to be ruled from Jerusalem and not from Samaria (or any other site to the north). This cannot mean anything other than very strong anti-Samarian propaganda. Yet the Samarians share the torah! A recent study, again by Graeme Auld, may help to explain this.[13] His analysis of the material common to Kings and Chronicles leads him to suggest that, rather than Chronicles having copied from Kings, both copied from an earlier source but one that nevertheless told the story up to the Babylonian deportation and therefore is to be dated after that event. On this view, the Deuteronomistic revision of this earlier account added material about the "northern kingdom" that was not in its *Vorlage*. If so, we are left with an originally pro-Judean but not necessarily anti-Samarian account, which (in Auld's view) the Chronicler rather more closely reflects in this instance. The "Deuteronomistic" rewrite of this introduced, among other things, a rather anti-northern subplot. If Auld is right, then also the dating of at least the book of Kings should be placed well into the Persian period at the earliest. Auld's thesis is likely to meet with firmly entrenched opposition, but it is consistent with the arguments put so far in this book; and whether or not he is correct, the fact remains of a negative appraisal of Samaria, and that must not be overlooked.

But explicit condemnation of Samarians is in fact perhaps less outright than a complete rift might warrant. According to 2 Kings 24, the population of Samaria was displaced by foreign settlers ("to this day"); and because lions are killing the people (due to their ignorance of the "law of the land") the Assyrian king sends a priest carried away from there to teach them. He resided in Bethel: but despite his efforts, many other nationalities practiced their own cults. But "they also worshiped Yahweh . . . to this day, they continue to practice their former customs" (vv. 32, 34). The plausibility of the story need not detain us. But the account leaves us with the acknowledgment of a Yahweh-worshiping community in Samaria which, if only it would learn from its wicked past and acknowledge the authority of Jerusalem, might rejoin "Israel." In this respect its attitude, though more overtly hostile than Chronicles, is less so than Nehemiah.

WHY IS THERE A
PROPHETIC SCROLLS CANON?

The existence of a canon of historical scrolls telling the story of the nation from the death of Moses to the end of the "old order" does not require even a paragraph of explanation. The existence of a second account in Chronicles is more of a problem, but in any case neither will be discussed here. The interesting problem lies in the four prophetic scrolls of Isaiah, Jeremiah, Ezekiel, and the Twelve—all of them, as I have suggested, capable of being understood as canons in their own right and, indeed, each one entirely independent of the others. However, being archived together and being dated, as far as possible, on the guidelines developed from the canon of History (or whatever it was called), it became a larger canon of scrolls.

But *why* are there these prophetic scrolls in the first place? Why were they written, why preserved, and why copied and (in some cases) so grossly expanded? We have seen that once canonized, they were linked to history and to torah, and that the institution of prophecy became an important issue for the canonizers. In the case of the Moses torah or the books of Joshua–Kings, however, we can readily identify both the political and the intellectual interests of the scribal class at work, creating a national ideology and, indeed, a ruling class ideology as well. In the case of some of the books finally embraced in the "Writings" canon (see chapters 8 and 9), we can also deduce plausible reasons for both authorship and readership: for private pleasure or moral instruction or religious reflection. But the prophetic books are something of a problem (Jonah apart, for it is by any standards a very good read). The inherited view that these books emanate from individuals who had a message for their times, and that their disciples or schools wrote their words down, does not explain why they were preserved, nor, as pointed out, why so little historical context attaches to so much of it. And, as Barton has said, we should not assume that anyone read the larger prophetic books as wholes (any more than they do now, except for "canonical critics"). Rather, they were studies in excerpts.[14] This implies that they were understood to be structured as anthologies, as little canons of words attached to a name. That seems to explain Isaiah and Jeremiah and the Twelve—up to a point, but not entirely, for there is some evidence of chronological and thematic organization, and we ought to ask what notions about the point of these scrolls induced the canonizers to edit them in the way they did.

Why did prophetic scrolls, which are a unique form of ancient literature, come to be produced? What, after all, is their purpose? Prophetic scrolls on the whole seem to comprise political and social criticism, and deal not only with the fate of Samaria but with the behavior of Judah and other societies, and always under the threat of political consequences and implications. Some of the major prophetic figures are active in political direction or intrigue, though the majority are not. This literature casts its eye beyond its own nation to the deeds of neighboring states both in the genre of "oracles against foreign nations" and in its presentation of foreign imperial expansion as punishment for Israel. It also focuses very firmly on the ultimate question of the destiny of history. In fact, if the Latter Prophets have any uniting theme, it is what we call "eschatology." Will Israel finally vanquish the other nations (Ezekiel), or will a golden age supervene in which all nations will come to Jerusalem to worship Yahweh (Isaiah)? Are the other nations on a par with Judah/Israel, to be punished like them (Amos), or are they to repent and be forgiven (Jonah)?

These prophetic books, taken as a whole, explore a theme that also dominates the book of Deuteronomy and the "former prophets": the understanding of history in the light of the destiny of "Israel." The problem is addressed by a number of perspectives. In Jeremiah the covenant plays a major role; in Isaiah it is Jerusalem that features; in Ezekiel the significance of the temple. But the impact of *monotheism* is everywhere apparent. Behind all these texts lies the question of the status of Judah as a society wedded to the one universal deity; and correspondingly, the rather narrower issues addressed by the historiography—of the demise of the old monarchy as a result of monarchs breaking the covenant—are inadequate. What is the political role of Judeans in their god's historical scheme? What, indeed, *is* the scheme? Understanding the past is one important effort, but writing the history of the future is more difficult. Both, however, seek to discern and apply the meaning of history in terms of the political and moral character of Judean society.

The observation that the structure of the prophetic books creates a focus on eschatology has been made often before.[15] Will Judah go the way of Israel—scattered by divine fury (Amos)? Or is Israel always to be loved by its god (Hosea)? Will the nations come to Jerusalem to worship its god (Isaiah)? Or will they be vanquished as a demonstration of his power (Ezekiel, Nahum)? Or be spared through repentance (Jonah)? Will the final divine punishment include Judah (Joel)? Or only its enemies (Obadiah)? The clearest sign of overall editing in this direction is the ending of the book of the Twelve, where we find a promise of the return of Elijah, a figure that unites the Twelve not only with the History but perhaps also with Deuteronomy's "prophet like Moses." Blenkinsopp has also suggested that the combination of three major and twelve minor books represents, deliberately, the twelve tribes and the three patriarchs. Another possibility exists, however: like the three priests and twelve nonpriests of the Qumran Community Rule 8.1, they perhaps represent the tribes and the sons of Aaron. Both Jeremiah and Ezekiel are said to be priests (of

Isaiah we do not know). The suggestion would be more plausible if we knew of other prophetic scrolls that had been rejected. But of course it is entirely possible that the number was conceived from an early stage and all prophetic material canonized deliberately within three scrolls.

The canonizing process, then, moves the political and social critique of the prophetic scrolls in the direction of a debate about the movement of history, internationalizing and universalizing it just as the cult of Yahweh was the cult of the one high god. However, and perhaps quite deliberately, no consensus is being encouraged. The future is not something on which agreement can or should be reached. Within this canon, then, exists a range of scenarios. They are, however, coupled to warnings and promises concerning lifestyle, which makes them not at all incompatible with the Torah canon. This said, the idea of an inexorable world order, one not driven solely by the state of Judean morals, is also put on the agenda.

The process of canonizing prophetic books, then, generated a literary institution called "prophecy,"[16] but also notions of what prophecy was about. This institution was the means by which the deity had informed Judeans—or indeed, humanity at large—of the meaning of its history and its future. The very fact that these books became canonized means, I think, that they were regarded as being of contemporary relevance. The story in Daniel 9, for example, construes a statement of Jeremiah as a sign needing interpretation, which is duly given. This is a mantic hermeneutic. Manticism is the culture of divination, the belief that the natural world contains clues to things otherwise known only by the supernatural, such as dreams, marks on the entrails of sacrificed animals, or unusual meteorological or astronomical phenomena. In Daniel 5, the sign is writing on a wall; in chapter 9 it is a fragment of prophecy.

But before reaching that, or any, conclusion, let us ask by whom and why these scrolls were read, and try to work backward. Ben Sira's inclusion of the prophecies in the scholar's curriculum tells us only that they should, like all Hebrew literature, be studied, but does not tell us exactly why. The ending of the book of Hosea (14:9) is a little clearer:

> Those who are wise understand these things; those who are discerning
> know them. For the ways of Yahweh are right and the upright walk in
> them, but transgressors stumble in them.

Perhaps this "wisdom" language disguises an admonition to study the Mosaic torah, and it may just mean that the prophets were understood as being ethical teachers. But the "wise, who understand these things" reminds us of Dan. 12:10 (though with *maskil* for *ḥakam*) and suggests that prophecy might contain hidden meanings. The idea that in the prophetic scrolls one found hints about the *future* makes these scrolls a congenial companion to the history of the "old regime," and perhaps provides the sort of link between the two that led both Joshua–Kings and Isaiah–Twelve Prophets to be referred to as "prophecy." But, as with so many issues related to canonizing, we can only exercise our minds over the clues that have been left. The recesses of the scribal school, the archive, and most of all the Judean scribal mind are not as readily accessible as we would like, or as textbooks are supposed to make them.

CHAPTER 8

Canons of
David and Solomon

It is a widely shared belief among readers of the Bible that the author of the
Psalms is David and the author of Proverbs Solomon. In fact, although these
two texts do not themselves entirely support that notion, we can nevertheless
see evidence that psalm composition was canonized under the name of David,
and texts of instruction under the name of Solomon. Stories about David and
Solomon in the books of Samuel and Kings have also been developed with
an eye to emphasizing their role as producers of a certain type of literature.

Consequently, it appears reasonable to pursue the suggestion that there
developed, during the Second Temple period, the notions of Davidic and
Solomonic works of literature, such that works of a certain kind were composed for this canon, attracting the names of these kings. In *In Search of
'Ancient Israel'* I sketched out, with some, but not total, seriousness, the notion of scribal "colleges" of David and Solomon, in which psalms and wisdom texts were written and copied.[1] Here the idea is being redefined into
a notion of distinct Davidic and Solomonic canons (though the idea of
scribal "colleges" is not necessarily being abandoned!).

DAVID AS MUSICIAN
IN SAMUEL

The portrait of David as a musician takes a secondary role in the books of
Samuel, but is firmly enough established. Into the (composite) narratives of
the anointing of Saul and of David, and of the meeting between the two, is
a brief section (16:14–23) that describes how Saul sent for David as one who
could play the lyre. This gift is once again mentioned in 1 Sam. 18:10, when
Saul throws a spear at David while the latter is playing. In 2 Sam. 1:17, after the death of Saul and Jonathan:

> David sang this lament over Saul and his son Jonathan. He instructed it
> to be taught to the Judahites. It is written in the book of Yashar.[2]

126

David also sings another song, an elegy for Abner, in 2 Sam. 3:33–34, and in 2 Samuel 22 utters a psalm of thanksgiving for military success over the Philistines, of which Psalm 18 is another version. Its place alongside the "last words of David" (23:1–7) may suggest that it is part of an appendix: Noth regarded it as subsequent to the composition of his "Deuteronomistic History."[3] Thus, while in the Samuel books there is no great importance attached to David as a musician, and, indeed, he has no connection with the composition of songs for worship (since he plays no part in the establishment of the Jerusalem temple), there are clear signs of such a trait, even if, as is possible, they have been brought in under the influence of other literature about David as singer.

DAVID IN CHRONICLES

In Chronicles the portrait of David as cultic musician is central. Neither the lament for Saul and Jonathan nor that for Abner are included (Chronicles covers this period very briefly). But David's solo dancing before the ark in 2 Sam. 6:16, which does not include any mention of music or indicate musical gifts, reads in 1 Chron. 13:8 "David and all Israel were dancing before God with all their might, with song and lyres and harps and tambourines and cymbals and trumpets." Although the divine refusal to allow David to build a sanctuary is narrated in Chronicles (chap. 17) as well as 2 Samuel (chap. 7), the Chronicler, as is well known, proceeds to have David make the preparations for the building of the temple in Jerusalem (1 Chron. 22). In 1 Chronicles 16, David has already appointed Levites, and specifically the family of Asaph, to perform the musical worship, inaugurating this commission with a psalm (vv. 17–36). Having appointed the levitical and priestly temple service in chapters 23–24, David then proceeds to organize the musicians (chap. 25), before attending to gatekeepers and other officials and then noncultic officers.

A case can be made for considering the book of Chronicles itself to have been associated with (if not part of) a "David" canon. Here are a few reasons:

1. 1 Chronicles commences its narrative with the death of Saul and accession of David, and makes David the architect of the temple service.
2. The names of persons and groups in the headings of psalms correspond with names of levitical persons or groups in Chronicles:

Name	Psalms	Chronicles
Asaph	50; 73–83	1 Chron. 15:16–19; 16:4–5, 7, 37; 25; 2 Chron. 5:12; 20:1; 29:13; 35:15[4]
Korah	42; 44–49; 84–85; 87–88	1 Chron. 1:35; 2:43; 6:22, 37; 9:19;[5] 12:6; 26:1; 2 Chron. 20:19
Jeduthun[6]	39, 62, 77	1 Chron. 9:16; 16:38–42; 25:1–6; 2 Chron. 5:12; 29:14; 35:15 (exclusive to Chronicles)
Heman	88	1 Chron. 15:17, 19
Ethan	89	1 Chron. 15:17, 19

3. Chronicles quotes from the Psalms collection, as follows:

1 Chron. 16:8–22	from Ps. 105
1 Chron. 16:36	from Ps. 106
1 Chron. 16:23–33	from Ps. 96
2 Chron. 6:41–2	from Ps. 132 (8–10)
2 Chron. 20:1	from Ps. 29

These correspondences do not of course prove direct literary dependence between the two texts. But insofar as they refer to the same groups, we may reasonably assume that the production and canonizing of the books are both the products of these circles, leading to the same conclusion. The Mosaic canon, however, does not incorporate levitical singing into the list of levitical arrangements. While Deuteronomy does not distinguish priests and Levites, Numbers assigns the "service of the Tabernacle" to them. But no specific details of the cult as reflected in Chronicles are offered.

The Moses-David axis in Chronicles is actually quite interesting: Chronicles is aware of the "book of Moses" and Moses' dispositions regarding Levites, yet more than balances this by his attribution to David of their precise cultic duties. Equally, he plays down the role of Moses as begetter and savior of the nation and its constitution, making no reference to the exodus, but rather promoting David in that role. It would seem that whatever the authority of Mosaic torah at the time of composition of Chronicles, the authority of Moses was not paramount to the extent that it seems to have been in other circles, and especially in Alexandria. That being said, Moses was assigned to the tribe of Levi (as recalled in 1 Chron. 23:14, for example).

THE STRUCTURE OF THE PSALMS CANON
AND THE DEVELOPMENT
OF ATTRIBUTION TO DAVID

The Masoretic Psalms collection contains five divisions, the same number as scrolls in the Mosaic canon, perhaps another reflection of the Moses-David axis just referred to. The sections, moreover, appear to reflect in sequence the order in which five collections were crystallized. This process is, in fact, an illuminating model of the way in which canonization seems often to have worked. From a large collection, one canonized collection is classified, the remainder having no classification, then a second collection is listed, and so on. While all the psalms that were regularly copied, then, were undergoing a process of canonizing, the completion of that process was accomplished in stages. The five psalms collections that make up the Masoretic book are 1—41; 42—72; 73—89; 90—106; and 107—50. Each of them closes with an almost identical doxology, except for the last psalm—though that may be explained if Psalm 150 is intended as a doxology to the fivefold collection, just as Psalm 1 constitutes an introduction to it.

The evidence from Qumran (as well as the slight variation in the Greek Psalter) shows that the fivefold division was not imposed at a single stage, nor perhaps uniformly accepted. But the evidence from Qumran (see further in chap. 10) does suggest that at least the first three books may have been standardized, for variations in order in the Cave 11 Psalms scroll only occur in psalms beyond this point. Thus the statement "the prayers of David, the son of Jesse, are ended," at the end of Book Three (Ps. 72:20), most likely means that unless the fivefold division was imposed very late, the first three collections of psalms were regarded as a Davidic canon.

Not all the headings of these psalms assign them to David. But this is a problem only to the mentality which assumes that in the ancient world authorship was understood as modern copyright laws understand it. Of the first 72 psalms, in fact, the superscriptions of the Masoretic text identify the following as "to/for/of David": 3—9; 11—32; 34—41; 51—65; 68—70. There are additionally another 18 with this heading in the remainder (86; 103; 108—10; 122; 124; 131; 133; 138—145). The clustering of these, especially in the first three books, shows some care in the arrangement, though we must beware (as will be discovered shortly) of assuming that the superscriptions necessarily predate the classification.

Other superscriptions, however, make it fairly clear that smaller canons/ collections were developed at some stage before being incorporated. There is an Asaph collection in 73—83, comprising most of the final Book Three; a Korahite collection is represented in 42—49 (opening Book Two), the rest in 84—85 and 87—88 (completing Book Three). Other individual psalms are assigned to various persons, mostly mentioned in Chronicles as temple singers, though two are ascribed to Solomon (72, 127) and one to Moses (90). There is also a collection of "Psalms of Ascent" (120—34).

Whether Psalms *as a whole* has a "canonical shape" is disputed. Gerald Wilson has argued for this in several publications,[7] finding indications of strategically placed psalms at the junctures of the five books, and a progressive theme throughout. Walter Brueggemann has also explored the possibility of a canonical reading of the whole book.[8] On the other side, Norman Whybray has vigorously denied that Psalms as a book has any intended coherence.[9] As in many disputes of this kind, one can find *some* evidence of coherence. The question is whether such signs are evidence of occasional opportunism on the part of a scribe here and there or the outcome of systematic organization. There is probably too little evidence to confirm the latter alternative.

But whatever the origin or classification of the individual psalms or the smaller collections, the larger collections, as we have just seen, clearly came to be associated with the name and authority of David. The collection of Psalms represents a Davidic canon. This Davidic connection continued to be enhanced, even after the collection (or collections) was made, by extending the superscriptions both numerically and in their detail. The Greek Psalter (which has 151 rather than 150 psalms) attaches a Davidic superscription to 85 against the Masoretic 73 psalms ascribed to him. The Qumran text 11QCompDav makes clear what is not perhaps yet explicit in Psalm 72:20, that the entire collection is to be assigned to David's own hand:

> 2 Now David was the son of Jesse, wise, and a light like the light of the sun; [and] a sage
> 3 learned and perfect in all his ways before God and humans. And Yahweh
> 4 gave him a spirit of intelligence and enlightenment, and he composed psalms:
> 5 three thousand six hundred; and songs for singing in front of the altar at the *Tamid*
> 6 offering every single day, every day of the year, three hundred and sixty-
> 7 four; and for the offering on sabbaths: fifty-two songs; and for the offering at the beginnings
> 8 of the months and all festival days and for the day of atonement: thirty songs.

9 And all the songs that he composed totaled four hundred and forty-
six. And songs
10 to be sung over those afflicted: four. And the total was four thousand
and fifty.
11 All these he composed by the spirit of prophecy which had been
given to him from before Elyon.

By comparing the Masoretic with the Greek and Qumranic Psalms collections
we can also detect a variation in the propensity of the transmitters to identify
certain psalms with incidents in David's life that are recorded in the books of
Samuel and Kings (or Chronicles). In the MT the following 13 (14?) Davidic
psalms contain biographical allusions in their headings: 3; 7(?); 18; 30; 34; 51;
52; 54; 56; 57; 59; 60; 63; 142.[10] In the Greek Psalter, the number increases to
21 (22?): 3; 7(?); 17 [18]; 26 [27]; 28 [29]; 29 [30]; 33 [34]; 50 [51]; 51 [52]; 53 [54];
55 [56]; 56 [57]; 58 [59]; 59 [60]; 62 [63]; 70 [71]; 95 [96]; 96 [97]; 141 [142]; 142
[143]; 143 [144]; 151. The number of such notices increases in the Cave 11
Psalms scroll. But these increments to the headings do not matter very much
in themselves, since we know in any case that once the entire Psalm collection
was regarded as Davidic, a tendency to relate some of those that appear to refer to events in an individual's life to the life of David is almost certain to follow. We need only observe that the Davidic character of the psalms is taken
more literally, and the Davidic collection becomes bigger, as part of the process
of canonizing.

LEVITES AS CANONIZERS

We are fortunate in the case of the Psalms collection to be able to identify
with some confidence the circles among whom it was canonized: the Levites
of the Jerusalem temple. It is also probable, as already stated, that the writer
of Chronicles was a member of the same scribal circle. The details given in
Chronicles about the structure of the temple administration can probably be
relied upon as a broad reflection, though not necessarily accurate in detail,
of the contemporary situation—perhaps in the third century B.C.E. According to this account, the Levites, divided into three levitical "tribes," were responsible for all the administration of the temple, except for the actual
sacrificing itself, which was reserved for the descendants of Aaron. In particular, the descendants of Asaph, Heman, and Jeduthun were responsible
for the music, presumably both composition and performance. We can only
speculate as to why there are psalms of Korah, because in Numbers Korah
is a villain who (Num. 16) confronted Moses and was swallowed up.[11]

In chapter 5 the very large number of Levites listed in Chronicles was noted

(38,000 over 30 years old attributed to the time of David: 1 Chron. 23:3). Of these, 24,000 were assigned to running the temple; 6,000 as administrators and judges; 4,000 gatekeepers and 4,000 musicians. According to 1 Chronicles 24, the priests were divided into twenty-four courses, each serving for a week twice a year (the figure in the Qumran texts e.g., 1QM2; 4Q320–1; 4Q327 is twenty-six, to accommodate the longer year); while according to 1 Chronicles 27, David's lay administration was divided into twelve administrative shifts, each serving a month. The priestly system may well have been in effect during the late Second Temple period: there were more priests than the temple needed for its administration, and the system is attested in various sources (Chronicles, Qumran scrolls, Mishnah, Josephus). But a political administrative system can hardly have functioned in this way, for administration, unlike priestly service, does not consist of a regular repetition of identical rituals. Still, the Chronicler described it in this way. Moreover, the distribution was extremely generous: we are told (1 Chron. 26) that the gatekeepers were assigned as follows: six Levites on the east gate(s), four on the north, four on the south, and four on the west, plus two for the *parbar* and four more for the storehouse. We do not need to anguish over the details: the main point to make is that the Chronicler supposed there to be too many Levites, as well as too many priests, than were necessary for the work assigned to them. Regardless of the actual numbers given by the Chronicler, the perception is important because it betrays the existence in the Chronicler's day of a numerous class with the leisure to devote itself to writing, copying, and archiving.

In fact there are three statements in Chronicles that identify Levites with the scribal class, or as an important part of it. First, 2 Chron. 24:11:

> Now whenever the chest was brought unto the king's office by the Levites, when they saw that there was a lot of money, the king's scribe and the high priest's officer came and emptied the chest, and took it back to its place again. This they did again and again, and gathered a great deal of money/silver.

The procedure resembles, in a quite startling way, the procedure suggested in chapter 4 for the collection of taxes under the Persians, in which the temple carried the responsibility for collecting and delivering to the royal official the amounts due. The story of 2 Chronicles 24 relates in fact to a special collection—raised by an approved king, Joash, and invoking a Mosaic law—for restoring the temple. The point is not that the Chronicler is describing regular tax collection, but that he assumes the king would raise the money through the Levites. The responsibility for maintaining the financial records, then, on the Chronicler's view, falls to Levites. Such bookkeeping was, as we saw earlier, one of the earliest and most basic functions of the scribal class.

We find the same revenue-raising procedure in 2 Chronicles 34, when Josiah is refurbishing the temple. Again, it is the Levites who had collected the money and delivered it. Moreover, they were in charge of the work itself: according to vv. 12–13, those Levites "skillful with musical instruments"

> were also in charge of the bearers of burdens, and overseers of all that carried out the work in any kind of operation: and some of the Levites there were scribes, and officials, and gatekeepers.

As we observed in the case of Egypt especially, the scribal class were responsible for the oversight of any official work anywhere in the land; and here some of them are also explicitly designated as "scribes" (*soferim*). Finally, in 2 Chron. 35:3 the function of the Levites is to "teach all Israel."

The same levitical functions are paralleled in Ezra and Nehemiah: in Ezra 8:30–33 Levites weigh out the revenue; Neh. 8:7–8 has Levites instructing the people in the law. We should add to this the fact that Moses is a Levite, and that the Chronicler presents Levites as heirs to the prophets in 1 Chron. 25:1–3 and 2 Chron. 20:13ff. The conclusion then seems hard to escape that it is not only the transmission of the Davidic canon that is owed to Levites but of the Mosaic canon, the Joshua–Kings canon, and the canon of prophets, as well as the books of Chronicles. But this bald statement is not quite as adventurous or decisive as it seems! For the Levites are an extraordinarily slippery entity. They appear through the canonized writings now as a tribe, now as priests, now as not-quite-priests. If the term refers to temple scribes, who of necessity would have to enjoy some priestly status in order to allow them to handle the holy things, it probably also refers to any temple staff who were not members of the priestly caste, not authorized to offer sacrifices. Thus, to say that "the Levites" are the main producers of the canon is only to say that the temple scribes, to whom we would in any case accord that privilege, were de facto assigned to membership of the tribe of Levi—or at any rate, were recognized as such by most of the canonized writings. It follows (and the Chronicler also makes it clear) that these "Levites" are not necessarily a homogeneous group at all, but embrace all kinds of functions and interests.

If we see "Levite" as the generic term for the temple scribes, the "para-priests," we will not be surprised to find that the Psalms are not entirely (even if they are in large part) songs for cultic occasions. Certainly, one may reconstruct a number of cultic genres, in the manner of Gunkel, and reconstruct a cult itself, in the manner of Mowinckel. But a large number of psalms seem to be intended for an individual, and many psalms are what we would call "wisdom psalms." Nor should we overlook the strong hint from Psalm 1 that the collection was intended not for liturgical use but for private reading (though this is not indisputable). This use of canonical writings parallels, after all, what the ending of Hosea suggested for the canon of prophets too. There may be some public liturgical impetus behind the canonizing of some or all of these psalms, but that is far from easy to prove. It seems much more likely that the books of psalms, arranged as they are by authorship and title more evidently than by genre or theme, are precisely a *collection* of religious poetry. But this does not rule out the possibility of a core reason (or perhaps at least a function) for such a collection, which was no doubt housed somewhere in the Jerusalem temple. Private cultic occasions, such as the giving of vows, offering of sacrifices in thanks or in hope of healing or ease of distress, presumably called for off-the-peg formulas. And no doubt the person offering the psalm, the reciter of the psalm, and the author of the psalm were usually each different persons (so much for the "I" of the Psalms![12]). A levitical collection may well have served a purpose connected with the life of the temple. But the Levites obviously also collected (and presumably composed) religious poetry with no immediate cultic use, and may well have lent scrolls for private edification.

SOLOMON AND WISDOM

As in the case of David, we find the required profile of Solomon in the narratives (Kings and Chronicles). Solomon's portrait here, once assumed to be almost entirely favorable, has recently been questioned, and it has been asked whether in fact the narrators wished to present a more nuanced picture. Certainly his many wives are cited as the reason why a large part of his kingdom was taken from his successor.

He is, nevertheless, presented as an enormously rich ruler who asked for wisdom and got riches as well: a perfect example of the benefit of wisdom and the need for wisdom to be driven by piety (as well as the other way round). But in particular "he composed three thousand proverbs, and his songs numbered a thousand and five" (1 Kings 4:32). The sentence is very reminiscent of the list from Qumran Cave 11 of David's songs, and, we may take it, points toward the collection of proverbs in his name. But the songs? Here we have two possible interpretations, which are not mutually exclusive. One points to the psalms attributed to him, 72 and 127. The attribution of the first of these is almost self-explanatory, with the reference to "kings of Tarshish," "kings of Sheba," and "gold of Sheba" in v. 15 [16], as well as less explicit references. Since the parallels between this psalm and the story of Solomon in 1 Kings are not exact (he was visited by a queen, not a king, from Sheba) we might pause before concluding that there is direct dependence of psalm on narrative; it is conceivable, especially since there is no reference to "wisdom" in the psalm, that it was attributed to Solomon only because of the allusions. The reason for the attribution of Psalm 127 to Solomon is attributable to the opening mention of the building of the "house of Yahweh." Perhaps this connection was also reinforced by the fact that the psalm is composed entirely of proverbs, and of the sort we find in the book of Proverbs.

Perhaps, then, the "songs" of Solomon did not originally include any of the canonical psalms. But one factor does suggest otherwise. The book of Chronicles creates a tension (whether deliberate or not) between David and Solomon in effectively making the temple David's rather than Solomon's, as the book of Kings indisputably maintains. Is there, then, a hint in 1 Kings 4:31 of a slight retaliation—not at either of the great legendary monarchs, but at a pro-David tendency? "He was wiser than anyone else, wiser than Ethan the Ezrahite, and Heman, Calcol, and Darda, descendants of Mahol." Ethan the Ezrahite and Heman, whom we have met earlier in this chapter, are mentioned in 1 Chron. 15:17, 19, and to them are attributed respectively Pss. 89 and 88. In 1 Chron. 2:6 they appear again, this time with Calcol and Dara. Note the different spelling of this last name,[13] while "Mahol" is presumably the "Hamul" of 1 Chron. 2:5![14]

A claim on behalf of Solomon to have written psalms is consistent with this little jibe, though there may be more about these four putative descendants of Zerah than the extant canons have preserved. In any case, there is another candidate for Solomon's canticular oeuvre: the "Song of Songs," which may itself be understood as a collection of poems. We shall consider this presently. For the moment, we can attend to Proverbs.

In Proverbs, as in Psalms, there are signs of smaller collections still present, indicated by the presence of seven headings. These are as follows:

1:1   "The Proverbs of Solomon, son of David, king of Israel." (Perhaps this was in time taken to be a superscription for the entire book, or perhaps expanded to serve that purpose)

10:1   "The Proverbs of Solomon"

22:17 (if we follow the Greek and identify a new heading, "The Words of the Wise," at this point, as is commonly done, supported by the next heading)

24:23 "These also are the words of the wise"

25:1   "These too are the proverbs of Solomon which the men of Hezekiah king of Judah copied"

30:1   "The Words of Agur, son of Jakeh. The oracle (Heb; המשׂא)"

31:1   "the words of Lemuel, king of Massa. An oracle (משׂא again) that his mother taught him" (if we disregard the Masoretic vocalization)

A little more can be said about these seven collections. Proverbs 1:1–9:18

consists of what we would recognize not as proverbs (such as we find in other sections of the book) but of longer and more sustained advice (Whybray calls them "discourses" and identifies ten of them[15]). The closest parallel here is afforded by Egyptian instructional literature. Characteristic of this is the second person address, the imperative, and the identification of the speaker as a parent (see the opening verses of the first seven chapters).[16]

The section 10:1–22:16 is a collection of single sayings, which do not exhibit any obvious order (nor is there any reason why they should). Chapter 22:17–24:22 contains the statement (22:20), "Have I not written for you these thirty sayings?" It is not beyond the ingenuity of a scholar to count thirty in this section!, and many of them are more than a single line. Chapter 25:1–29:27 is another collection of single sayings. The "words of Agur" contain (possibly as an addition) a set of numerical sayings from 30:15 onward (except for the concluding proverb, vv. 32–33). The words of Lemuel also break into a 22-verse praise of a "good woman" (however we translate the wisdom ideal of אשת חיל), composed as an acrostic. However, while this may be an addition either to the Lemuel collection or the entire book, such praise does seem appropriate coming from a mother, especially given the sorts of details that are described. Descriptions of women by men in wisdom literature tend to focus on sexual rather than domestic matters.

Taking the Proverbs scroll itself as a product of canonizing, we have an example of a set of collections, some ascribed to Solomon, copied together onto a single scroll for obvious archiving reasons, and stored with the label "proverbs" or "proverbs of Solomon." Putting all the "Solomonic" literature onto a single scroll and archiving it, then copying it, is nothing more or less than canonizing.

SECULAR AND RELIGIOUS
VIEWS IN PROVERBS

One of the keenest debates in scholarship on Proverbs has been the tension between a secular and pragmatic view of life on the one hand and a religious ethic on the other. McKane, regarding the former as "Old Wisdom," suggested that it had been overlaid with "Yahwistic piety," in which a concept borrowed from Egyptian literature is identified as belonging to Yahweh and indeed as equivalent to "fear of Yahweh." The idea that wisdom in Judah progressed from a secular ethic developed by and taught to the scribal-administrative class to a specifically pious ethic, in which Wisdom was harnessed to torah, seems to be supported by the writings of ben Sira (and a number of psalms, notably 119). It also seems to be supported by additions to the writings of Qoheleth, though the problem here is that this third-century sage (see below) seems to be writing in a secular tradition.

The mixture of secular and religious occurs throughout nearly all the sections, although all of them are predominantly secular. (For religious sayings in a secular context, see, e.g., 2:6; 3:5, 12; 8:13 in the first section; 18:10 and 21:30 in the second section; 22:19 in the third; 28:5, 25 in the fifth; 30:5, 9 in the "words of Agur"; and 31:30 in the "word of King Lemuel.") But there is little sign of editing toward a specifically theological view of wisdom except in chapters 1—9. Here the address given by Dame Wisdom (chap. 8) identifies the secular belief in the rational order of the universe with the divine plan, potentially equating empirically derived knowledge with obedience to the torah. But, whereas torah and wisdom are equated in a few places outside Proverbs, Proverbs itself does not use the word in that sense. In fact the usage is quite interesting. There are thirteen occurrences, of which six (1:8; 3:1; 4:2; 6:20, 23; 7:2) refer to parental teaching. In 3:1; 6:20; 6:23; and 7:2 torah is actually paralleled (linked in 6:23) with "commandment" (מצוה). In 13:14 the torah is that of the wise. In chapter 28 "law" is used in an absolute sense, and a case can be made for a Yahwistic or a secular meaning. In the absence of any clear hint of a Yahwistic meaning, and particularly of a phrase such as "law of Moses" or "law of Yahweh" or "law of Elyon" the secular is probably to be favored, but the usage is nevertheless odd. Equally problematic is 29:18: "Where there is no vision, the people perish: but happy are those who keep the law." The phrase "keeping (שמר) the law," despite the generally nontheistic tone of the rest of the section, may imply that Yahweh's torah—whatever that means—is in mind. Finally, in 31:5, 26, the usage is secular.

The conclusion is, I think, permissible that Proverbs remains essentially a secular collection, though of course the references to Yahweh, and the presence of chapter 8, make it entirely possible for this secular wisdom to be understood in a religious—even Yahwistic—sense, as it presumably came to be.

A final observation concerns the place of the feminine in Proverbs. Both Folly and Wisdom are personified as females, and the book ends with praise of a good wife. The possible origin of this device in a goddess figure (whether an Israelite/Judean consort of Yahweh or the Egyptian Maat) is beyond our concern here.[17] In any case, it seems appropriate that a father or mother giving a male adolescent advice on curbing passion, avoiding temptation, and choosing rationally should select the image of a woman, her dangerous charms and indispensable virtues, for what else occupies a male adolescent's thought as much as the opposite sex? But it is the association of Solomon and women in the Kings narratives that is important here. He is visited by a famous queen (a "foreign woman," 1 Kings 2:16; 5:3) and his marriages with foreign women are named as the cause of his kingdom's fission. The theme of women in the Solomonic canon, highlighted by the parallels in Proverbs and Kings, may also partly explain the attribution to him of the Song of Songs.

ECCLESIASTES

But first to another book of wisdom. The "words of the preacher, the son of David, king in Jerusalem" (1:1) do not quite mimic the opening of Proverbs, but they are close. Like ben Sira (which, however, has no Solomonic connection) this writer is an individual, and constructs for himself an identity as the wise king (see 1:12–18). However, my including this scroll as part of a "Solomonic canon" requires some justification. It is certainly a rather special aspect of the canonizing process, one that we might even call parodic, where a deconstructive reversal is appended to a canon or an icon. The author appears antagonistic as much to the secular ethos of wisdom as to the religious, and his Solomonic mask is surely ironical, since he claims that the only true wisdom is that there is no wisdom! But quite apart from the (circumstantial) evidence that the work was included in the Masoretic canon, there are signs that this book was itself edited. Thus, framing the first-person narration of the writer (by means of which he stresses the empirical rather than traditional source of knowledge) are third-person references. The twin statements "vanity of vanities, says Qoheleth" in 1:2; 12:8 (and notice the phrase "says Qoheleth" in 7:27), suggests a narrator other than the Preacher himself, and there is an epilogue (12:9–14) that undercuts Qoheleth's thesis in several ways. First, it removes the Solomonic guise: retaining the title "Qoheleth," it reduces him to the level of a less illustrious mortal than Solomon. Also, while he is said to have taught, studied, and arranged proverbs, he is not credited with having composed any. Again, while this epilogue affirms the wisdom of "Qoheleth," it appears to issue its own warning about how seriously to take the "words": they are "like goads." And whether it constitutes a comment on Qoheleth or a more general warning to the reader, "much study is a weariness of the flesh" is less than an enthusiastic endorsement of what precedes. Finally, vv. 13–14 give the "sum": "Fear God and keep his commandments," for every secret deed (including the reading of Qoheleth?) will be judged by God. Hardly an accurate précis!

The problem is, of course, not to appreciate why the words of Qoheleth are packaged in this way, but why it was necessary. I take it, as do most scholars, that the author is writing not within a scribal school and for the education of the scribal classes, but for the individual, the one seeking wealth and knowledge, undergoing a private education—for it is widely agreed that the date for this writer is in the Ptolemaic period, when, it seems, the growth of such a class spread education beyond the confines of the scribal classes. Such a reader may have been advised by his scribal tutor to study Proverbs, but the rivalry between the scribal teachers and the new Judean "sophists" like our "Qoheleth" explains the attitude toward traditional wisdom, and even the mocking appropriation of the patron of wisdom, Solomon. The book, then, is a deliberate comment on the Solomonic canon, and as such is part of it, at least in the author's mind. But it did not enter any Solomonic canon by virtue of being adopted by the guardians of that canon; nor was it taken into the Masoretic canon because it was genuinely believed to be from Solomon. Yet it was bowdlerized, and this operation itself suggests its popular status, its potential canonicity. Like other works we shall consider in chapter 9, however, it seems to have been composed as a private work or perhaps a private school text, and adopted in school curricula. Having found its way into the classics, it was reluctantly (on the evidence of the epilogue) shelved in Judean libraries, including no doubt the temple libraries. And where else would it be archived but alongside Proverbs?

THE SONG OF SONGS

As with Ecclesiastes, the connection with Solomon (but not necessarily his authorship) is not imposed on the work after its composition by pious tradition or in an attempt to justify its status among the classics of Jewish literature: it is embedded in the work. The woman appears to be a lover of Solomon—she knows his furnishings ("curtains of Solomon," 1:5); that he "made himself a chariot of the wood of Lebanon" (3:9, admittedly not necessarily private knowledge); she knows "the crown with which his mother crowned him on the day of his marriage" (3:11); of his vineyard at Baal-hamon (8:11); and in 8:12 she addresses him directly: "My vineyard, which is mine, is before me: you, Solomon, must have a thousand." It is no doubt Solomon who has "brought me into his chambers" (1:4). Finally, and not least, she is called a "Shulamite" (6:13) which, regardless of the geographical speculations, makes her Solomon's female counterpart.

As to the origin and nature of this book, whether an anthology of independent poems or a montage depicting a narrative of some kind, the variety of views is too great, and probably too well-known to need rehearsing.[18] There are no clear reflections of the book in other canonical writings, nor references to it until the second century C.E.—unless we count the reference to Solomon's "songs" in 1 Kings 4:32, mentioned earlier (and discounted). It is a work inspired by Solomon.

As with Ecclesiastes, we can hardly look to any institutional scribal

communities for the creation of this work. Whether its contents are of folk origin or are literary compositions in traditional styles (such as the *wasf*) does
not matter for the question of canonizing: only that it has been written down.
And for what purpose? Conceivably for private reading, but also as part of the
curriculum of a private school, in which a native Judean king who also
resembles a Hellenistic king (the wealth, the women!) is celebrated in love
poems. It would be easy to point to the many parallels in Greek and Arabic
literature to such poems, which are typically the product of an educated male
lifestyle, especially at court—or to the Egyptian and even Tamil parallels that
have been suggested, hinting at a far from rustic origin for the poems.[19] But
the arguments that the woman's songs may be female compositions cannot be
ignored. Women's roles as mourners and singers are well enough attested in
the Jewish scriptures themselves,[20] but the issue in this case is one of women's
education. If some of the poems here are women's, have they been heard and
transcribed by men, or written by women? The possibility of educated women
in the Hellenistic period is strong enough, and generalizations about the canon
being that of a "patriarchal society" may need a little qualification. It seems natural that women should be among the beneficiaries of the wider opportunities
for education at this time and would regard it as plausible that these poems
found their way into the curriculum of texts studied, learnt, and read by
educated men and women.

PSALMS OF SOLOMON,
WISDOM OF SOLOMON

These texts deserve at least a mention here: the *Psalms of Solomon,* from the
first century B.C.E., afford no intrinsic evidence of having been composed as
Solomonic. Moreover, they did not, as far as we know, become canonical anywhere. By contrast, the "Wisdom of Solomon" was canonized in the Christian
Old Testament and almost certainly in some Jewish circles before then. As in
the case of Qoheleth, the author assumes the identity (though more seriously)
of Solomon and narrates his quest for Wisdom (as the courting of a bride!). The
work, Greek in language and literary form, is generally agreed to have been
composed in Egypt. The value of these (and other) works for our understanding of canon is to show that certain themes as literary styles become "canonized" in connection with certain figures, though not exclusively: the proverb
and the wisdom instruction with Solomon, but also, to a lesser extent, the
psalm. Thus, the attribution of a composition—where no hint of it is present
in the text—to a particular figure is an illustration of one of the classificatory
techniques by which canons are compiled, as well as a recognition that a canon

exists. Were these works, then, composed in order to be canonized as Solomonic? Were they classified in libraries and school as "Solomonic," alongside other texts bearing the label? We do not know: but by such processes canons are formed. Here is one important, and undervalued, explanation for the explosion of pseudepigraphic writing in the late Second Temple period: the habit refracts the process of canonizing that has already created the categories (authorship, literary form) to which these works conform or which they manipulate.

CHAPTER 9

Serious Entertainment

There are a number of canonized writings, including Daniel (including Susannah), Esther, Ruth, Jonah, Tobit, and Judith, which are stories apparently written largely for pleasure. To these readable works of fiction we might wish to add once-independent tales such as the Joseph story (Genesis 37ff.: the original ending is uncertain); the family history of David (the so-called "Succession Narrative," again with uncertain limits but mainly 2 Samuel 2—20, 1 Kings 1—2); and the stories of Daniel 2—6. Where do these stories originate? How were they preserved, and how did they become classics of Jewish literature?

Whether or not we wish to understand these stories primarily in terms of a specific motivation (which is both unfashionable and probably wrongheaded as well), such as opposition to the exclusivity of Ezra and Nehemiah in the case of Ruth or Jonah, or an explanation of the origins of Purim in the case of Esther, the important question is the use of the novel form. Stories of this kind may well have an oral background, though an oral origin for those so far mentioned seems unlikely (except possibly for the Daniel stories).

The earliest heroes of tales were generally courtiers (i.e., scribes), tales of whose adventures go back at least to twentieth-century B.C.E. Egypt with the story of Sinuhe, who flees his native Egypt for fear of a civil war and lives with foreigners before being welcomed home. From a millennium later is an account of the travels of Wen-Amun. Both of these scribal compositions probably became classics in scribal schools, being intended for the instruction—but not without entertainment—of the pupils.

From the beginning of the Persian period some instructional writings acquire a narrative framework or addition. The earliest example of this, the story of Ahiqar from Elephantine, is first attested in Aramaic (its original language) in a Jewish environment, at the colony in Elephantine (end of fifth century B.C.E.). The story, which tells of a wise courtier (a royal scribe) of Esarhaddon and Sennacherib—who is tricked by his heir, escapes execution, and finally returns to royal favor and serves the king by his wisdom, turning the tables on his betrayer—is accompanied by a collection of his wise sayings. It evidently continued to be enjoyed by Jews, since Ahiqar is coopted in the story of Tobit as his nephew. Indeed, the work was so widely translated in antiquity that it must have been extremely popular.[1] The mixture of narrative and instruction is also present in the Egyptian *Instruction of Onkhsheshonq,* from the same period.[2] The hero is thrown into prison as a result of intrigue and is rescued when a conspiracy against the Pharaoh is uncovered. So perhaps it might not be too rash to suggest that the earliest stories we have from the ancient Near East have some clear didactic purpose and tell of people in royal service. Wills has suggested, however, that the story form lends itself readily to irony and ambiguity. He believes that where a set of instructions was attached, in some cases the stories actually undermine the teaching, showing how "wisdom" is not necessarily of paramount value in everyday life. Such a view makes problematic the suggestion that such stories were intended to be educative, though it does not dispose of it. For the scribe being trained for a career in court life had to be aware of the limits of his own rational philosophy in the face of the irrationality of rulers as well as the envy of rivals. In fact, Wills's suggestion is illustrated by a good deal of the literature discussed in this chapter (and some not discussed): Jonah, Job, Ecclesiastes, Ruth, Esther, David's family history, and the stories of Solomon—not to mention many of the stories of the Judges, if not the entire book of Judges itself—display a use of irony that recent literary study of the Hebrew Bible has brightly illuminated, and which ought not to be overlooked in any historical study of classical Jewish literature.

But this does not mean that stories unconnected to instructions are not didactic. There are very strong links of motif between *Onkhsheshonq* and both Joseph and Daniel stories. The Jewish tale of Joseph might, with von Rad, be interpreted as having a didactic element, while the Daniel stories (perhaps excluding Susannah and Bel and the Dragon) are certainly presented as an example of upright and successful living in foreign service.

Yet the (possible) origins of the short story genre do not prescribe its subsequent development. With the spread of literacy comes a wider audience for scribal stories, and the existence of such an audience (I should say "readership") in turn has an effect on the nature of the genre. For instance, while a scribal school may seek to inculcate class values as well as professional skills, if one is serving not scribes but merchants or landowners less didactic and more entertaining forms of literature may be offered for their patronage. However, in considering these stories individually we may as well begin with those dealing with scribes and their adventures.

DANIEL

Perhaps there is a case for considering the scroll of Daniel, in its various forms, to be the product of a canonizing process in which stories of a certain kind clustered around a figure. We can glimpse this process of accretion through the addition in the Greek versions of two stories that seem quite clearly to be later additions: the tales of Susannah and "Bel and the Serpent (or Dragon)." The texts from Qumran contain a number of further texts associated with a Daniel cycle, including one (4QPrNab) that looks like a version of Daniel 4, but replaces Nebuchadnezzar by Nabonidus and Daniel by an unnamed Jewish captive. It is not difficult to suppose that the change from the little-known Nabonidus to the better-known villain, and the giving of the unknown captive the name of Daniel are processes that attend the creation of a canon. The composition of the book of Daniel itself, then, presents evidence of a cycle of tales collected under the name of Daniel. Furthermore, this little canonical collection is supplemented by a series of visions, perhaps added in sequence, and the whole finally brought together as a more or less unified statement for a specific historical context, thereafter to be frozen: a perfect canonical history within a short space of words and of time.

The scribal character and background of the Daniel collection is indisputable: the mantic culture, in which the secrets of the universe are encoded in written signs (chaps. 5, 9, 12); the emphasis on writing and books;[3] the belief that intellectuals (*maskilim*) constitute the religious leadership of Judaism (chap. 12). But these features are concentrated in the second part of the book, where the Daniel cycle is exploited to a more serious purpose. What of the stories themselves? Whether or not the setting in the foreign court points to a foreign origin for the stories is hard to say: it is not impossible that some of them do, though such an exotic backdrop is a commonplace of this genre, whether the court be in Persepolis or Susa, in Alexandria or Antioch (one thinks of the country house and the English detective novel). These stories are entertaining; their message, that by dint of loyalty to his own (Jewish) god, the clever Jewish official can outwit other non-Jewish courtiers and even convert the king, is fanciful but pleasurable. Müller has argued that these stories are originally *Märchen* ("folktales," or "romances"[4]) in which poor and insignificant people rise to power. Possibly: yet Daniel is hardly a poor Jew but a very privileged one, noble and well educated. His disadvantage is also his advantage: his status as Jewish exile and his worship of the "real" god. The stories are well in the tradition of courtier tales, though with a strong Jewish twist. They are "serious entertainment" and, like most examples of the court genre, written in Aramaic.

The reasons for the translation/composition of chapters 1 and 7—12 into Hebrew will never be clear, but the switch does correspond to a change of orientation, in which Daniel becomes a seer of history and a teacher of the contemporary generation. The book was so popular and perhaps regarded as so important in the Hasmonean period that there was never any doubt that it quickly found its way into the Judean literary canon. It may have been regarded at the time as one of the "prophets" collection; certainly Daniel was regarded by contemporary sources as a prophet. Yet it is usually understood that the scribes who produced the Daniel scroll were of quite a different sort from ben Sira. They were interested in the end of history, which they thought to be predetermined and capable of being understood, through revelation, by the "wise." There is an element of truth in this: Daniel's wisdom is revealed and not acquired by experience. Certainly the scribes of Daniel stand intellectually closer to those who produced the Enoch canon, but we cannot be sure that ben Sira would not have regarded the prophets as having imparted secrets that study would repay. And, given the dramatic change in circumstances between ben Sira's time and the 160s B.C.E., it is easily possible to exaggerate the differences. Both ben Sira and the compilers of Daniel pursued the same profession, at any rate: they were teachers in Jerusalem, perhaps of rival schools?

ESTHER AND RUTH

Esther and Ruth belong together as short stories about women who married out without being blamed for it, and who were known for having connections with kings (and so we may add the Shulamite of the Song of Songs). Indeed, it is tempting to think of these three as constituting a "female canon," although the first two women conform in many respects to the requirements of patriarchal society, seeking the protection of their husbands and perpetuating the survival of the family or the *ethnos*. This superficial conformity may, of course, be part of the stories' guile.

Esther is an example of the well-known Jewish court tale. Its lack of reference to God is often remarked on, but in that respect the Joseph and Ruth stories are little different; the deity is not an agent in any of these. The absence of Esther from the Qumran texts may or may not be significant, in view of the fact that several other books are represented by only one or two manuscripts. But it has some unique peculiarities: its hero is a woman in the impossible category of wife of a Persian king, and the plot ends with an equally impossible scenario—Jews massacring opponents. The impossibilities, like Jonah's fish and Nineveh's repentance, are an indispensable part of what is an ironic tale. The tale points out the fragility of the much-vaunted "law of the Medes and Persians," which can be used (as in Daniel) to trap rather than to protect minorities (even to trap the king himself). The king is made a fool of by his wife Vashti; the courtier Haman is caught, not by the wiles of Mordecai but by the plain speaking of Esther and simple expedient of letting Esther catch him in a compromising position. Perhaps the name "Mordecai" (from the Babylonian god Marduk: think of the number of times *baal* is changed to *bosheth* in the Masoretic text!) is also deliberately chosen?

Also disputed is its place and purpose of composition. The story reads, as do the tales of Daniel and the Joseph story, as an affirmation of the potential of Jewish life in the Diaspora. But it is an originally Hebrew text (as far as we know), and the story could as well be relevant to Palestinian Jews living under Persians, Ptolemies, or Seleucids. The exotic royal court setting need be nothing more than a device for dramatizing and focusing the issue of Jewish identity in an imperial (or colonial) context. In any case, the story of Esther exists in a number of forms, and an "original" shape is impossible to reconstruct.

The Greek version(s) constitute a more explicitly religious story. Six additional passages tell, among other things, of Mordecai's dream (and its interpretation), and both Mordecai and Esther offer prayers. The word "god" is also liberally sprinkled through these additions, but also injected into the rest. One of the two Greek texts gives the date of its translation as the fourth year of Ptolemy and Cleopatra, either 77 B.C.E. or 114 C.E., and Josephus at the end of the first century C.E. already knows the story of Esther with the additions. But even the MT version of Esther probably does not represent the original form (or at least the only Hebrew form), for the Greek translation known as the A text is based on a different Hebrew text (though it was adjusted to the Greek version of the story by inserting the additions from Text B). The MT story seems, in any case, to have evolved from a number of originally separate elements and through various textual stages; it is not, as are Ruth or Jonah, the product of a single storyteller. Possibly separate stories about Esther and Mordecai have been merged, but even then, the Masoretic version has been revised by the addition of three successive appendices which in different ways shift the emphasis of the story. The first (9:1–19) basically expands the restrained ending in 8:15–17 by magnifying Mordecai's honor and turning the threat of Jewish reprisal into a fact. It also extends the revenge on Haman to the execution of his sons, and finally specifies the date of the celebration as the 13th and 14th of Adar. The second appendix (9:20–32) formalizes this feast day through a letter from Mordecai and identifies its name as Purim, which is explained as meaning "lots," while the third appendix (10:1–3) is a celebration of Mordecai, probably inspired by the notices of kings in the book of Kings.[5]

The origin of the feast of Purim, which these appendices introduce, is also obscure. The earliest reference to this feast outside the book is in the *Megillat Ta'anit,* a first-century C.E. list of religious festivals. It is not mentioned in any of the liturgical texts from Qumran, and there is complete disagreement among scholars as to its origin. The connection between Esther and Purim, as we have seen, is secondary. The history of Esther revealed by this analysis throws light on the interplay (in this case quite dramatic) between the popularity of a book and its canonization. The changing forms of this story show awareness of a need somehow to *accommodate* it as a classic work of Hebrew literature, but betray the fact that it was already popular enough to need such revision, and thus was already canonized.

Although the story of Ruth is set "in the days of the judges" and ends with a genealogy of David, it was not, as was the Joseph story, incorporated into, or written for, the same canon as the stories of either the judges or David, but remained a separate work. Like all canonized Jewish novellas, it is set in a historical context (in this case, the one provided by the books of the prophetic canon). If it was produced within scribal circles for the instruction of their pupils (as I suspect Daniel was) there is no unambiguous evidence of it, though the motif of the *'eshet hayil* at the end of Proverbs and that book's warnings against foreign women may suggest that, like other stories referred to a little earlier, it has an irony, which the Davidic genealogy perhaps lays on too heavily (though a hint of David's foreign ancestry remains in 1 Sam. 22:3–4). Its membership of the Masoretic canon may—like other insidious writings like Esther, Song of Songs, and Ecclesiastes—have more to do with its liturgical use (see next chapter), though such use presumably implied a status, already achieved, as a classic Hebrew story. It is written in good classical Hebrew (which gives us no clue as to its date), and it does not understand the regulations given in the Mosaic torah about the possession or transfer of land and title, hopelessly confusing levirate marriage and *ge'ullah.* It seems likely that this story about women was written by a woman: as with the Song of Songs it describes a woman as active in the pursuit of a man, even to the point of seduction, but without any censure on the narrator's part. Nor is there censure on the marriage of Mahlon and Chilion to Moabite wives, unless it is implied in their early deaths.

The feminine perspective of the book is sustained by the end of the narrative:

> And all the people that were at the gate, and the elders, said, "We are witnesses. May Yahweh make the woman who has come into your house like Rachel and like Leah, who both built the house of Israel. May you produce children in Ephrathah, and leave a name in Bethlehem. And let your house be like the house of Perez, whom Tamar bore to Judah, from

the children that Yahweh will give you by this young woman." So Boaz
took Ruth, and she became his wife: and when he went in unto her, Yahweh made her conceive, and she bore a son. And the women said unto
Naomi, "Blessed be Yahweh, who has not left you this day without a
go'el, and may his name be famous in Israel. For he shall be a restorer of
your life, and a nourisher of your old age: for your daughter-in-law, who
loves you, who is better to you than seven sons, has borne him."

And Naomi took the child, and laid it in her bosom, and became his
nurse. And the women, her neighbors, gave it a name, saying, "There is
a son born to Naomi."

(Ruth 4:11–17)

The ending seems symmetrical: it is the women (the counterparts of the
"daughters of Jerusalem" in the Song of Songs?) who pronounce the last word,
and Naomi with whom the story ends, for the story is her story; as widow of
Elimelech she brings him, as it were, back to life and at the same time recov-
ers her place in Judean society. Boaz is blessed, Ruth is blessed, and then
Naomi is blessed (thus the original order of appearance is reversed). Then the
child is finally blessed and joined with Naomi. Last of all, the son is named as
born *to Naomi,* not to Boaz or to Ruth. The episode is also placed within the
context of Israelite matriarchs Rachel and Leah, and with the matriarch of Judah, Tamar. Tamar also provides the foil for this story, which is also about the
raising of children to a dead husband (in less enchanting circumstances), but
with more dramatic consequences for the existence of the tribe of Judah.

But at this point it ceases to be a woman's story. The "naming" provides
a pretext for the following:

They called him Obed: he is the father of Jesse, the father of David.
    These are the generations of Perez: Perez was the father of Hezron,
Hezron the father of Ram, Ram the father of Amminadab, Amminadab
the father of Nahshon, Nahshon the father of Salmon, Salmon the father
of Boaz, and Boaz was the father of Obed. And Obed was the father of
Jesse, and Jesse was the father of David.

(Ruth 4:17–22)

The writer of Chronicles (1 Chron. 2:12) was acquainted with a shorter version of this:

And Boaz was the father of Obed, and Obed was the father of Jesse.

Possibly a case of haplography; probably not. At any rate, the compiler of
the male appendage has done a little research into the Mosaic canon: Gen.
46:12 and Num. 26:21 give Perez to Hezron; Num. 1:7; 2:3; and 7:12, 17 give
Amminadab to Nahshon. The other links are made up or lost.

The setting of the story in Elimelech's town of Bethlehem=Ephratah provides a pretext for the link with David, and it can be argued that the final genealogy always belonged to the story. However, as with Esther, it is perhaps justifiable to see the story as having been supplemented in order to provide it with a more substantial "message."

Indeed, all three of the books just reviewed, to which we could add Ecclesiastes, are cases where a work has been edited in order to convey a more pious message and thus a more weighty *point d'appui*. In the case of Daniel the stories arguably have a strong theological message in the first place, and the addition of the visions merely dramatizes and contemporizes that message. But in the case of Esther and Ruth (as with Ecclesiastes) a slight or nonexistent religious "message" has been compensated by some light editing. The significance of this observation is that the popularity of these works has led to their being adapted to serve in a *religious* canon. Whether this slight pious editing succeeded in imposing itself on all the editions of these texts is hard to say, but their various versions of Esther display varying degrees of explicit religious sentiment (including none at all in the Masoretic edition!). We may well be confronting evidence here of a distinct canonizing move in which already canonized writings are dressed up for the purposes of fitting better into what was being seen as a *religious* collection. Works originating outside the institutional scribal orbit were occasionally amended in the process of being incorporated into the collection of what were coming to be seen as religious writings. A similar explanation might account for the poem of Job, based around a foreign character and comprising a conversation about divine justice, but turned into a story about the Judean god Yahweh and his justification.

But why should the Judean canon undergo this religious/orthodox coloring? The answer points to a specifically religious interpretation of the essence of Judaism on the part of the literary establishment in Jerusalem, which will be explored in chapter 11.

OTHER WORKS OF
"SERIOUS ENTERTAINMENT"

Mention should be made briefly of other compositions of "serious entertainment" which have *not* been edited for increased religious value. Many of them have some satirical elements. The story of the later history of the legendary warrior and womanizer has David indulging in sex while his general fights his wars (2 Samuel 11), and fleeing from the city when his son usurps his throne (2 Samuel 15). His ability to rule a kingdom exceeds by far his ability to rule his family. But the story (which I take, with Van Seters and Auld,[6] to be a late addition and not deliberately left out by the Chronicler) is not so much anti-Davidic as critical, or quizzical, about his character, presenting him as more ambivalent rather than less sympathetic. The book of Jonah mimics the stock phraseology of prophetic books and of psalms (chap. 2), and mocks the operation of divine intervention (Yahweh "appoints" fish, storms, plants, etc.). Its ending (apparently untouched by any editor) is a celebration of the holiness of cows. But Jonah was buried within a single book of twelve prophets, perhaps to make up the numbers, while the David story was slotted into what would become the book(s) of Samuel.

Berquist[7] has pointed out that many of these stories—Joseph, Jonah, Ruth, Esther, Daniel—deal with questions of ethnicity, very often to the suppression of piety. They do, of course, diverge: for Jonah and Ruth, non-Jews are not to be shunned; for Esther and Daniel, Jewish identity is something to be preserved from threatening foreigners, even though foreign rulers are not necessarily bad. Issues of gender, which have already been noted, may be related: the question of *identity,* which was identified as a matter of national importance, of class importance, in the Torah and prophetic books, becomes a more *personal* matter. Alongside the personalization comes a personalization of piety too: what does it mean *for an individual* to be a Judean, a Jew? We ought not to consider this purely a diaspora matter, for diaspora Jews did not write in Hebrew: it is a matter of ethnicity *within Judah itself.*

These stories (as Berquist again notes) ascribe little importance to the temple or cult. The visions of Daniel contrast sharply here with the stories. Jonah mocks it in his psalm; it has nothing to do with Esther or Ruth; and certainly Solomon's antics in the Song are unconnected with his temple building. There are, then, a number of writings, many featured in this chapter, that betray an interest in individual identity. The factors promoting this are several. First, the reading classes are concerned with their own individual careers: their fortunes depend less on cooperation with others. But in the wider cultural world they inhabit, their own social identity is important. It is, after all, a label they have to wear. Jonah, Esther, Ruth, and Daniel all deal with the image of a Jew (or "Hebrew") among non-Jews. In this they point not only to a diaspora world but also to a Judah that is becoming much more cosmopolitan. Their travels, too, force them to face the question of their ethnic identity. Jonah, asked who he is, answers "I am a Hebrew and worship Yahweh the god of heaven." Precisely what that identity entailed was what Judean schools would try to teach, but they would not necessarily all have the same answer.

In what circumstances do such writings move on the path toward canonization? How is a hitherto scribal canon opened up to such works? Is it simply that they are widely read? There are two possibilities: one is that these works were used very widely in the school curriculum. Indeed, Jonah, Ruth, and Esther are still used as college texts to teach classical Hebrew, because they are short and grammatically simple. Another factor may be a concern deliberately to loosen the control of one class on the canon and to sanction a wider range of literature held in the temple libraries.

Chapter 10

Canons and the
Dead Sea Scrolls

Until the discovery of ancient manuscripts at Qumran (and elsewhere in the nearby Judean desert, at Naḥal Ḥever) our earliest copies of Jewish scriptural texts in Hebrew were little more than a thousand years old and represented the standardized Masoretic text, the product of centuries of fixing and annotating. Since 1947 we have been able to jump almost another millennium backward. The manuscripts from Qumran date mostly from the second century B.C.E. to the first century C.E. Just over two hundred of the eight hundred or so manuscripts preserved (mostly in fragments) from Qumran are of books from what we now call the "biblical" canon. From them we can discover the state of fixity of the texts of these scrolls at the turn of the era and also try to discover whether or not the writers of the scrolls were aware of a canon, or canons, of scripture.

This is not, of course, the most important question: we would rather know what the scrolls tell us about canonizing in general than about any particular canon. In any case, there are three problems to be faced. One is that on the narrow definition of canon as a fixed list of books, it is very hard to decide whether a "scriptural canon" was recognizable in the Qumran archive. It is possible, however, to recognize that the *notion* of a canon was present, and that certain canons can be identified (see below on Psalms). The second factor is the extent to which one may extrapolate from the Qumran manuscripts to other Judaisms. Do the canons recognized at Qumran reflect a wider consensus (or indeed a more widely fixed closed canon), or are they peculiar to a certain group or groups? Here the answer will differ from one instance to another. The third factor is really the most important for our purposes. Does this archive represent, as perhaps most scholars think, a library—whether written by a particular group or groups; or (an intermediate position) held by a specific group or groups, but contain writings from other groups as well; or, yet a third view, represent the contents of a number of Jewish libraries? The scrolls, then, can tell us a lot about canonizing processes in Judaism, but not necessarily a great deal about Jewish *canons* in general.

"LAW AND PROPHETS"

We can begin by looking at canons already encountered. As in other contemporary sources, we find Torah and prophets both together and separately, though we should certainly make no presumptions about "prophets" as comprising only the Masoretic selection, nor indeed as being a finally fixed list. A certain unity of "law" and "prophets" is also evident: In 1QS 1.3 we find "as he [God] commanded by the hand of Moses and all His servants the prophets," while a similar conjunction of Moses and the prophets occurs in 1QS 8.15–16 and in CD 5.21–6.1. But the two can also be mentioned separately: the phrase "law of Moses" occurs in 1QS 1.2–3; 5.8; and 8.22; 4QDibHam^a 3.12–13; CD 15.2; 9.12, etc., while in CD 7.17 the "books of the prophets" are mentioned on their own. And while "prophets" may be linked to Moses as sources of divine command, we shall presently see that they are also treated in a quite different way as predictors of the end of time. Both these understandings of "prophecy" we have seen elsewhere. We can also assume with some certainty that the Qumran canon of prophets was little different from the rabbinic-Masoretic one, unless perhaps Daniel was included in it. All "biblical" prophetic books are present, and (Daniel apart) not others that we can readily identify as part of that canon.

Because Qumran is a relatively large archive with multiple copies, and a large number of "biblical" texts, we can weigh a number of factors that enable us to identify a canonized writing. The presence of multiple copies is obviously one of these. Another is citation of contents as authoritative—and here we can make the useful distinction between works canonized by many groups and those probably canonized only within some group or groups. The *kind* of authority and the use to which different writings were typically put will have differed. In arguing with opponents, for example, some authors of Qumran texts use works that both they and their opponents accept as canonical; in matters of internal discipline or esoteric lore one appeals to one's own texts. But we shall still expect to find that the widely recognized canonical texts will be used, among other things, to advocate and support one's own "Judaism." In any given time and place in middle to late Second Temple Judaism one will find canonizing of different books and collections of books at different stages and levels, and so it will be here.

Another factor is the extent to which the text has been fixed, and, finally, the extent to which a writing has generated interpretative literature. Together these factors will give us a list of texts canonized (perhaps to varying degrees), though certainly not a definitive "Qumran canon." Let us deal with these criteria first.

Number of copies

The presence and number of copies of texts at Qumran is only one factor in assessing what might have been canonized, and it is far from reliable. By "copy" is meant an original manuscript. Since the majority of the scrolls survive only as small fragments, a "copy" in this context may very well be represented by a few phrases, words, or even letters. However, it is more usual to find a manuscript in several fragments, and from the physical quality and handwriting of a fragment it is usually possible to decide whether or not it belongs with other fragments, in which case a single "copy" is reconstructed. It is probably well known to most biblical students and scholars that all of the books of the Masoretic canon are represented among the Qumran texts with the exception of Esther and Nehemiah.[1] But since Ezra and Chronicles have only one copy each, with Proverbs and Joshua only two, absence is only a relative indicator. The numbers of copies so far listed are as follows, in order of frequency:

> Psalms (36)
> Deuteronomy (29)
> Isaiah (21)
> Exodus (17)
> Genesis (15)
> Leviticus (13)
> Numbers, Twelve Prophets, Daniel (8)
> Jeremiah, Ezekiel (6)
> 1–2 Samuel, Song of Songs, Ruth, Lamentations (4)
> Judges, Ecclesiastes (3)
> Joshua, Proverbs (2)
> Ezra, 1–2 Chronicles (1)

In addition, there are fragments of an Aramaic translation of Leviticus and two of Job. The Job translations are not hard to explain: the book contains some very difficult Hebrew!

Among the multiple copies of texts of the five scrolls there are fragments of three manuscripts that appear to have contained more than one Torah book (though no fragment actually contains the end of one book *and* the beginning of another), showing the possibility of a single Torah scroll, and reinforcing the suggestion that canons were sometimes represented by the contents of single scrolls. Also present are scrolls written in the old Hebrew script, though only in the case of Torah. This might attest either a greater veneration for the Mosaic writings or a belief that they were much older than other texts.

But we ought to put alongside these figures the numbers of some other texts not in the rabbinic-Masoretic canon: Jubilees (15) and Enoch (11). There are also several copies of works that appear to have been authoritative within a certain community only, such as CD or 1QS. But whether compilations such as 1QS or CD count as literary rather than documentary texts is hard to answer. A text may be authoritative in governing the behavior of a group without being "canonized." On a strict definition of "canon" it is thus impossible to say whether disciplinary or reference texts qualify. But collections of hymns and commentaries, if believed (it is a big "if") to have been composed by a religious leader (such as the "teacher of righteousness") could well have become canonized by the time the archive was deposited in the caves.

Citations

The formula "as it is written" attached to a citation has been taken by some scholars as an indication of the canonical status of the source. It is used with citations from all of the books of the Mosaic canon; also from the "former prophets" (Joshua is thus cited once and the books of Samuel perhaps twice); also of the "latter prophets," where citations occur from Isaiah, Ezekiel, Hosea, Amos, Micah, Zechariah, and Malachi; and indeed of other literature in the received canon, such as Psalms and Proverbs. But it is doubtful how useful this information is. The texts that contain the total of seventy or so such citations are actually rather few (CD, 1QS, 4QFlor, 4QTestim, 11QMelch, and 1QM) and hardly give us a comprehensive view. There is also at least one such citation of a book that is not in the Masoretic canon (CD 4.15 of a statement of Levi son of Jacob). Again, it is not established that a specific formula for citing canonized books was actually required: CD 16.3–4 refers the reader to the Book of Jubilees (of which fragments of at least fifteen copies have been found at Qumran). The number of allusions to books simply without the use of a citation formula is also very large. We really cannot, on the basis of citation formulae, automatically spot what was regarded at Qumran as canonized and what was not. The use of such formulae does betray the presence of a notion of canonical authority, but that is hardly surprising.

Fixed texts

A work, during its canonization, may undergo a great deal of development. But at some point (and not necessarily when it can only just fit on a single scroll), it tends to stabilize. We have seen that in the Hellenistic schools the authority of the writings of Homer, for example, led to the comparison and control of variant texts. According to Ulrich,[2] Genesis and Leviticus display a virtually complete uniformity—at least so far. But Exodus is attested in the two versions known to us from the Samaritan Pentateuch and the MT (though the Samaritan text's insertion at Exod. 20:17 of a command to build an altar on Gerizim is not included). Numbers also appears to have existed in at least two basic editions, while Deuteronomy has the most fluid text of all the Mosaic books.

Little can be said about the textual fluidity of many of the books from the prophetic canon because of too little material. But one of the fragments of Joshua (4QJosh[a]) is of particular interest, because it includes a passage that is differently placed. At the end of chapter 8 in the MT is an account of the building of an altar on Mt. Ebal. In the Greek this episode occurs a little later (chap. 9) while in 4QJosh[a] it is set at Gilgal as soon as Joshua enters the land. This latter sequence also seems to be the one known to Josephus (*Antiquities* 5.20).[3] In the case of Samuel, too, there are passages differently located, and one intriguing variation is in the story of David and Goliath. Some 21 manuscripts of the book of Isaiah were put into the caves, ranging from one still completely preserved (1QIs[a]) to one in thirteen fragments, extending intermittently from chapter 7 to chapter 66 (1QIs[b]). None agrees in its text exactly with any other, nor with the existing Masoretic text, though 1QIs[a] is very close. Qumran has also provided a Hebrew text of the shorter edition of Jeremiah, previously known only from the Greek translation.

What does the non-fixity of these texts imply? The "prophets" texts show rather less stability than the Torah scrolls, and this might suggest that we are toward the end of a process of scribal formation and adaptation of the prophetic texts, and not yet at a point of textual fixation. But even the torah texts are not totally fixed. Some Torah texts are written in the ancient Hebrew script,[4] but even these do not exhibit uniformity of text. If the Qumran texts are the products of a single group, that of course entails a fairly high degree of tolerance of textual variety within such a group; even if they represent the *library* of a single group, the same conclusion should be drawn. Variety of texts and even editions clearly does not bring into question their authority as scripture. Indeed, we shall presently encounter a case in the Habakkuk *pesher* where textual fluidity has actually been exploited in interpretation. The Qumran scrolls underline very boldly that canonization does not presuppose a fixed text. As the fate of Greek texts in the Hellenistic period also demonstrates, where a canon of texts is firmly established, having become objects of scholarly study, there is every reason why textual and grammatical scholarship should lead to the establishment of a "critical" and thus a standard text, so that the continued proliferation of "bad" texts should not deform the canon itself. We should therefore be careful not to assume that the standardizing of the Masoretic text in Judah arose from essentially religious motives rather than scholarly ones. Fixing texts, then, is a consequence of canonizing, not an ingredient of it.

Interpretative activity

The authority of the "law of Moses" is taken for granted by the writers of the Qumran texts (or some of them at least). Indeed, the authority of the Mosaic law is understood to be accepted by other groups as binding. But the canonized corpus has already engendered conflicts of interpretation and variations in practice, not only between individual readers but between groups. Regulations governing a group lifestyle can now be based on a set of particular interpretations of the Mosaic Torah. While not suggesting that we are able to generalize in all respects as to "Qumran" attitudes to Torah, we can take the *Damascus Document* (CD) to illustrate all these points.

The first part of CD (the *Admonition*) argues that "Israel" (and specifically a group nicknamed "builders of the wall") had been led astray by Belial. In 4.12–5.11 these are condemned for, among other things, (a) marrying more than one wife during their lifetime and (b) marrying one's niece. However, both charges concern not the *letter* of the law but an interpretation of it. For there is no law about monogamy, and CD has to argue from the divine command "male and female he created them" (as in Matt. 19:4–6; Mark 10:4–9), to which it adds that Noah only took pairs of animals into the ark. As for the marrying of a niece: Lev. 18:13–15 explicitly forbids aunt-nephew sexual relations, but not uncle-niece. Therefore, the principle is introduced: "the rules of incest are written with reference to males, but apply equally to females" (CD 5.10–11). Within the "Damascus" community, then, there is already visible the application of hermeneutical principles to a canon that is taken to be a body of prescriptive law.

This hermeneutic is quite emphatically underlined. In rehearsing the historical foundations of the sect, CD 3.12–18 claims that those who were faithful to the first covenant made another covenant with God (or reaffirmed the old one; CD is ambiguous on this), in which matters about "his holy sabbaths and his glorious set times, his righteous testimonies and his true ways" were revealed. As Lawrence Schiffman has analyzed in detail, the lifestyle of the community was governed both by "revealed" laws (those in scripture) and "hidden" laws (those given exclusively to the community).[5]

The *Laws* section of CD accordingly presents a selection of laws, couched in the terminology of the scriptural laws ("let no one . . . "), which often reproduce the text of scriptural laws, though usually with additional nuancing or interpretation. But concern to rationalize scriptural law is also evident in other Qumran texts where practical application of such an exercise is less direct. The *Temple Scroll* represents an attempt at such a systematization, reordering scriptural contents into a clearer sequence but also combining texts from different places so as to present a fuller version. One interesting facet of the *Temple Scroll* is that it sometimes changes scriptural texts from third person to first person so as to present what is *reported* as divine speech in Deuteronomy as direct speech. But whether this constitutes a claim to be an authoritative work—whether it was seen, for example, as belonging to the Mosaic canon—is dubious. It might perhaps be loosely comparted with something like Tatian's *Diatessaron,* a work designed to harmonize canonical texts, though it is more selective and follows its own structure. There is no evidence from other texts at Qumran that it was regarded as an authoritative torah text, although some scholars have raised the possibility. Jubilees would be a likelier candidate in this regard (see below).

Concern for the systematization and clarification of purity laws, and differences in interpretation, are also clear from 4QMMT,[6] part of which is a statement of differing principles in which the writers' view is expressed by "we consider that" (ואנחנו חושבים, e.g., B29) or "we say" (אנחנו אומרים, e.g., B55), with regular appeal to "what is written" (without specific citation). Here again, both sides agree that what is in the *torah* of Moses must be performed. But each side, believing that it does in fact carry out the written law, employs or advocates different practices. Both sides, however (one explicitly, one implicitly), believe that their practice (or theory) is the correct application of Mosaic law. The canon has become authoritative for group practice, but, of course, only when "interpreted."

The abundant evidence of interest in the scriptural law as a system to be developed for either practical or theoretical purposes, illustrates a further aspect of the authority of the Mosaic canon. And while the claim of a new revelation of law is clearly expressed in CD, there are few (if any) new laws (as opposed to communal disciplinary regulations) that do not emerge as an extension or interpretation of the canonized laws. There is no body of supplementary law distinct from the scriptural. The contrast with the rabbinic "dual torah," in which the scriptural canon is extended, if not overlaid, by a written corpus of laws represented as Mosaic "oral torah," may be illustrative of a greater reluctance on the part of the rabbis to mix interpretation with scriptural text. But we cannot be sure.

A great deal of interest has recently been stirred by the publication of "parabiblical" texts in which a biblical story is retold with added or changed details.[7]

These texts include the *Genesis Apocryphon,* in which the birth of Noah and the adventures of Abraham are retold in Aramaic, with expansion; 4Q252, in which the flood story is retold with revised chronology in accordance with a solar calendar, and several other texts. There are also fragments of what may have been a very extensive "rewritten Pentateuch" (4Q364–7) containing some additions to the canonized narrative, but on the whole following its contours. What the existence of these retellings tells us about the status of the canonical texts at Qumran is hard to say. Perhaps modern analogies are helpful. Even those who adhere most strictly to the literal words of the Bible are usually quite content to have their stories expanded or improved, whether in children's versions, in hymns, or via the medium of Hollywood. Canonized laws acquire one form of authority: canonized stories another. Especially in a culture that is predominantly oral, the idea of a story having a fixed authoritative textual form may be absent. Thus the attempt in the Qumran scrolls to create a practical or theoretical *system* out of biblical law without rewriting the text may have been paralleled by an effort to rewrite the *stories,* not by altering the text but by, as it were, "writing over" different versions of the narrative. This desire is itself a testimony to the canonicity of the stories and probably also in a more or less standardized form. The "parabiblical" texts were not attempts to re*place* the canonical texts, but rather to re*present* the canonical stories in a more "correct" manner. Stories are most easily exegeted by being retold.

Interpretation of prophets

The best-known feature of interpretation of the prophets are the *pesharim,* which are section-by-section treatments of a continuous scriptural text with a view to deciphering the eschatological meaning. Just as the canonized Law of Moses was, according to CD, made clear to the sectarian group through inspired interpretation, so is the meaning of the prophetic texts, which have become signs or codes. The hermeneutic is explicitly set out in the commentary on Habakkuk from Qumran cave 1:

> And God told Habakkuk to write that which was to happen to the final generation, but he did not reveal to him when time would come to an end. And as for the statement "He who reads it may run," its interpretation refers to the Teacher of Righteousness, to whom God revealed all the mysteries of his servants the prophets.
>
> (1QpHab 7:1–5)

The authority of the canonical texts, in conjunction with the inspired interpretation, is used to confirm the significance of the events alluded to as part of the divine plan, and to argue that the authors' group is the rightful heir to the scriptures that all Judaisms share, the true Israel. What is clear from these *pesharim* is that the literal and sequential meaning of the passages is not important: each statement is to be taken as an isolated "oracle." The prophetic texts are not being read as "literature" but as a collection of cryptic statements. We saw in chapter 7 that the prophetic books are not composed on the whole as "literature," and thus this "atomistic" procedure is not quite as strange as it may seem to moderns. We also considered there the techniques of mantic exegesis. Here, then, will be noted just one intriguing feature of the Habakkuk *pesher*: the exploitation of textual variants. Two places in the Habakkuk *pesher* are potentially quite instructive in showing us the degree of freedom in varying the written text. In 2:15 the Masoretic text reads as follows:

הוי משקה רעהו מספח חמתך ואף שכר למען הביט על מעוריהם שתה גם־אתה והערל

> Woe to him who makes his neighbor(s) drink, mixing in your wrath/poison even until they are/he is drunk, so as to look upon their nakedness . . . drink yourself, and play the uncircumcised!

The *pesher* reads slightly differently (1QpHab 11:2–3, 9):

הוי משקה רעיהו מספח חמתו אף שכר למען הביט על מועדיהם שתה גם אתה והרעל

> Woe to him who makes his neighbors drink, mixing in his wrath/poison even until they are/he is drunk, so as to look upon their *feasts* . . . drink yourself, and *stumble!*

and in the following "explanation" we find (11:13):

כיא לוא מל את עורלת לבו
For he did not circumcise the foreskin of his heart. . . .

There is a significant change from "nakedness" to "feasts," though it only involves changing two very similar letters and switching the order. But the change is probably not accidental: the reading in the *pesher* is not attested elsewhere, and "feasts" is an important topic in the subsequent explanation (we saw how important feasts were in the context of calendrical differences earlier in a passage from CD). A deliberate change has been made, then, in the text before the scribe, in order to accommodate the desired interpretation. The second change involves transposing two consonants, changing the meaning from "be uncircumcised" to "stumble." (This is actually the reading preferred by the NRSV!) However, since the interpretation alludes to the reading given in the MT, we either have a deliberate change or, much more probably, a play on the variant. If so, we can see that the author, like a good Alexandrian scholar, is both aware of and concerned about the existence of variant texts. But he takes a different tack: these variations are clues to hidden meanings.

Interpretation of
"law and prophets" together

I noted earlier that in a few passages among the Qumran scrolls we find "law and prophets" together as a combined source of divine commandments. But in the Melchizedek midrash from Cave 11 (11QMelch) we find law and prophets combined in a different literary form. For while the hermeneutics are basically the same as in the *pesharim,* and indeed small sections of this work follow the *pesher* technique over a single verse so that texts are taken out of their canonical context, this midrash weaves texts from different writings into a coherent argument. This is an important development because it already implies, as the rabbis were to accept, that scriptural texts form a unity, and that the meaning of one text may be elucidated by another, even a text from another canon. What this process attests of course is the *amalgamation of canons,* and it confirms that "law and prophets" was already, at least somewhere at this time (first century B.C.E.) being regarded in this way. The rabbis were to take the principle of the canon explaining itself to a considerable degree.

The preserved text, of which the beginning is lost, opens in the middle of an explanation of the jubilee year, citing Lev. 25:13 and Deut. 15:2, focusing on the release of slaves and debts. This law is then expanded by means of Isa. 61:1, which also speaks of the release of prisoners. Therefore the text is referring to a jubilee. Since debts to God take the form of sins (we may loosely say), and these are atoned for on a national basis by the high priest at the Day of Atonement, the agent of this final release will be the heavenly High Priest on the final day of atonement. This figure is identified as Melchizedek, and the date is "the end of the tenth jubilee," i.e., after 490 or 500 years (depending on whether one counts a jubilee as 49 or 50 years). Texts from the psalms and Daniel (both regarded as belonging to "prophets") are used to develop the plot which deals, as do the *pesharim,* with the end, though not with events peculiar to one group, but to the nation and world.

Finally, there are also a number of works of a "predictive" and hortatory kind: testaments or visions attributed to Pentateuchal figures, mostly patriarchal but including Moses; and a range of unfortunately only minutely preserved texts associated with Joshua, Samuel (first person), Jeremiah, Ezekiel, and Daniel, which serve sometimes to give more color to these characters and their stories (as in the biblical paraphrases of Pentateuchal books, mentioned earlier) or to add words of consolation or prediction, in the familiar manner of pseudepigrapha. Here again we can see that a similar treatment is being accorded to figures from both canons, reinforcing the impression that they are being effectively treated as a single canon.

PSALMS:
CANON WITHIN A CANON?

The relevance of all these factors is clearly illustrated in the case of the collection of Psalms. The following text (11Q CompDav) has already been referred to in chapter 8:

> 2 Now David was the son of Jesse, wise, and a light like the light of the sun; [and] a sage
> 3 learned and perfect in all his ways before God and humans. And Yahweh
> 4 gave him a spirit of intelligence and enlightenment, and he composed psalms:
> 5 three thousand six hundred; and songs for singing in front of the altar at the *Tamid*
> 6 offering every single day, every day of the year, three hundred and sixty-
> 7 four; and for the offering on sabbaths: fifty-two songs; and for the offering at the beginnings
> 8 of the months and all festival days and for the day of atonement: thirty songs.
> 9 And all the songs that he composed totaled four hundred and forty-six. And songs
> 10 to be sung over those afflicted: four. And the total was four thousand and fifty.
> 11 All these he composed by the spirit of prophecy which had been given to him from before Elyon.

Here is a perfect instance of a Qumran canon of Davidic compositions. Of one thing we can be reasonably sure, too: the totals imply a 364-day (exactly 52-week) calendar, such as we find very widely followed in the Qumran texts (and elsewhere).[8] If such a canon were also recognized where a lunisolar calendar of about 354 days was practiced, the number of *Tamid* songs and sabbath offerings would be reduced accordingly. Elsewhere, as we have seen, the Davidic canon is represented only by collections of psalms, of which the Masoretic canon has 150 and the Greek 151, though they share the same sequence. Now, of all the "biblical" books, Psalms is represented by the largest number of Qumran manuscripts (36, ahead of Deuteronomy with 29).[9] In most of these manuscripts it is impossible to detect the order of the psalms, because so little of the text of the fragment has been preserved. But some of the psalms contain additional material and a different sequence from the Masoretic, including the Cave 11 scroll, the most extensively preserved, which includes "David's Last Words" (2 Sam. 23:1–7), Psalms 154—155 of the Syriac canon, the Greek Psalm 151, and ben Sira 51:13–30.[10] No Qumran text irrefutably supports the Masoretic and Greek order against 11QPs[a], though many may have exhibited that arrangement. (Flint has suggested that the Qumran texts represent "at least four collections."[11]) The suggestion that the Cave 11 scroll is not meant to be a scroll of canonical Psalms but a liturgical text[12] has no positive evidence and does not take account of the fact that for Psalms 1—89 the order in MT and 11QPs[a] agrees. The likely conclusion is that some collections had achieved a fixed order, while the remainder had not (this was the view adopted in chapter 8).

It should be noted, finally, that 11QDavComp's attribution of a "spirit of prophecy" to David fits well with the fact that of the Qumran *pesharim,* the only ones not based on one of the named prophetic books are on Psalms (1QpPs, 4QpPs[a] and [b]). This would not have to mean that psalms were assigned to a "prophetic" canon; it should be remembered that according to Chronicles the spirit of prophecy continued into the liturgy: Levites could, and did, sing and prophesy at the same time (1 Chron. 25:1).

A CANON OF ENOCH?

In chapters 8 and 9 were mentioned one or two works that were not adopted into the rabbinic-Masoretic canon. Among the Qumran scrolls a number of candidates for this category might be mentioned, the most obvious of which are the Enoch writings. A book of Enoch is in fact canonical in the Ethiopic church and was best preserved in Ethiopic (into which language it was translated from Greek) until Aramaic Enoch texts were found at Qumran. Here, then, seems to be the logical place to discuss the texts.

Enoch (which should be referred to as 1 Enoch) is, in its Greek/Ethiopic form, a book which scholarly analysis shows to be made up of five books. These are the "Book of the Watchers" (1—36); the "Book of Parables (Similitudes)" (37—71); the "Book of the Heavenly Luminaries" (72—82); the "Book of Dreams" (83—90); and the "Epistle of Enoch" (92—105). But this fivefold book is the result of development that continued to occur later than the Qumran stage, and the Aramaic texts allow us to reconstruct an earlier form.

The importance of the Enochic literature is that its earliest components seem to be at least as early as the third century B.C.E., making it contemporary or near-contemporary with a great deal of the "law and prophets." It is also remarkable in paying little attention to either law or prophets, but focusing instead on an antediluvian figure mentioned in Genesis 5:21–4, of whom it is there said "and he was not, for God took him." To this mysterious statement can be added the length of his earthly life: 365 years. Enoch, like Noah, seems to have been modeled on a Mesopotamian figure,

Enmeduranki, also said to have lived before the Flood, and one endowed with wisdom from the gods.[13] The contents of the Enoch books are revelations received by Enoch and passed on to his son Methuselah. These revelations deal with the nature of the world (metaphysics) and the end of the righteous and the wicked (ethics). In the tradition of much wisdom literature, the two are intrinsically connected.

The earliest Enochic composition is generally agreed to have been the Astronomical Book (72—82), probably datable to the Persian period, in which Enoch travels through the heavens and explains their working. The account also embodies an argument for a calendar ruled by the sun, not the moon, i.e., a calendar of 364 days, the same principle found in many of the Qumran texts (remember Enoch's earthly lifespan according to Genesis). The "Book of the Watchers" deals with the origins of sin: not, as in the Mosaic canon, something attributable to human actions alone but brought to earth from heaven by rebellious angels ("Watchers," cf. Dan. 4:13, 23) who also bring knowledge of metalworking (for weapons and jewelry). This story is reminiscent of the Greek Prometheus legend of the origin of fire, and may be hinted at in Genesis 6:1–4 (and the Cain story). Although this part of Enoch is usually taken to be a rewriting of Genesis, we should probably regard it as roughly contemporary if not older than Genesis, since its dating is widely thought to be from the third century B.C.E. at the latest. The thrust of this presentation is that goodness can only come about through a heavenly restoration, when the righteous will live in a restored world and the rebellious angels will be eternally punished. For the meantime, their leader is buried under a rock in the wilderness (see Leviticus 16!). Again, Enoch is taken to heaven, then to the West, where he witnesses the place of punishment of the wicked angels, and then back toward the East, where he sees the place of the spirits of the dead, the divine throne, the Tree of Life, paradise, and the sources of luminaries and winds. The "Book of Dreams" contains two visions, one of the Flood, the other of the course of world history from Adam to the end, with humans represented by animals and angels as humans (again, as in Daniel 7—11). The righteous are represented as sheep (the Watchers); the ending comes after the Maccabean success, enabling this section (or this part of it) to be dated to the second century B.C.E.

The Epistle of Enoch contains an account of the history from exile to eschaton in weeks (see again Daniel 9), culminating in oppression of—and then deliverance of—the righteous and the rebuilding of the temple. The date of this section is perhaps in the second or first century B.C.E. The "Book of Parables" is not attested at Qumran: debate rages over whether it exhibits any Christian influence, but that need not concern us. It seems that whether or not the Enoch literature also persisted elsewhere, it has clear connections with other Qumran writings and with Jubilees (also found at Qumran) and is plausibly to be associated with whatever social and ideological developments led to the circles responsible for many, if not all, of the Qumran texts. The solar calendar, antagonism to the priesthood in charge of the temple (which is evident throughout Enoch), the calendar of weeks, the emergence of a dualistic worldview in the notion of the "elect," are common features. But one must be reserved in identifying the Enochic canon as exclusively a Qumranic one. The apocalyptic genres of Enoch are not developed in these texts: the Mosaic torah is prominent in the Qumran texts. Connections with the book of Daniel have also been noted above. Genesis and ben Sira both betray knowledge of Enoch as an important figure, which should warn us about relegating the Enochic canon to one circle only.

The Enoch writings are a distinct, continually evolving corpus which I would readily define on my terms as a canon. The final fivefold structure has been suggested as an imitation of the Mosaic canon, though Milik has in fact suggested that even the Qumran Enoch canon had five books, with the incorporation of a "Book of Giants."[14] Perhaps the popularity of Enoch with circles hostile to the Jerusalem priesthood explains why this canon was not incorporated into the rabbinic scriptures. But other reasons may also be offered (see chapter 11). Like an early collection of Daniel stories, Enoch is an Aramaic canon.

Another important issue is to what extent the Enoch canon and the Mosaic canon interacted. I have suggested (following an assertion by Milik) that the story in Genesis 2—4 is a deliberately manufactured alternative myth to the prevailing Enochic one—which still contains traces elsewhere in the Mosaic and prophetic canons—and that the angelic arch-villain Semihazah/Asa'el/Azazel was replaced by the human Cain. This development is quite consistent with the view of the evolution of the canons offered in this book, but there is no space to argue it again here.[15]

QUMRAN AND CANONIZING

Of the canons that may have been acknowledged by the original owners of the Qumran we can make some educated guesses. In addition to those already considered, two small fragments of the (non-Solomonic) book of ben Sira from Cave 2 (the Masada scroll of the work may also have come from Qumran) and five of Tobit (four Aramaic and one Hebrew) show that further texts canonized by Greek Jews (and Christians) are also to be brought into consideration.

In the matter of canon, as in other respects, the Qumran literature can be compared with that of the early Christian communities. The existence in the

Qumran caves of a number of texts of value only to a certain group or groups alongside texts enjoying wider canonical recognition should cause us to reflect on the equivalent process within those groups that formed the Christian church(es). Here, alongside a (more or less) inherited collection, a secondary collection was also emerging. Just as the Christian "scriptures" developed as a set of already canonized writings (Jewish scriptures) alongside another set that was being canonized (letters of Paul, gospels), so it was in the Qumran collection(s). In the case of Qumran, the comparison is complicated, however, by our uncertainty as to how to interpret the collection and the site. We need to discover whether these scrolls constitute a library or libraries, and if so, whether of one or more scribal schools, or one or more sects; or indeed, if they are simply a collection of texts from certain private or public libraries, hidden for safety. In other words, if there are canons among these texts, whose canons are they? Views about these options range from one extreme to the other. At one end is Norman Golb's opinion that the contents of the caves are deposits of several libraries, probably in Jerusalem, which were taken from the city in the face of the imminent siege by the Romans during the war of 66–70 C.E.[16] On that view, the ruins of Qumran are unconnected with the production or copying of the texts, and we are dealing with multiple origins for texts which, taken as a whole, represent a spectrum of Jewish beliefs, texts, and, we would add, canons. At the other end of the spectrum is the more longstanding view that the texts were composed by and for a community (usually considered Essene).[17]

How much easier it would be to regard all Qumran texts as emanating from a single source. But one fatal problem with this conclusion is the very large number of different hands that wrote the scrolls. In a single community, especially if it wrote its own scrolls, one would have to expect that each scribe wrote many scrolls. But although the figures vary, no scholar who has investigated the handwriting concedes that there are more than a handful that can be said to have been written by the same person. Accordingly, the older standard view has become modified: while the texts formed an Essene collection, not all of them were Essene compositions—and the majority were written outside Qumran.[18]

Yet another view, recently put forward by Hartmut Stegemann, is that Qumran was a purpose-built library, and that the Essenes, far from being one of a number of smaller movements within Judaism, constituted a major and mainstream movement.[19] The Essenes were "spiritually the leading group of Palestinian Judaism in their times."[20] Stegemann proposes that these "Damascus Covenanters," the *Hasidim,* the temple establishment, and the Maccabees represented the four main Jewish groups in the years around 159 B.C.E., the year of the decease of the high priest Alcimus, who succeeded in uniting all the groups except the Maccabees but was ousted by the Hasmonean Jonathan. This Zadokite high priest founded the Union or *yahad,* with branches throughout Palestine. Alas, many of the *Hasidim* withdrew from this Union to become Pharisees, while the (Hasmonean) temple establishment formed the Sadducees.

Stegemann continues by suggesting that Qumran was specially built by the Essenes at the end of the second century B.C.E. as a study center, a place of retreat for its members, with or (usually) without their families, but not their birthplace or their original home. He includes an unusually detailed account of the layout and function of the buildings at Qumran: the main building comprised a hallway and staircase, with an arsenal and emergency stores under the tower (in case of marauders), while on the upper floor lay the "scriptorium," beside which were living quarters for about forty people. Below on the lower floor was, perhaps, a workroom where the scrolls were prepared, sewn, and cut. Also on the lower floor was the library, consisting of three rooms, in the largest of which the approximately one thousand scrolls later found in the caves would have once been housed. To the left of the entrance to this reading room was a small hole into which the user would drop a small stone inscribed with his name. New members of the order studied biblical books; more senior members were allowed other books of the Union. Further on was a small hatch, through which the librarian would hand a requested scroll to an approved reader. There was also a specially constructed platform for the unrolling of particularly long scrolls, to prevent damage to them when being consulted. By Stegemann's calculations, between 150 and 300 Essenes inhabited this retreat.

This hypothesis, then, is an ingenious defense of the Essene/Hasmonean hypothesis, which even copes with the plurality of scribal hands—if the Essene scribes, of whom there may have been many, only spent a short period of time here before returning to their own "camps." It also manages to remove the issue of sectarianism. But it is less comfortable, perhaps, with the range of biblical text forms and of religious ideas in the Scrolls, and can afford no place for the Copper Scroll, that list of buried treasure found in Cave 3 to which Golb attaches a good deal of importance. But in regarding the scrolls as the products of a library of a mainstream Jewish movement Stegemann is agreeing to one aspect of Golb's position. Both see the scrolls as the contents of a library, and one in which mainstream views are represented.

If the scrolls are indeed the contents of a library or libraries rather than the working texts of a religious community, it would seem likely that the copies were produced for the sake of editing, reading, and consultation. Suppose, for instance, the copies of the *Community Rule* from Caves 1 and

4 were both documentary texts detailing how the community was to be run; why are they not identical? And why is there such clear evidence that 1QS has been compiled from a number of different sources? Why, indeed, its incoherent shape? And why is it written on the same scroll as other compositions (1QSa, 1QSb)? Were the three compositions thought to be closely enough related to be written on a single scroll? If so, here again is an activity related to archiving, and pointing either to a library copy (in which similar texts were archived together) or perhaps a private scroll.[21] If many (or all) of these texts really are (whatever their immediate provenance or ultimate origin) library *copies,* the great value of the Qumran texts, then, will be this: to have frozen, for our inspection, a Jewish library (whether public, sectarian, or personal), containing a collection of texts in different stages of being canonized: some hardly past the autograph stage; others recognized by every Judaism as canonical for a long time; and yet others already having been copied, edited, and combined with other texts on a single scroll. Can the importance of these texts for our understanding of Jewish canonizing possibly be overestimated?

CHAPTER 11

Holy Books

THE RABBINIC-MASORETIC CANON

Why have Jews inherited a single canon of "scriptural" books? What forces led to the need to declare that such a canon existed? For even if such a canon was not as important in Judaism as it has become to Protestant Christianity, and if, indeed, rabbinic canonizing continued to take place, the rabbis nevertheless did take into their Judaism a canon of texts, which the Masoretes then set about, as we shall see, decorating and transforming into a sacred icon.

Two observations are basic. First, the rabbis did not *create* a scriptural canon. They inherited a more-or-less agreed set of writings. Second, they set about defining the meaning of this canon in terms of their own system. We can ask, then, what part this canon plays in the rabbinic system, and the answer will explain why rabbinic discussion of the canon is as it is. But first of all we have to ask: how was it that the rabbis came to inherit, from the many writings that we know Judaism had been producing, a relatively small set of Hebrew scrolls? To answer this we need to look to the period before rabbinic Judaism developed.

Let us first underline that the rabbis inherited a collection of "holy" writings, rationalized this collection according to their own priorities, and imposed divisions. The fabled "council of Yavneh (or Jamnia)" used to be cited as the occasion on which the "rabbinic canon was decided." Certainly, after the fall of Jerusalem the rabbis under Yoḥanan ben Zakkai went to Yavneh on the Mediterranean coast and sought to transform and extend some of the roles once exercised in the temple cult. There are references in the Mishnah to a court and a school "in the vineyards at Yavneh" (e.g., m. Sanhedrin 11:4; m. Ketuboth 4:6), while ben Zakkai is mentioned in m. Yadayim 4:6 as having participated in the discussion about scriptures, and 3:5 (see below) refers to a "decision." But this is thin evidence for a "council," and such a body looks suspiciously like an equivalent of a Christian council of the kind that would meet to set doctrines and define heresies. There is abundant evidence that the contents of the "holy books" were largely already set before this time, and hints that the discussion continued for a while later on. But it has to be emphasized that a record of a discussion in a rabbinic document does not tell us that an issue was solved, nor when and where. Most discussions recorded in rabbinic literature are artificially constructed, attestations notoriously unreliable. The rabbis did not always narrate discussions in the service of a decision, but sometimes to raise a methodological issue. Indeed, discussion about the order of the scriptural scrolls is a particularly good example. Except in a codex, after all, order has little meaning, and there is enough evidence in the rabbinic literature and in medieval manuscripts to show that an absolutely fixed order of prophets and writings was not in place. Only the advent of printing and with it the creation of a Jewish "Bible" would do that.

A better way to proceed with analysis of the rabbinic "canon" is to consider the function of holy books within the rabbinic system. Let us begin with the rabbinic definition of what is *scripturally* canonical, namely what books "defile the hands." "Defiling" brings us within the domain of clean and unclean, holy and unholy, a basic rabbinic categorization. As Neusner has observed regarding the Mishnah:

> [T]he Mishnah is made up of lists; these lists are composed of things that exhibit shared traits of an intrinsic order . . . the inner structure set forth by the hermeneutics of a logic of classification sustains the system of ordering all things in proper place and under the proper rule.[1]

This citation is worth making also because it sets rabbinic thought so clearly in the context of scribal behavior generally: classification, as we saw in chapter 2, is a characteristic activity of ancient Near Eastern scribalism. The victory of rabbinism is the victory of the scribe over the king and over the priest: the victory of the intellectual, rational, and ethical turn of mind over the political or the cultic. Nothing characterizes rabbinic thought better than its systematization, its rationality, its concern with minutiae and their place in the scheme of things, their wish to archive the whole of creation in terms of its intrinsic structures: the will of the god of Israel and the nature of the people of Israel. But the main point to be made here is that books, like everything else, have to be divided into categories, and the major category of the rabbinic taxonomy of the world is holiness. Inevitably, then, with an inherited category of "holy books," the rabbis could not but address the question of what belonged in it and what did not. Those books that were not holy, forming the largest category, were simply "outside books."

Thus the rabbis do not use the term or the concept "canon" but deal with the taxonomy of scrolls. Why the formula "defile the hands"? The view that it marks out these artifacts as "holy" is probably correct. Mishnah Yadayim 3:5 is the *locus classicus:*

> All the holy scriptures (כתבי הקדש) defile the hands (מטמאם את ידים). The Song of Songs and Ecclesiastes defile the hands. R. Judah said, "the Song of Songs defiles the hands but there is a dispute about Ecclesiastes." R. Jose said, "Ecclesiastes does not defile the hands but there is a dispute about Song of Songs" . . . according to the words of ben Azzai they decided.

And, as already discussed, the issue is not about "canonicity" but about the handling of these artifacts. For each of the disputed scrolls (and Esther and Ruth were also disputed, see b. Talmud Megillah 7a) came to be read on a particular feast day. For that reason, the five scrolls and the torah are often linked together in rabbinic literature (e.g., in the Midrash Rabbah). So the issue seems to be about books publicly read. But some perspective must be retained. That the rabbis continued now and then to argue about the status of certain books does not mean a great deal: this is characteristic of rabbinic debate, even over matters already established.

None of the explanations given for why "defile" is the term used is entirely satisfactory. Haran thinks it goes back to a pre-rabbinic folk custom;[2] Beckwith that it goes back to the sanctity of books in the temple court, noting that while the holy books there did not defile the hands, these books did if handled outside: or indeed, that holy books taken into the temple still made the hands unclean.[3] On this view there was something irregular about the handling of these holy objects outside the temple. But the important issue is that the rabbis did not form or change a canon, but addressed the question of holy and unholy books. And with the exception of the creation of the "dual torah," by means of which torah was turned into halakhah by the development of the Mishnah and then the "oral torah" theory, all the issues related to hermeneutics and authority of scriptural writings had been anticipated.

Why these books were deemed "holy" is an intriguing question. The simplest answer is that they were inherited as a special collection, and their status was defined in terms of rabbinic categories. Can we go further? Those scrolls whose "holiness" was questioned (Ruth, Song of Songs, Esther) do not contain the divine name: was it thought that on this ground they could not "defile the hands"? Perhaps; but if so, the argument did not persuade. Could it be that holiness was connected to liturgical use? Only for some: a number of these scrolls were not so used. The important point to make here is that to examine rabbinic discussion in order to find out why the canon was formed as it was is mistaken. The rabbis did not form it, but only sought to rationalize what others had already formed.

They may, however, be responsible for its present divisions. A great deal of discussion has taken place over the distinction between the Prophets and Writings sections, for it is here that rabbinic decisions seem to have been made. The standard view (established by Ryle[4] and maintained by the influential works of Leiman[5] and Beckwith[6]) is that the canon was created in three stages, with Prophets canonized only after Torah was closed and Writings only after Prophets was closed. This would mean that the rabbis were involved only with the extent of Writings. But, as reviewed in chapter 7, the evidence and arguments assembled by Barton make it more likely that some books in both Prophets and Writings divisions were accorded equal status, and indeed that the term "Prophets" did not denote a fixed list before the rabbinic period. Yet this has little to do with the actual scrolls in question, only about their classification. We cannot perceive a formal distinction between "Writings" and "Prophets" before the rabbinic period. But what is the rationale behind it? Barton has suggested that it may be due to the practice of reading from the prophetic books in synagogue liturgy but not from the "Writings," and he ponders a possible distinction at some point between "read prophets" and "written prophets" as a basis for the partition.[7] The attraction of this suggestion (one which Barton does not follow up) is that it simultaneously explains the division between "former" and "latter" prophets, since parts of only the "latter" prophets are read out in the synagogue.

But in that case, why were the "former prophets" not moved to the "Writings" also? In reply, it might be suggested that the "former" and "latter" prophets were already seen to be firmly connected by means of overlapping passages and chronological cross-references, so that it was deemed inappropriate to separate them: or that the "former prophets" were understood to be a record of the deeds of the prophetic institution to whom the "latter prophets" belonged. In both cases we are guessing, and whether this issue has to do with canon *formation* is rather dubious anyway.

The *contents* of the books that "defile the hands" is quite another issue and has nothing to do with *rabbinic* canon. For the rabbis, the holiness of the books attaches to their physical form, not their contents. We are dealing with a canonization of objects, not of discourse. As W. S. Green has pointed out, many treatments take it as axiomatic that the "rabbinic thought" is centered on the scriptures.[8] But as he points out, it was not such scriptures that created rabbinic Judaism but the loss of temple and then land: and thus of cult, the locus of divine presence, priesthood, and the structure of holiness. The structure of the earliest rabbinic writings displays a concern to replicate the system that the cult represented, which was itself a regular, well-ordered celebration of communication with the deity. Rabbinic Judaism is concerned with behavior: the observance of sacred times and places, and sacred distinctions. These were not derived directly from the scriptures but were developed systematically according to indigenous categories and then linked to scripture.[9]

The place of the torah scroll in synagogue worship, kept in an "ark" and regularly read, shows that it functioned as a continuation of the "holy of holies" and indeed as the text of the law given by Yahweh to Moses, which did belong in the temple and was supposed to have been read out to the people. It was therefore accorded a very high degree of holiness: it was a "holy book," though we shall see presently that the holiness of the Mosaic torah was not of itself a rabbinic innovation. But rather than text to be *read* (despite its liturgical recital every Sabbath), it was an *object;* it could not be touched or destroyed, and it had to be prepared according to very strict rules. In Green's words, the *sefer torah* was the "stable center for rabbinism's system of piety."[10] That was probably the reason why every (male) Jew was required to possess a copy.

The *authority of the contents of Torah,* which is a doctrine so dear to Protestant Christianity, is precisely what is *not* promoted by rabbinic Judaism. For the *meaning* of the torah, and thus the duties laid upon every Jew, are the product of rabbinic scholarship. The torah is not to be interpreted directly: it is not a primary source for doctrine or practice. That authority lies with the rabbis, and rabbinic exegesis is not a matter of deciding what the text means but deciding what the system is that it implies. The torah, then, was always a *pretext;* and that is why (*pace* Green on this particular point) it could be allowed to have multiple meanings. The meaning depended not on the intrinsic sense but on the sense yielded when a particular problem or discourse was applied to it.

The fixing of the text in the rabbinic and post-rabbinic period (here is meant the post-Talmudic period, beginning at about the end of the sixth century C.E.) likewise has something to do with a process that had already begun, but which was also fed by the rabbinic attitude toward holy writings as artifacts. The way in which a scroll had to be written, the materials, the script, and so on, were all aimed not at the integrity of the contents but of the physical scroll. How else would it matter whether the scroll was written by a Gentile, or written on papyrus, or in a particular script?

However, the physical sanctity of the torah scroll (for it is this scroll that sets the norm) of necessity dictated that each copy be an exact replica. That in turn means a single uniform text. Such a text was never achieved, of course, though a standard Western Masoretic text was finally established by Jacob ben Ḥayyim, the editor of the second rabbinic Bible which Daniel Bomberg published in Venice in 1524/5. But the thousands of small variations that ben Ḥayyim found were not the result of carelessness with the form of the text, but arose in spite of and partly because of it; for a concern to copy exactly leads to the preservation of "errors" as well. We shall see presently that the process of standardizing a text, well known from the Hellenistic world, was already influencing the scribes of the Second Temple period. The work of the Masoretes, undertaken much later, is a logical extension of the rabbinic concern for a standard text and for standardization in its liturgical use. It is also an exercise in the sort of textual criticism known to us from the Hellenistic schools, including the noting of unusual grammatical forms and unique vocabulary.

But what took place *after* the rabbis had appropriated a canon of "holy writings" into their system is a topic that deserves a separate treatment. Most of the canonizing processes were essentially complete by the end of the first century C.E.—indeed, by the end of the Second Temple period: a more-or-less agreed collection, a recognition of certain writings as "holy," and a move toward standardizing texts had already taken place.

THE HASMONEAN INITIATIVE

The evidence from Qumran underlines very boldly that there were many more writings than were taken over into the rabbinic canon; and indeed that a Jewish library would contain a much larger number of books. The central problem is to understand the emergence of a relatively small collection. The answer to this question involves other phenomena: the emergence of the notion of "Judaism" in its many definitions, and specifically as a religious culture, leading to the designation "holy books"; and the creation of institutions (libraries, schools) that would support the idea of "Judaism" through the promotion of a restricted canon of literature.

Although it will be argued that the "Hasmonean initiative" plays a central role in all of these developments, it should be remembered that history is not merely a sequence of great moments or epochs. Events both generate and are generated by processes, and while ancient historiography and ancient sources are explicit about events, they do not concern themselves much with processes. Indeed, the tendency is to assign processes to events (like the arrival of Ezra). The "Maccabean wars" and the subsequent rise of the Hasmonean dynasty (see chap. 4) was not a sudden irruption into the history of Judah of a tyrannous regime, nor did Hellenism first hit Judah in the early second century B.C.E. But since our sources shine most clearly on this period, we can discern there as in no preceding period some of the basic ingredients that made up the category of "holy writings." Additionally, the emergence of independent political power created an agenda for both external and internal initiatives that did not exhibit themselves in earlier periods.

JUDAISM AS A
PERSONAL RELIGION

A lot of writing from the ancient Near East is "religious" in the broad sense of the word, because temples dominated society; belief in the existence of transcendental causes for harvests, history, and wars was ubiquitous; and religion was used to create and maintain the social status. The "religiosity" of the books of the Jewish canon is not surprising in this context. Indeed, since Judah was refounded under the Persians as a temple province and (we are surmising) with a Judean law officially recognized, it does not seem surprising that a Judaism should be regarded as a religious phenomenon. But at this point the term "religious" is too imprecise. Both temples and law codes address the matter of social identity, define a person as a member of a social body: the cult not so much in respect of inner religious belief as of corporate behavior. Laws, too, in an imperial system define the citizen as a member of a particular *ethnos,* for (beyond whatever imperial laws apply to all) their jurisdiction applies only to those who acknowledge it.

The seed of the Mosaic torah was a book laying out a portrait of an ideal postmonarchic state centered on a sanctuary, with a divinely revealed written law and levitical priests to guard it. To this was added the biography of the great lawgiver and inventor of this constitution, Moses, telling how he not only gave the laws but founded the nation and brought it to its territory. The colonial ideology that lies at the core generated a justification of its rights to the land and invented itself in a past that, with the addition of the Genesis materials, reached back to the very beginning. It is the canon of a nation-society, showing how it came into being and what its constitution is. It is not about personal values. The remaining books, which were generally referred to as "prophets," dealt with Moses' succession and the history of the occupation of the land by the predecessors in the days of the kings, explaining why the land was lost despite the efforts of prophets to educate people and monarchs. Again, these writings address a corporate nation (always conceived as in the past). It is in the Psalms and Proverbs, in Jonah, Job, and Ecclesiastes that one finds the individual addressed. The "wisdom" literature, precisely because of its logical detachment from either law or cult, provides the nucleus of an individual ethic. It is not surprising, therefore, that the signs of development of a personal religion identified with "Judaism" come about in connection with what we can call "wisdom." In some of the psalms and in ben Sira we see "torah" being brought closer and closer to the ideal of *personal* uprightness: we see evidence in the epilogue to Hosea of prophecy treated as moral instruction; and we find ben Sira advocating the study of the law, prophets, and sayings of the wise. Thus in 41:8 he condemns those who have "forsaken the law of the Most High God," where "law" approximates to the Stoic meaning of *nomos* (something like a natural world order, physical and moral, and not dissimilar to the meaning of "wisdom" in some Jewish writings), and "wisdom" consists in discovering and living according to it: a personal ideal.

In his celebrated study of ancient classical religion, A. D. Nock[11] noted how in the Hellenistic world religion became more of a matter of personal choice—something to which one could attach personal commitment. This is especially true of Judaism. And the development of private religion goes hand in hand with the medium of literature as its vehicle. There are no private "mysteries" to rival the national temple cult; instead, these mysteries are found in ancient writings. Nor are traditional ways of life so deeply entrenched that they cannot be adapted to living outside Judah or doing business with non-Jews. Indeed, the spread of Jewish societies across the Hellenistic world tended to make Judaism more a matter of personal lifestyle. It is not surprising that the view that so many ancient writers had of Judaism was of a philosophical school.

Already by ben Sira's time Jewish writings were being studied as part of a school education that was offered and taken beyond the scribal classes. The aims of this education, as far as we can glean, were to impart a knowledge and understanding of the world, good manners, and an ethical code. Just as the Greeks read the once-aristocratic ideal of Greek citizenship into Homer, so Jews were taught the literature of Judah. The century and more of Hellenistic culture that the wealthier and more privileged of Judeans had witnessed—and, no doubt, their knowledge of Greek institutions of education—must have induced many to acquire a Greek education. But some elements of that education were certainly hard to reconcile with traditional Judean behavior. A Hebrew-language curriculum and due attention to the law of Moses make it clear that in Jerusalem already there was a conscious attempt to create and sustain a notion of "Judaism." For education was, as was explained in chapter 3, the main source of sustaining and spreading Greek culture, alongside the gymnasium and the theater. But in Judah Hellenism had the effect of creating "Judaism," a term that we first find being used (several times) in 2 Maccabees, where it "parallels and contrasts with 'Hellenism' (*hellenismos*) and even 'foreignism' (*allophylismos*)."[12]

Teachers such as ben Sira, or those inculcating the Enochic science, or those cynics such as Qoheleth, all peddled their versions of Judaism, in Hebrew and/or Aramaic, while Greek-speaking Jews perhaps enjoyed reading (or performing?) tragedies featuring Moses[13] alongside Greek translations of the Mosaic books. But, as argued in chapter 9, it also embraced new forms of literature, inspired by non-Judean models but expressing Judean values and, in particular, the importance of Jewish ethnicity.

JUDAISM AS A
POLITICAL ISSUE

The significance of the Maccabean revolt is that it took the form of a *religious* war, and thus made the definition of "Judaism" an issue that could no longer be avoided. The success of the Hasmoneans, moreover, gave an opportunity (and a demand) that "Judaism" should be officially promoted. Whatever the root causes of the Maccabean conflict, which were at least as much economic and political as religious, Antiochus IV was seen by the Judeans who resisted him to have attacked the foundation of Judaism, its major symbols of national identity, the high-priesthood. But alongside the nationalistic-xenophobic account of 1 Maccabees (an apology for the Hasmonean dynasty) another is discernible, between "apostates" and "pious" within Judea. Naturally, right-eousness lies with the victors: a dispassionate assessment is no more to be ex-pected than historical accuracy in a historian of this period. Among the fundamental symbols of this struggle are circumcision, diet, sabbath, and holy books. Apart from the obvious case of the temple cult, these are identified as the targets of Antiochus's policy. But while the narrative of the victors repre-sents an "orthodoxy" attacked by a heresy, it is likely that no such orthodoxy really existed: "Judaism" had no public definition, nor, in Judah, did it need one. Thereafter, until the success of the rabbis in creating an orthodox Judaism, there was to be no consensus, but the lack of consensus itself was a political issue.

The Hasmoneans inherited a victory in which they emerged as the de-fenders of "Judaism," but they had done so with the help of various groups. It was therefore difficult for them, as a native regime, to support particular practices without taking sides. The history of the period shows that they did, in fact, sway between supporting Sadducees and Pharisees. What other ne-gotiations they had to make we do not know for sure, but it is possible that the Qumran scrolls give us further information about other groups who were either favored or rejected by the rulers.

Apart from the contentious issues of cult and calendar, the issue of language and literature was one such dilemma. 1 Macc. 1:56-7 refers to the burning of books by the Syrian forces, while 2 Macc. 2:13-15 communicates as follows:

> The same things are reported in the records and in the memoirs of Ne-
> hemiah, also that he established a library and collected the books about
> the kings and the prophets, and the writings of David and letters of kings

> about offerings. In the same manner, Judas also collected all the books
> that had been lost because of the war that had broken out over us, and
> they are in our possession.

This is not evidence of the activities of Nehemiah, but it points to a deliberate collecting of scrolls, presumably to establish a library also, possibly by Judas, but at least by his immediate successors. We should of course assume that there had previously been collections of scrolls in the temple, where the composition, copying, and editing also took place. That library, presumably, was destroyed. But now, whatever might have been the collection of books previously, a decision was needed about what books to include. What were the writings sacred to Judaism? Which were authoritative and holy? (Re)creating this library was not a matter of collecting anything and everything deemed worthwhile, however, because certain books had become symbols of Judaism. The (re)establishment of a library by the Hasmoneans should probably be seen as a political act, made, as it was, in the aftermath of a book-burning campaign and now carefully scrutinized by the various groups who had fought for the kind of Judaism they wanted (which was not, of course, identical).

We have, alas, to jump over two centuries (in which a great deal can happen) to find further witnesses to a restricted collection, and we cannot be certain that the restrictions go back to the Hasmoneans; it is just an informed hypothesis. In the late first century c.e., the book of 4 Ezra tells a story of Ezra's reconstitution of the lost scrolls of the Jews. (This may be a deliberate response to the Nehemiah legend in 2 Maccabees). The story goes that Ezra dictated ninety-four "tablets," of which twenty-four were to be made public and seventy reserved for the "wise among your people" (14:19–48). The contents of these twenty-four books are described as follows (14:21–2):

> Your law has been burned, and therefore no one knows the deeds that
> have been done and are to be done by you. If then I have found favor
> with you, send the Holy Spirit to me and I shall write down all that has
> happened in the world from the beginning, the things which were writ-
> ten in your law, that humans may be able to find the way and those who
> wish to live in the last days may live.

It seems, if the text is correctly transmitted, that the twenty-four books are all referred to as "the law" (we have seen this fluidity already in other references) but also described as books of *historical* content (which we have also encountered earlier).

In Josephus (*Against Apion* 1.37–43) the picture is only slightly different:

> It therefore naturally, or rather necessarily follows (seeing that with us
> it is not open to everybody to write the records, and that there is no dis-
> crepancy in what is written; seeing that, on the contrary, the prophets

alone had this privilege, obtaining their knowledge of the most remote and ancient history through the inspiration which they owed to God, and committing to writing a clear account of the events of their own time just as they occurred)—it follows, I say, that we do not possess myriads of inconsistent books conflicting with one another. Our books, those which are justly accredited [*ta dikaiōs pepisteumena*] are but twenty-two and contain the record of all time. Of these, five are the books of Moses, comprising the laws and the traditional history down to the death of the lawgiver. . . . From the death of Moses until Artaxerxes who succeeded Xerxes as king of Persia, the prophets subsequent to Moses wrote the history of the events of their own times in thirteen books. The remaining four books contain hymns to God and precepts. From Artaxerxes to our own time the complete history has been written, but has not been deemed worthy of equal credit with the earlier records because of the failure of the exact succession of the prophets.

We have given practical proof of our reverence for our own writings. For, although such long ages have now passed, no one has ventured either to add, or to remove, or to alter a syllable; and it is an instinct with every Jew, from the day of his birth, to regard them as the decrees of God, to abide by them, and, if need be, to die cheerfully for them. Time and again ere now the sight has been witnessed of prisoners enduring tortures and death in every form in the theaters, rather than utter a single word against the laws and the allied documents [*tas meta toutōn anagraphas*].

Josephus claims that the Jews have twenty-*two* books, which are regarded as "decrees of God." There are, he admits, other books, but these are not "justly accredited" since they were not written under inspiration, which means they were not written by prophets.

There are marked similarities between the two near-contemporary passages. Both note a fixed total (24 or 22); both refer to other books as well—though Josephus regards these as of lesser value and the author of 4 Ezra as of greater value! Both regard the contents as broadly historical but also think of them as "law" (Josephus refers to "the law and allied documents"). Both also regard the writings as very old and having divine sanction ("decrees of God" in Josephus, and dictated by the Holy Spirit in 4 Ezra).

Josephus elsewhere (*Ant.* 3.38; 5.61) refers to these books as being "held in the temple." Such a collection cannot be imposed except by an appropriate authority, nor easily maintained except through an "official" archive, and the temple is the only institution with sufficient authority to maintain a canon of holy books. What is "in" the Jewish "scriptures" can henceforth mean what is housed as such in a designated temple library. Hence, while Josephus says that the Jews do not possess "myriads" of books, and claims that there is no reliable history once the succession of prophets ceased, he

certainly not only knows of, but uses such books. One of his sources for the
Maccabean war is 1 Maccabees!

Establishment of such a list of holy books probably achieved more-or-less
universal consent, though it did not prohibit the existence of further canons. It
does, moreover, provide the means for a stabilization of the text. Between the
time of writing of the Qumran scrolls and the end of the first century C.E. efforts had begun to standardize a text of these books. The earliest evidence is
the existence of a Greek scroll of Minor Prophets from Naḥal Ḥever, a few
miles from Qumran, but very probably not connected with the site.[14] This manuscript, dating from the first century B.C.E., represents a revision of a Greek
translation and anticipates the later (second-century C.E.) Greek translations of
Aquila, Symmachus, and Theodotion, which all render the Masoretic text. This
text, as is now clear, is not a superior text, nor one with a uniform tradition. It
means only the text that became canonized, and its characteristics differ among
the various books. No text-critical work was applied to establish it. It is highly
probable that the standardized text represents the text of a single copy of each
canonized scroll, and is not the outcome of a scholarly comparison such as the
scholars of Alexandria carried out. If the standardizing of the text can be assigned to the period of the Hasmoneans, it was a deliberate attempt at conformity and not a necessary expedient given the loss of scrolls during the
Maccabean war. The Qumran texts, many dating from the first century B.C.E.,
witness to a very fluid text, and, incidentally, make it unlikely that there was a
great shortage of scrolls as a result of Antiochus's measures.

The most dramatic indication of a Hasmonean initiative in establishing a
library with the "official" version of the holy books comes from the chronology system now evident in the Masoretic text. The chronology through the
Torah and Prophets has been edited at some point so as to highlight key
events. This explains the well-known differences in certain dates and periods between the MT, the LXX, and the Samaritan Pentateuch. In a study of
such chronologies, a number of scholars have demonstrated the following
chronologies for MT (dates are from the creation of the world):[15]

Event	MT
Flood	1656
Abraham	1946
Entry into Egypt	2236
Exodus	2666
Foundation of First Temple	3146
Destruction of Temple	3576
Foundation of Second Temple	3626

The figure of 2666 is two-thirds of 4000, and that from the date of the destruction of the temple (587/6 B.C.E.) to the rededication of the temple under Judas Maccabeus (164) are 422/3 years, making that dedication fall in the year 4000 (or 3999). Such a delicate chronology really requires a fixed text! It also entails control over the transmission of a number of scrolls. This exercise of dynastic ideology is at least consistent with the establishment of a canon of holy books, reflecting a desire for a canonical account of national history, and one, of course, that bolsters the divine right of the Hasmonean kings.

One can go further. Not only does the new archive promote an official national history, a national archive, and potentially a normative literature for religious purposes, but, as revised by the Hasmonean scribes, the literature is presented as being now fulfilled. The constitution of the biblical laws is being realized through the patronage of the Hasmonean king-priests (latter-day Melchizedeks), the history of "Israel" being brought to a glorious climax in the establishment of Judaean/Israelite hegemony in the Promised Land, including the reunification of the territory of the "twelve tribes" and the re-creation of the legendary empire of David. If it is true (as was suggested in chap. 3) that the Hellenistic Greek canons are a symptom of the feeling of a classical age that is gone, we would have to acknowledge that the Hasmoneans were interested in invoking it as a model for the present. The writer of 1 Maccabees, inspired by this program, presents his narrative as a story of a latter-day family of judges, raised up to save the nation from the oppressive nations "all around" (see, e.g., 1:11; 5:62), and Judas is given an epitaph fit for the book of Kings (9:22). Indeed, this book was very probably originally written in Hebrew. For the Hasmoneans encouraged not only the use of the Hebrew language (not that it was dead), but also the use of the old Hebrew script (to distinguish it from Aramaic and the Aramaic "square script"). 2 Maccabees mentions that the mother of the seven martyred sons encouraged them "in the language of their ancestors" (7:21). One can see from this that the Hasmonean canon could be in no other language than Hebrew (with a dash of Aramaic).

The encouragement of spoken Hebrew (which had probably never died out entirely as a living language) may account for the curious bilingual form of the recently written Daniel, some of which was likely translated from Aramaic. It is impossible to imagine that anyone who knew Hebrew at that time did not also know Aramaic, so that the translation must have had something to do with Hebrew as a more appropriate medium for a putatively ancient text, or even, perhaps, for a text belonging to a Hebrew canon. (Why chapters 2—7 were not translated into Hebrew will probably remain forever a mystery.) This canon now officially recognized a number of popular but non-scribal works (Song of Songs, Ruth, Ecclesiastes), not only because the Hasmoneans were anxious not to be too partisan, but also because, having forcibly "Judaized" most of Palestine that was not already Jewish, they also encouraged a Jewish education based on the holy books, some of which needed to be interesting and relevant to a wider readership in ways that, say, Leviticus, Numbers, Isaiah, Jeremiah, and Ezekiel (to name only a few) were surely not! Having reversed the changes that Antiochus made to "times and seasons," the Hasmoneans introduced Hanukkah and may have added Purim (who else had the power to introduce a new feast, and what more appropriate than one celebrating a massacre of Gentiles?). They may have been responsible also for the practice of linking the other "festival scrolls" with the national holidays (a practice which we know only for a later date). It is just as likely, however, that this was a rabbinic innovation.

For the fact is that we do not know why a canon of 22 or 24 (or some such figure) religiously authoritative books was created, though we may reasonably assume that its establishment was a political act, intended to create consensus, counter deviance and establish authority. Between the time of the Hasmoneans and the rabbis no body, as far as we know, had the power or the motive for such an act. The idea that such a canon imposed itself is nonsense, given the lack of any unified Judaism and the existence, as has been argued, of several canons.

The likely creators of the canon that the rabbis inherited were, therefore, the Hasmoneans, who appropriately blended a veneration of stories of the past with a knowledge of (and liking for) Hellenistic monarchy and even alliances with Greeks and Romans. "Judaism" as defining a religious system was in a sense a product of Hellenism, and so was its canon. Both are of course related to each other and came about through a combination of imitation of, and reaction to, the foreign culture. The Hasmonean bequest was national identity but also internal dissent. It was in the name of their "Israel" that the Judeans fought Rome and lost the temple, with the result that the rabbis again reconstituted a different "Israel," and having iconized the scriptures set about canonizing all over again.

POSTSCRIPT:
THE OLD TESTAMENT

The formation of the Christian Old Testament, though not the topic of this book, is of course relevant to Jewish canonizing, because, rather like the rabbis, the early Christians inherited a collection of scriptural writings. Although some Christian communities very probably inherited the Hasmonean Hebrew collection that also formed the basis of the Masoretic canon, it was a collection of writings in Greek (mostly translated from Hebrew) that came to be regarded by Christians as the Jewish scriptures. The same was presumably the case for most diaspora Jewish communities, until the rabbinic canon succeeded in being imposed. The theory once dominant—that the earliest Old Testament canon of the church was the Jewish canon of Alexandria—has been abandoned.[16] In its place two major views have emerged: that of Sundberg, that there was a rather fluid canon among non-Palestinian Jews; and that of Beckwith,[17] that the "Hellenistic" canon was identical with the Palestinian one, and that Christians gradually added other books.

The two positions are not entirely incapable of accommodating each other. The existence of a Hasmonean canon did not mean the abolition of all other canons, as the Qumran scrolls suggest. Ben Sira, at least, was surely regarded as a scriptural text by many Jews as well as Christians. But the growing authority of the Hebrew collection and a standardized Hebrew text led to the production of new Greek translations from that text. This process did not extend formally to Christian communities, but since Christians had a less clearly fixed canon of scriptures, and because Christians and Jews were for some time in debate over the scriptures, the effect may well have been to accommodate the scriptures used by Christians to those embraced by Jews. That there are not many patristic citations of books outside the rabbinic canon (which Beckwith makes a major argument) is not particularly significant.

For if, as Sundberg plausibly argues, Christians had a rather fluid canon, with the consequence that the collection of "Jewish scriptures" would vary from one Christian community to another (while increasingly, Jewish communities were standardizing their own text and canon), some influence in the direction of standardizing the Christian scriptures toward the one fixed (Jewish) canon is likely to have been felt.

However, the great Christian biblical codices from the fourth and fifth centuries (Alexandrinus, Sinaiticus, and Vaticanus) contain what are now called the "apocryphal books." Beckwith is obliged to argue that this betrays a process of Christian enlargement, which seems improbable. It is more likely that these betray a tendency to preserve a larger number of inherited Jewish scriptural books, despite the discrepancy with the Jewish canon. The result of the two contrary influences, toward a larger and a smaller canon, explains quite well the final compromise: in which certain writings were retained, though with a lesser status, forming, in the Protestant canon, a separate semibiblical Apocrypha (which was sometimes omitted altogether).

We have been considering so far, of course, only the evolution of the Western Old Testament(s). But each of the major Christian churches has its own: the Catholic and Protestant, Orthodox, Armenian, Ethiopic, and Syrian each have a different Old Testament canon. What the Old Testament contains, then, depends on where you are and whose Bible you are reading. A dramatic instance of how easily an Old Testament can change is the result of the decision several centuries ago to translate the Old Testament into modern European languages from the Hebrew (where available). This meant replacing one version of Jeremiah, Esther, and Daniel with another. At a stroke Christian scriptural *books* (not just texts) were replaced by Jewish ones. The modern Christian Old Testament is actually, from the historical point of view, not a Christian Old Testament at all, but a Jewish-Christian one. For that we thank not church leaders or even theologians, but translators and publishers, who nowadays decide what is "biblical" and what is not. (This can be instructively proved by a comparison of recently published new Bibles.)

Nothing, in fact, can underline more effectively the need to look at canon and Bible in historical as well as in theological terms than the following paradoxes. The Jewish *canon* is older than the Christian, while the Christian *Bible* is older than the Jewish. Judaism has one standard scriptural canon and text, while Christianity does not. Therefore Christian canonical criticism understandably prefers to deal with the "Hebrew Bible" than with an "Old Testament" whose earliest form is Greek, not Hebrew, that has no fixed text and no universally agreed list of canonical contents. The "Old Testament" is today still fluid, and still developing, just as when it began. Canonizing lives!

Abbreviations

ABD	*Anchor Bible Dictionary*
AJSL	*American Journal of Semitic Languages and Literature*
BA	*Biblical Archaeologist*
BETL	Bibliotheca Ephemeridum Theologicarum Lovaniensium
BJRL	*Bulletin of the John Rylands Library*
BZAW	Beihefte zur Zeitschrift für die alttestamentliche Wissenschaft
CBQ	*Catholic Biblical Quarterly*
CBQMS	Catholic Biblical Quarterly Monograph Series
CRINT	Compendium Rerum Iudaicarum ad Novum Testamentum
DJD	Discoveries in the Judaean Desert
ET	English translation
ET	*Expository Times*
HUCA	*Hebrew Union College Annual*
IDB	*Interpreter's Dictionary of the Bible*
JAOS	*Journal of the American Oriental Society*
JBL	*Journal of Biblical Literature*
JCS	*Journal of Cuneiform Studies*
JJS	*Journal of Jewish Studies*
JSOT	*Journal for the Study of the Old Testament*
JSOTS	Journal for the Study of the Old Testament Supplement Series
LAI	Library of Ancient Israel
OBO	Orbis biblicus et orientalis
SBLDS	Society of Biblical Literature Dissertation Series
SBLMS	Society of Biblical Literature Monograph Series
SFSHJ	South Florida Studies in the History of Judaism
VT	*Vetus Testamentum*
VTSup	Supplements to Vetus Testamentum
WUNT	Wissenschaftliche Untersuchungen zum Neuen Testament
ZAW	*Zeitschrift für die alttestamentliche Wissenschaft*

Notes

Introduction

1. Wilfred Cantwell Smith, *What Is Scripture? A Comparative Approach* (London: SCM Press, 1993), 18–19.

1. The Dimensions of Canon

1. The issues are succinctly put in J. N. Lightstone, "The Formation of the Biblical Canon in Judaism of Late Antiquity: Prolegomena to a General Reassessment," *Studies in Religion* 8 (1979), 135–42. See also David M. Carr, "Canonization in the Context of Community," in R. D. Weis and D. M. Carr, eds., *A Gift of God in Due Season,* JSOTSup 225 (Sheffield: Sheffield Academic Press, 1996), 22–64.

2. For a defense of such a canon (and a definitive list), see Harold Bloom, *The Western Canon: The Books and School of the Age* (New York and London: Harcourt Brace Jovanovich, 1994).

3. For a fuller treatment of what follows, see Jan Gorak, *The Making of the Modern Canon* (London and Atlantic Highlands, N.J.: Athlone Press, 1991), 9–43.

4. The definition "the recognized genuine works of any writer" fits this fairly well, combining the often related meanings of "authority" and "authorship." Authorship is frequently an issue in matters of canonicity.

5. In Islam, while the Qur'an is a single-work canon, certain verses also "abrogate" others.

6. "Canon and Power," in R. von Hallberg, ed., *Canons* (Chicago: University of Chicago Press, 1984), 65–83 (quote from p. 67).

7. This is well expressed by James Barr, *Holy Scripture: Canon, Authority, Criticism* (Oxford: Clarendon Press, 1983), 2–4.

2. Canons in the Ancient World

1. Still indispensable for an understanding of the ideological mechanisms of society and their links to economic systems is G. E. Lenski, *Power and Privilege: A Theory of Social Stratification* (New York: McGraw-Hill Book Co., 1966). See especially pp. 189–296 on agrarian societies.

2. See Lenski, *Power and Privilege,* 245–6; W.V. Harris, *Ancient Literacy* (Cambridge, Mass.: Harvard University Press, 1989); Susan Niditch, *Oral World and Written Word,* Library of Ancient Israel (Louisville, Ky.: Westminster John Knox Press,

1996), 39–45; J. Baines, "Literacy and Ancient Egyptian Society," in *Man* (London: Royal Anthropological Institute of Great Britain and Ireland, 1983), 572–99.

3. See Niditch, *Oral World and Written Word,* 39–59, for discussion of the oral-written "continuum."

4. A fuller account of their social world and intellectual profile, especially in ancient Israel and Judah, is given in Joseph Blenkinsopp, *Sage, Priest, Prophet,* (Library of Ancient Israel, Louisville, Ky.: Westminster John Knox Press, 1995), 9–65. For a broader assessment, see John G. Gammie and Leo G. Perdue, eds., *The Sage in Israel and the Ancient Near East* (Winona Lake, Ind.: Eisenbrauns, 1990); Lester L. Grabbe, *Priests, Prophets, Diviners, Sages: A Socio-Historical Study of Religious Specialists in Ancient Israel* (Valley Forge, Pa.: Trinity Press International, 1995), 152–221.

5. As Lenski points out (*Power and Privilege,* 211) a good deal of surviving state records are concerned with military campaigns, which were generally written according to strict literary conventions. On the military language of Joshua, see K. L. Younger, Jr., *Ancient Conquest Accounts: A Study in Ancient Near Eastern and Biblical History Writing,* JSOTSup 98 (Sheffield: JSOT Press, 1990).

6. F. Posner, *Archives in the Ancient World* (Cambridge, Mass.: Harvard University Press, 1972), 3ff.

7. For a reconstruction of shelving at Ebla, for example, see G. Pettinato, *The Archives of Ebla* (Garden City, N.Y.: Doubleday, 1981), 49; for Mari, see J. M. Sasson, "Some Comments on Archive Keeping at Mari," *Iraq* 34 (1972): 55–67.

8. L. Oppenheim, "The Position of the Intellectual in Mesopotamian Society," *Daedalus* 104/2 (1975): 34–46.

9. W. G. Lambert, "Literary Style in First Millennium Mesopotamia," in E. Bender, ed., *Essays in Memory of E. A. Speiser,* American Oriental Series, 53 (New Haven: American Oriental Society, 1968), 123–32, 123.

10. Lambert, "Literary Style," identified it as "Old Akkadian" (123).

11. The phrase, though not the verdict, comes from Benjamin R. Foster, *Before the Muses: An Anthology of Akkadian Literature,* 2 vols. (Bethesda, Md.: CDL Press, 1993), 3.

12. For an excellent collection of Akkadian literature, with introduction, see Foster, *Before the Muses;* also P. Michalowski, *Letters from Mesopotamia,* SBL Writings from the Ancient World (Atlanta: Scholars Press, 1993).

13. For a survey of the contents of this library, see A. Oppenheim, *Ancient Mesopotamia: Portrait of a Dead Civilization,* 2d ed. (Chicago: University of Chicago Press, 1977).

14. Details in Posner, *Archives,* 46.

15. See Posner, *Archives,* 32–35.

16. R. J. Williams, "The Sages of Ancient Egypt in the Light of Recent Scholarship," in J. M. Sasson, ed., *Oriental Wisdom, JAOS* 101 (1981): 5.

17. Posner, *Archives,* 71.

18. The standard collection of these is A. Gardiner, *Ancient Egyptian Onomastica* (Oxford: Oxford University Press, 1947).

19. R. J. Williams, "The Sage in Egyptian Literature," in Gammie and Perdue, *The Sage in Israel,* 27.

20. J. Assmann, "Egyptian Literature," *ABD* 2, 386.

21. H. Marrou, *A History of Education in Antiquity,* trans. G. Lamb (London: Sheed & Ward, 1956), 6.

22. The references are taken from R. Pfeiffer, *History of Classical Scholarship* (Oxford: Clarendon Press, 1968), 28.

23. Plato's attack on the classic literature can be found in his *Republic,* especially books 2, 3, and 10.

24. The Greek tragedians seem to have used literary sources in their works. Aristophanes pokes fun at Euripides for having used literary sources in composing his tragedies (*Frogs,* 943), but may well have done the same himself.

25. According to Diogenes Laertius 4.1; 5.51.

26. Pfeiffer, *History of Classical Scholarship,* 102.

27. Called *pinakes.* See Pfeiffer, *History of Classical Scholarship,* 127–33.

28. The following account is based on Hallo's essay, "The Concept of Canonicity in Cuneiform and Biblical Literature: A Comparative Appraisal," in K. L. Younger, Jr., W. W. Hallo, and B. F. Batto, eds., *The Biblical Canon in Comparative Perspective,* Scripture in Context 4 (Lewiston, N.Y.: Edwin Mellen, 1991), 1–19. Sarna's views are found in "The Order of the Books," in C. Berlin, ed., *Studies in Jewish Bibliography, History and Literature in Honor of I. Edward Kiev* (New York: Ktav, 1971), 407–13.

29. W. G. Lambert, "Ancestors," 1–14, discerns from some texts the notion that all revealed knowledge had been given to the antediluvian sages, and sees in this a parallel to the Jewish notion of all divine revelation being contained in the Torah.

30. Pap. Chester Beatty 4.2.5ff. For the text, see A. Gardiner, *Hieratic Papyri in the British Museum,* vol. 1 (London: British Museum, 1935). Cited by R. Williams, "The Sage in Egyptian Literature," in Gammie and Perdue, eds., *The Sage in Ancient Israel,* 24–25.

31. James C. VanderKam, *Enoch and the Growth of an Apocalyptic Tradition,* CBQMS 16 (Washington, D.C.: Catholic Biblical Association, 1984).

3. Canon, Canonizing, and Canonical Criticism: Approaches to Jewish Canonizing

1. Philadelphia: Westminster Press, 1983.

2. London: Darton, Longman & Todd, 1986.

3. J. N. Lightstone, "The Formation of the Biblical Canon," 135–42; *Society, the Sacred, and Scripture in Ancient Judaism: A Sociology of Knowledge* (Waterloo, Ont.: Wilfrid Laurier University Press, 1988).

4. D. M. Carr, "Canonization in the Context of Community," 22–64 (quote from p. 25).

5. M. Haran, האסופה המקראית (The Biblical Canon) (Jerusalem: Magnes Press/ Mossad Bialik, 1996).

6. Sundberg's refutation of the notion of an "Alexandrian canon" (*The Old Testament of the Early Church* [Cambridge, Mass.: Harvard University Press, 1964]) is correct only in terms of a narrow definition of canon. That Jews in Alexandria recognized a canon or canons of Jewish scriptures seems clear enough; at the very least the torah was a canon to Philo.

7. Shaye J. D. Cohen points out that the canonizing of *Tanak* "did not stifle the creative spirit as much as it redirected it" and makes the point that "ancient Judaism has left us few works that are secular or non-religious," and later, that "several non-

Jewish writings of the Greco-Roman period do not appear to make the scriptures central to their theological concerns" (*From the Maccabees to the Mishnah,* Library of Early Christianity [Philadelphia: Westminster Press, 1987], 193, 204).

8. Martin Noth, *Überlieferungsgeschichte des Pentateuch* (Stuttgart: Kohlhammer, 1948); ET, *A History of Pentateuchal Traditions,* trans. B. W. Anderson (Englewood Cliffs, N.J.: Prentice-Hall, 1973).

9. F. M. Cross, *Canaanite Myth and Hebrew Epic* (Cambridge: Harvard University Press, 1973).

10. See M. Noth, *The Deuteronomistic History,* trans. H.G.M. Williamson, JSOTSup 15 (Sheffield: JSOT Press, 1981 [German original, 1943]).

11. R. N. Whybray, *The Making of the Pentateuch* (Sheffield: JSOT Press, 1987).

12. William McKane, *Jeremiah,* vol. I (chaps. 1–25), ICC (Edinburgh: T. & T. Clark, 1986).

13. For which tribute has to be made above all to Norman K. Gottwald.

14. "How the Books of the Bible Were Chosen," in Harvey Minkoff, ed., *Approaches to the Bible* (Washington, D.C.: BAS, 1994), 108–12 (quote from p. 110).

15. M. Smith, *Palestinian Parties and Politics That Shaped the Old Testament* (New York and London: Columbia University Press, 1971).

16. J. W. Miller, *The Origins of the Bible: Rethinking Canon History* (Mahwah, N.J.: Paulist Press, 1994).

17. See note 4 above.

18. (Oxford and New York: Clarendon Press/Oxford University Press, 1985).

19. M. Haran, האסופה המקראית (The Biblical Canon) (Jerusalem: Magnes Press/Mossad Bialik, 1996). Haran's book appeared, unfortunately, too late to be taken as fully into consideration in this volume as it deserves.

20. M. Haran, "Book-Scrolls in Israel in Pre-Exilic Times," *JJS* 33 (1982): 161–73; "More Concerning Book-Scrolls in Pre-Exilic Times," *JJS* 35: 84–85.

21. M. Haran, "Book-Scrolls at the Beginning of the Second Temple Period: The Transition from Papyrus to Skins," *HUCA* 54 (1983): 111–22.

22. Cohen, *From the Maccabees to the Mishnah,* 192f.

23. Only a selection of the numerous recent writings on canon can be addressed here, namely those treatments in which the historical evolution of the canon is explicitly or implicitly considered. Theological approaches that begin with the final form and deal rather with the reception of the canon are omitted, though R. Rendtorff, *Canon and Theology: Overtures to an Old Testament Theology,* Overtures to Biblical Theology (Minneapolis: Fortress Press, 1993) issues an important warning against a purely Christian canonical reading.

24. Sanders's position is set out in his *Torah and Canon* (Philadelphia: Fortress Press, 1972); *Canon and Community: A Guide to Canonical Criticism,* Guides to Biblical Scholarship (Philadelphia: Fortress Press, 1984); *From Sacred Story to Sacred Text: Canon as Paradigm* (Philadelphia: Fortress Press, 1987). For a statement of his own position relative to Childs, see *From Sacred Story,* 155–74.

25. Sanders, *From Sacred Story,* 165.

26. See Sanders, *Canon and Community,* xv–xviii.

27. Sanders, *From Sacred Story,* 166.

28. Brevard Childs, *Introduction to the Old Testament as Scripture* (Philadelphia: Fortress Press/London: SCM Press, 1979), 41, 71.

29. Ibid., 41.

30. Ibid., 40.

31. A point made by M. G. Brett, *Biblical Criticism in Crisis? The Impact of the Canonical Approach on Old Testament Studies* (Cambridge: Cambridge University Press, 1991), 13–14.

32. Barr, *Holy Scripture,* esp. 49–104.

33. For a review of Childs on similar lines, though not unsympathetic to the possibility of a theological canonical-critical agenda, see Brett, *Biblical Criticism in Crisis?*

34. Sanders, *From Sacred Story,* 171.

35. Smith, *What Is Scripture?,* 2–3.

36. P. R. Davies, *In Search of 'Ancient Israel': A Study in Biblical Origins* (Sheffield: JSOT Press, 1992).

4. A Sketch of Israelite and Judean History

1. For a discussion of various definitions see C. Schäfer-Lichtenberger, "Sociological and Biblical Views of the Early State," in V. Fritz and P.R. Davies, eds., *The Origins of the Ancient Israelite States,* JSOTSup 228 (Sheffield: Sheffield Academic Press, 1996), 78–105; and on patronage, see N. P. Lemche, "From Patronage Society to Patronage Society," in the same volume, 106–20.

2. See H. Niemann, *Herrschaft, Königtum und Staat: Skizzen zur soziokulturellen Entwicklung im monarchischen Israel* (Tübingen: Mohr, 1993).

3. See Graeme Auld and Margreet Steiner, *Jerusalem I: From the Bronze Age to the Maccabees,* Cities of the Biblical World (Cambridge: Lutterworth Press/Macon, Ga.: Mercer University Press, 1996), 38–45.

4. 2 Kings 25; Jeremiah 40.

5. See H. Kreissig, *Die sozialökonomische Situation in Juda zur Achämenidenzeit* (Berlin: Akademie Verlag, 1973); Jon L. Berquist (*Judaism in Persia's Shadow: A Social and Historical Approach* [Minneapolis: Fortress Press, 1995]) has spelled this out and applied it to biblical literature. For an analysis of the extent of this province, see Charles E. Carter, "The Province of Yehud in the Post-Exilic Period: Soundings in Site Distribution and Demography," in Tamara C. Eskenazi and Kent H. Richards, eds., *Second Temple Studies 2: Temple and Community in the Persian Period* (Sheffield: JSOT Press, 1994), 106–45.

6. Hoglund, "The Achaemenid Context," in Philip R. Davies, ed., *Second Temple Studies 1: Persian Period,* JSOTSup 117 (Sheffield: JSOT Press, 1991), 54–72.

7. J. Weinberg, *The Citizen-Temple Community,* JSOTSup 151 (Sheffield: JSOT Press, 1992). See also the qualified approval given by J. Blenkinsopp, "Temple and Society in Achaemenid Judah," in *Second Temple Studies 1,* 22–53.

8. For an analysis of this process, see Hans G. Kippenberg, *Religion und Klassenbildung im antiken Judäa* (Göttingen: Vandenhoeck & Ruprecht, 1978; 2d ed. 1982).

9. On the "house of life" see Williams, "The Sage in Egyptian Literature," 19–30 (27–29).

10. On Persian lawmaking, see J. Blenkinsopp, *A History of Prophecy in Israel: From the Settlement in the Land to the Hellenistic Period* (Philadelphia: Westminster Press, 1983), 227; A. T. Olmstead, "Darius as Lawgiver," *AJSL* 51 (1935): 247–49, and *History of the Persian Empire* (Chicago: University of Chicago Press, 1948), 119–342.

11. The difference between "Samarian" and "Samaritan" is important. The canonized Judean view (2 Kings 17:24–41) that the Samaritans go back to Samarians is clearly wrong. The origins of Samaritans as a distinct sect is to be dated to the Hellenistic period.

12. See Olmstead, *History of the Persian Empire,* 297–99; Joachim Schaper, "The Jerusalem Temple as an Instrument of the Achaemenid Fiscal Administration," *VT* 45 (1995): 528–39.

13. See Kippenberg, *Religion und Klassenbildung,* 54–77.

14. The names of several governors have been extracted from bullae (seal impressions) by N. Avigad, *Bullae and Seals from a Post-Exilic Jewish Archive,* Qedem 4 (Jerusalem, 1976).

15. B. Porten, *Archives from Elephantine: The Life of an Ancient Jewish Military Colony* (Berkeley and Los Angeles: University of California Press, 1968).

16. Josephus (*Antiquities* 11.8) reports a marriage in the fourth century B.C.E. between the priestly families of Jerusalem and Samaria.

17. The process has been thoroughly documented by M. Hengel, *Judaism and Hellenism,* 2 vols. (London: SCM Press, 1974). See also V. Tcherikover, *Hellenistic Civilization and the Jews* (Philadelphia: Jewish Publication Society, 1959). For a review of the main points of discussion, see Grabbe, *Judaism from Cyrus to Hadrian,* 148–56.

18. For an analysis of the Hasmonean alliances and strategies, see J. Sievers, *The Hasmoneans and Their Supporters* (Atlanta: Scholars Press, 1990).

19. For the connections between Judean and Greek historiography, see John Van Seters, *In Search of History* (New Haven and London: Yale University Press, 1983).

5. Judean Scribes, Schools, Archives, and Libraries

1. The discussion of "The Sage" by Joseph Blenkinsopp in *Sage, Priest, Prophet,* 9–64, covers some aspects of the following.

2. Oppenheim (*Ancient Mesopotamia,* 230) classifies the purposes of Mesopotamian writings as follows: administrative recording, codification of laws, formation of a sacred tradition, for annals, for scholarly purposes.

3. E.g., Gammie and Perdue, *The Sage in Israel.*

4. M. Weinfeld, *Deuteronomy and the Deuteronomic School* (Oxford: Clarendon Press, 1972), 177–78.

5. The visitor to the tell of ancient Hazor is offered a dramatic verification of this: while the city once occupied two hills, the Iron Age citadel (popularly ascribed to Solomon) occupies a small part of only one of them.

6. See R. N. Whybray, *The Intellectual Tradition in the Old Testament,* BZAW 135 (Berlin: De Gruyter, 1974).

7. Blenkinsopp, *Sage, Priest, Prophet,* 11.

8. Stuart Weeks's *Early Israelite Wisdom* (Oxford: Clarendon Press, 1984), in arguing that "wisdom literature" does not arise from the education of administrators, does not explain from where it does arise.

9. E. W. Heaton, *The School Tradition of the Old Testament* (Oxford: Oxford University Press, 1994).

10. Heaton, *School Tradition,* 13, 15.

11. Heaton, *School Tradition,* 185.

12. M. Smith, *Palestinian Parties and Politics,* 157ff.

13. D. W. Jamieson-Drake, *Scribes and School in Monarchic Judah* (Sheffield: JSOT Press, 1991).

14. For the corpus (excluding Tel Dan) see G. I. Davies, ed., *Ancient Hebrew Inscriptions* (Cambridge: Cambridge University Press, 1991). A convenient collection of relevant Israelite, Judean, and Transjordanian texts, with discussion, is contained in K.A.D. Smelik, *Writings from Ancient Israel* (Edinburgh: T. & T. Clark, 1991).

15. J. W. Rogerson and P. R. Davies, "Was the Siloam Tunnel Built by Hezekiah?" *Biblical Archaeologist* 59 (1996): 138–49.

16. A. Biran and J. Naveh, "An Aramaic Stele Fragment from Tel Dan," *IEJ* 43 (1993): 81–98.

17. The view that a good deal of writing took place in Persian-period Jerusalem, despite the evidence of a rather poor material culture, is entailed even on the traditional view that places the beginnings of the Judean canonizing process in the Iron Age. For on this view, the *editing* of virtually all this supposedly earlier literature must be assigned to the Persian period.

18. A. Lemaire, *Les Écoles et la formation de la Bible dans l'ancien Israel,* OBO 39 (Fribourg: Éditions Universitaires, 1981).

19. E.g., R. J. Williams, "Writing and Writing Materials," *IDB* 4, 909–21; A. Demsky, "Writing in Early Israel and Early Judaism: The Biblical Period," in M. Mulder, ed., *Miqra,* CRINT 2:1 (Assen: Van Gorcum, 1988), 2–20; T.N.D. Mettinger, *Solomonic State Officials* (Lund: Gleerup, 1971).

20. J. Crenshaw, "Education in Ancient Israel," *JBL* 104 (1985): 601–15 (601).

21. Ibid., 602.

22. This is well argued by F. Golka, "Die israelitische Weisheitsschule oder 'des Kaisers neue Kleider,'" *VT* 33 (1983): 257–70.

23. The influence of the Egyptian *Instruction of Amenemope* on Proverbs at this point has long been suspected.

24. M. Haran, "On the Diffusion of Literacy and Schools in Ancient Israel," in J. A. Emerton, ed., *Congress Volume Jerusalem 1986,* VT Suppl 40 (Leiden: Brill, 1988), 81–95.

25. For an excellent recent discussion of orality and literacy, see Niditch, *Oral World and Written Word.*

26. See, e.g., A. Millard, "An Assessment of the Evidence for Writing in Ancient Israel," *Biblical Archaeology Today* (Jerusalem: IES), 301–12. A more chauvinistic assessment can be found in Demsky, "Writing in Ancient Israel."

27. This is a maximal figure, according to Baines, "Literacy and Ancient Egyptian Society," who gives 1 percent for Egypt "in most periods."

28. E.g., Josephus, *Against Apion* 1.60; Philo, *Legation,* 16.

29. P. S. Alexander, "How Did the Rabbis Learn Hebrew?" (unpublished). I am grateful to Prof. Alexander for a copy of the text of his lecture (given in 1996). Quote from p. 10.

30. The use of rabbinic sources tends to be a little uncritical in this regard. See S. Safrai, "Education and the Study of the Torah," in S. Safrai and M. Stern, eds., *The Jewish People in the First Century,* vol. 2 (Assen: Van Gorcum, 1976), 947–70; E. Schürer, *The Jewish People in the Age of Jesus Christ,* vol. 2, rev. G. Vermes, F. Millar, and M. Goodman (Edinburgh: T. & T. Clark, 1979), 417–22.

31. For a list and discussion of these cities, see Schürer 2:85–183.

32. These examples I have taken from R. T. Beckwith, "Formation of the Hebrew Bible," 39–86 (41).

6. The Mosaic Canon

1. S. Paul, *Studies in the Book of the Covenant in the Light of Cuneiform and Biblical Law* (Leiden: Brill, 1970); R. Westbrook, *Studies in Biblical and Cuneiform Law* (Paris: Gabalda, 1988), and *Property and the Family in Biblical Law* (Sheffield: Sheffield Academic Press, 1991).

2. M. Fishbane, *Biblical Interpretation in Ancient Israel* (Oxford: Oxford University Press, 1985), 95–96.

3. B. S. Jackson, "Ideas of Law and Legal Administration: A Semiotic Approach," in R. E. Clements, ed., *The World of Ancient Israel* (Cambridge: Cambridge University Press, 1989), 185–202.

4. Jackson, "Ideas of Law," 198; J. M. Sprinkle, *The "Book of the Covenant": A Literary Approach* (Sheffield: Sheffield Academic Press, 1994).

5. Lightstone, *Society, the Sacred, and Scripture,* has argued that Deuteronomy was the original "torah" and that the name gradually became transferred to the Pentateuch.

6. Joseph Blenkinsopp also takes Deuteronomy as his point of departure in *Prophecy and Canon: A Contribution to the Study of Jewish Origins* (Notre Dame, Ind., and London: University of Notre Dame Press, 1977); see esp. 24, where he quotes Wellhausen to this effect.

7. In a second covenant ceremony in chapter 24, Joshua *writes* in "the scroll of the *torah* of God"—perhaps in obedience to Deut. 27:1–4.

8. Haran has argued that the Pentateuchal books were by this time written on a single scroll ("Book-Scrolls at the Beginning of the Second Temple Period," 111–22) but this is speculative. The evidence from Qumran overwhelmingly disputes that, though there are four fragments that apparently contain more than one book: 4QpalaeoGen-Exod[l], 4QGen-Exod[a], 4QExod-Lev[f], and 4QLev-Num[a]. But only the first actually preserves the end of Genesis and the beginning of Exodus. See *Qumran Cave 4, VII: Genesis to Numbers,* DJD 12, E. Ulrich and F. M. Cross, eds. (Oxford: Clarendon Press, 1994), 7, 133, 153.

9. It would be interesting to know whether this is a conscious allusion to Jer. 36:22–23.

10. "Samarians" as the population of Samaria must be distinguished from "Samaritans," a religious sect closely related to Judaism. See chapter 4, note 11.

11. Not only is the Mosaic canon not pro-Judean; it is in many respects pro-Samarian: Joshua makes covenants at Shechem, while there is no hint of Jerusalem as a sanctuary. The prominence of Bethel, Hebron, and Beersheba in Genesis, of course, balances this slightly. But since the Mosaic canon is impartial regarding Jerusalem and Samaria, should we assume that it was, in fact, a Jerusalem product?

12. M. Noth, *Überlieferungsgeschichtliche Studien: Die sammelden und bearbeitenden Geschichtswerke im Alten Testament* (Tübingen: Niemeyer, 1943); ET, *The Deuteronomistic History,* JSOTSup 15 (Sheffield: JSOT Press, 1981).

13. Noth (*Deuteronomistic History*) argued for authorship during the exilic period, but in Palestine. The one major deviation from this has been the theory of Cross that

there were two recensions, an earlier one at the time of Josiah and a later one as an exilic revision (see F. M. Cross, Jr., "The Themes of the Book of Kings and the Structure
of the Deuteronomistic History," in *Canaanite Myth and Hebrew Epic,* 274–89).

14. M. Weinfeld, *Deuteronomy,* 168.

15. See James C. VanderKam, "Ezra-Nehemiah or Ezra and Nehemiah," in Eugene
Ulrich, John W. Wright, Robert P. Carroll and Philip R. Daves, eds., *Priests, Prophets
and Scribes: Essays on the Formation and Heritage of Second Temple Judaism in Honour of Joseph Blenkinsopp* (Sheffield: JSOT Press, 1992), 55–75.

16. See, e.g., T. C. Eskenazi, *In an Age of Prose: A Literary Approach to Ezra-
Nehemiah,* SBLMS 36 (Atlanta: Scholars Press, 1988); D.J.A. Clines, "The Perils of Au-
tobiography," in *What Does Eve Do to Help? and Other Readerly Questions to the Old
Testament,* JSOTSup 94 (Sheffield: JSOT Press, 1990), 124–64; J. C. VanderKam,
"Ezra-Nehemiah or Ezra and Nehemiah?," 55–75; D. Kraemer, "On the Relationship
of the Books of Ezra and Nehemiah," *JSOT* 59 (1993): 73–92.

17. CD and "Damascus Document" strictly speaking refer to the medieval manuscripts of a text known to have originated in the same way as many of the Qumran
texts. Unfortunately, it is impossible to reconstruct with certainty any supposedly
"original form" from the Qumran fragments, despite assertions to the contrary. Much
of the Qumran material simply does not overlap. For a survey of the Q material and
its readings, see M. Broshi, ed., *The Damascus Document Reconsidered* (Jerusalem:
Israel Exploration Society, 1992).

18. For fuller discussion see my *The Damascus Covenant,* JSOTSup 25 (Sheffield:
JSOT Press, 1982), 56–104.

19. Nehemiah 9; CD 2:4–3:12.

20. There is a convenient summary of the literature and issues in L. L. Grabbe,
Judaism from Cyrus to Hadrian; for this particular account see 216–18. Text, translation and discussion are in M. Stern, ed., *Greek and Latin Authors on Jews and Judaism,* vol. 1: *From Herodotus to Plutarch* (Jerusalem: Israel Academy of Sciences
and Humanities, 1986), 20–35; further discussion in Hengel, *Judaism and Hellenism,*
1:255–6; 2:169; and E. Schürer, *History of the Jewish People,* rev. ed., 3:671–7.

21. The ascription by Diodorus (or by Photius? Diodorus's text is preserved in
Photius's *Bibliotheca*) of these comments to Hecataeus of Miletus (ca. 500 B.C.E.) is
generally taken as an error.

22. *Contra Apionem* 1.183–204; see Stern, *Greek and Latin Authors,* 35–44, who
takes it as basically authentic, as does the revised edition of Schürer.

23. For the text and translation, see Stern, *Greek and Latin Authors,* 169.

24. D. Mendels, "Hecataeus of Abdera and a Jewish 'patrios politeia,'" *ZAW* 95
(1983): 96–110.

25. See R. P. Carroll, "Textual Strategies and Ideology," in *Second Temple Studies,* 108–24.

26. For a detailed analysis of the relevant prophetic texts, though in the context
of very conventional datings, see most recently R. Kessler, *Staat und Gesellschaft im
vorexilischen Juda, Vom 8: Jahrhundert bis zum Exil,* VTSup 47 (Leiden: Brill, 1992).
The implications of land tenure for the development of Judean society in the Second
Temple period are discussed by H. Kreissig, *Die sozialökonomische Situation;* and
H. Kippenberg, *Religion und Klassenbildung.*

27. *A History of Pentateuchal Traditions,* 208.

28. Note the ingenious suggestion of Thomas L. Thompson (*The Origin Tradition of Ancient Israel* [Sheffield: JSOT Press, 1987], 79–80) that the Babel story of Genesis 11 provides the basis for the movement of Terah's family from Mesopotamia toward Canaan.

29. Van Seters, *In Search of History,* 18–31.

7. The Canonizing of Prophets

1. Barr, *Holy Scripture.*

2. Barton, *Oracles of God,* 35–95.

3. Philo, *On the Contemplative Life,* 25.

4. I take this to be implied by the syntax: "kings and prophets" *may* be meant as a single designation, but if the genitive *prophētōn* is governed by or means "[books of] the prophets" (as in *ta tou Dauid*), the distinction is unambiguous.

5. For the argument and discussion, see A. Graeme Auld, "Prophets through the Looking Glass: Between Writings and Moses," *JSOT* 27 (1983): 3–23, and the responses by Robert Carroll, and H.G.M. Williamson, with a reply by Auld (pp. 25–44); also the renewed discussion in *JSOT* 48 (1990): 3–54 by Auld, T. W. Overholt, and R. P. Carroll. Finally, H. Barstad, "No Prophets? Recent Developments in Biblical Prophetic Research and Ancient Near Eastern Prophecy," in *JSOT* 57 (1993): 39–60.

6. Joshua 13:1–2, in which the dying Joshua is told that much conquering remains, may well be a trace of an earlier editorial link to the Judges scroll.

7. As examples of current thinking on the history of formation of Samuel and Kings, see S. McKenzie, *The Trouble with Kings* (Leiden: E. J. Brill, 1991); A. G. Auld, *Kings without Privilege: David and Moses in the Story of the Bible's Kings* (Edinburgh: T. & T. Clark, 1994); J. Trebolle-Barrera, "Redaction, Recension and Midrash in the Books of Kings," *Bulletin of the International Organization for Septuagint and Cognate Studies* 15 (1980): 12–35.

8. See Blenkinsopp, *Prophecy and Canon,* 39–53.

9. As has been done by K.A.D. Smelik, "King Hezekiah advocates true prophecy: Remarks on Isaiah xxxvi and xxxvii and II Kings xviii and xiv," in *Converting the Past: Studies in Ancient Israelite and Moabite Historiography,* OTS 28 (Leiden: Brill, 1992), 93–128.

10. The most recent (and most comprehensive) analysis of this chapter is by R. P. Carroll, "Manuscripts Don't Burn—Inscribing the Prophetic Tradition: Reflections on Jeremiah 36," in M. Augustin and K.-D. Schunck, eds., *"Dort ziehen Schiffe dahin . . .": Collected Communications to the XIVth Congress of the International Organization for the Study of the Old Testament, Paris 1992,* BEATJ 28: (Frankfurt: Peter Lang, 1996), 31–42.

11. Compare Jer. 51:59–64, which refers to another scroll, this time written by the prophet himself. But v. 62 makes it clear that its prophecies are regarded as the word of Yahweh.

12. The Samaritan book of Joshua is a composition in Arabic dating from not earlier than the fourth century C.E. Alan Crown ("Some Traces of Heterodox Theology in the Samaritan Book of Joshua," *BJRL* 50 [1967]: 178–98) has suggested that an older book of Joshua was extant among the Dositheans.

13. Auld, *Kings without Privilege.*

14. J. Barton, *Oracles of God: Perceptions of Ancient Prophecy after the Exile* (London: Darton, Longman & Todd, 1986), 141–51.

15. Blenkinsopp, *Prophecy and Canon*, 103–23; Davies, *In Search of "Ancient Israel,"* 120.

16. This statement is not intended to deny that intermediation was a common phenomenon in Judah throughout its history. The question is only whether such intermediation took the form of a "prophetic" institution distinct from other intermediation and, of course, distinct from the "false prophets."

8. Canons of David and Solomon

1. Davies, *In Search of "Ancient Israel,"* pp. 115–17.

2. Whether such compilations existed and what they may have contained we cannot say; if they existed, they also, of course, belong to the canonizing process.

3. Noth, *Deuteronomistic History,* 125n3.

4. Also in Ezra 2:41; 3:10; Neh. 7:44; 11:22.

5. The "sons of Korah" are mentioned twice in Exodus, and in Numbers there are extensive references to the wicked priest of that name.

6. Neh. 11:17 is the only other reference; compare the genealogy there with 1 Chron. 9:16.

7. G. H. Wilson, *The Editing of the Hebrew Psalter,* SBLDS 76 (Chico, Calif.: Scholars Press, 1985); "The Use of Royal Psalms at 'Seams' of the Hebrew Psalter," *JSOT* 35 (1986): 85–94; "The Shape of the Book of Psalms," *Interpretation* 46 (1992): 129–42.

8. W. Brueggemann, "Bounded by Obedience and Praise: The Psalms as Canon," *JSOT* 50 (1991): 63–92.

9. R. N. Whybray, *Reading the Psalms as a Book* (Sheffield: Sheffield Academic Press, 1996). Here a discussion of the various proposals for canonical shaping are reviewed.

10. Psalm 102, interestingly, gives an occasion ("for one afflicted, when faint and pleading before Yahweh").

11. It has been suggested that the Korah Psalms come from outside Jerusalem: see J. Maxwell Miller, "The Korahites of Southern Judah," *CBQ* 32 (1970): 58–68; Michael Goulder, *The Psalms of the Sons of Korah* (Sheffield: JSOT Press, 1982).

12. For more on this theme, see further Philip R. Davies, *Whose Bible Is It Anyway?,* 114–26: "Take It to the Lord in Prayer."

13. The Chronicles spelling may be in error: some of the ancient versions have "Darda." But these translations may be harmonistic, and the principle of *difficilior lectio* should perhaps apply.

14. The possibility of some rivalry between canons is intrinsically probable, though it should not be overplayed in the interests of making simplistic sociological deductions about "establishment" and "anti-establishment" groups. The tensions between Solomon and David or Moses and Abraham as canonical figures do not necessarily imply ideological divisions of this kind. Enoch, possibly, may constitute an exception (see chapter 10).

15. R. N. Whybray, *The Composition of the Book of Proverbs* (Sheffield: JSOT Press, 1994), 11–61.

16. The parallels with Egyptian instructional literature have been examined in de-

tail by W. McKane, *Proverbs,* OTL (Philadelphia: Westminster Press/London SCM Press, 1970), 51–150.

17. See, e.g., Bernhard Lang, *Wisdom and the Book of Proverbs: An Israelite Goddess Redefined* (New York, 1986).

18. Only a few need be cited. The traditional interpretations, Jewish and Christian, are allegorical—the poems tell of the love between God/Christ and Israel/the church. K. Budde, (*Das Hohelied* [Tübingen: Mohr, 1923]) thought of a collection of wedding songs; Marvin Pope (*Song of Songs: A New Translation with Introduction and Commentary,* AB [Garden City, N.Y.: Doubleday, 1977]) links the book with ancient Near Eastern funerary rites; M. Goulder (*The Song of Fourteen Songs* [Sheffield: JSOT Press, 1986]) sees it as tracing a coherent narrative, with a setting at Pentecost.

19. C. Rabin, "The Song of Songs and Tamil Poetry," *Studies in Religion* 3 (1973–74), 205–19; Michael V. Fox, *The Song of Songs and the Ancient Egyptian Love Songs* (Madison, Wis.: University of Wisconsin Press, 1985); John White, *A Study of the Language of Love in the Song of Songs and Ancient Egyptian Love Poetry* (Missoula, Mont.: Scholars Press, 1978).

20. For a review of these roles see Athalya Brenner, *The Israelite Woman: Social Role and Literary Type in Biblical Narrative* (Sheffield: JSOT Press, 1985). To Brenner we also owe the advocacy of female authorship of the Song. See conveniently her *The Song of Songs,* Old Testament Guides (Sheffield: JSOT Press, 1989), 63–66; and *A Feminist Companion to the Song of Songs* (Sheffield: JSOT Press, 1993).

9. Serious Entertainment

1. For a convenient discussion of the "courtier" tale, see Lawrence M. Wills, *The Jew in the Court of the Foreign King* (Minneapolis: Fortress Press, 1990), 39–74.

2. Wills notes (*The Jew in the Court,* 43) that there are narrative sections attached to earlier Egyptian works of instruction, but no fully developed narratives or narrative frames.

3. See Philip R. Davies, "Reading Daniel Sociologically," in A. S. van der Woude, ed., *The Book of Daniel in the Light of New Findings,* BETL 106 (Louvain: Peeters, 1993), 345–61.

4. H.-P. Müller, "Märchen, Legende und Enderwartung: Zum Verständnis des Buches Daniel," *VT* 26 (1976): 338–50.

5. The account of the evolution of the book presented here is basically that of D.J.A. Clines, *The Esther Scroll: The Story of the Story,* JSOTSup 30 (Sheffield: JSOT Press, 1984).

6. John Van Seters, *In Search of History,* 277–91; A. Graeme Auld, *Kings without Privilege.*

7. Jon Berquist, *Judaism in Persia's Shadow,* 230–31.

10. Canons and the Dead Sea Scrolls

1. A (possible) fragment from Ezra has been found in Cave 4. In rabbinic texts Ezra and Nehemiah are written as a single scroll, but it is not known whether the same was true at Qumran. The tendency to regard them still, in scholarly discussion, as a single composition has been rightly contested by VanderKam, "Ezra-Nehemiah or Ezra and Nehemiah," 55–75.

2. Eugene Ulrich, "The Bible in the Making: The Scriptures at Qumran," in Eugene Ulrich and James VanderKam, eds., *The Community of the Renewed Covenant: The Notre Dame Symposium on the Dead Sea Scrolls* (Notre Dame, Ind.: University of Notre Dame Press, 1994), 77–91, esp. 85–87.

3. For a detailed discussion of the fluidity of Joshua in the light of this fragment, see A. Rofé, "The Editing of the Book of Joshua in the Light of 4QJoahª," in *New Qumran Texts and Studies: Proceeding of the First Meeting of the International Organization for Qumran Studies, Paris, 1992* (Leiden: Brill, 1994), 73–80.

4. Patrick W. Skehan, Eugene Ulrich, and Judith E. Sanderson, *Qumran Cave 4 IV: Palaeo-Hebrew and Greek Biblical Manuscripts*, DJD 9 (Oxford: Clarendon Press, 1992).

5. L. H. Schiffman, *The Halakhah at Qumran* (Leiden: Brill, 1975). In CD 20.27–34 another authority is added: "the voice of the Teacher."

6. E. Qimron and John Strugnell, *Qumran Cave 4 V: Miqṣat Maʿaśe Ha-Torah*, DJD 10 (Oxford: Clarendon Press, 1994).

7. Harold Attridge et al., *Qumran Cave 4 VII: Parabiblical Texts Part 1*, DJD 13 (Oxford: Clarendon Press, 1994). This includes the Jubilees fragments.

8. See conveniently James C. VanderKam, *The Dead Sea Scrolls Today* (Grand Rapids: Eerdmans/London: SPCK, 1994), 60–62.

9. I take the figures from Peter W. Flint, "The Psalms Scrolls from the Judaean Desert: Relationships and Textual Affiliations," in *New Qumran Texts and Studies*, 31–52. Flint also provides a listing of variations from the Masoretic sequence; see also his "Of Psalms and Psalters: James Sanders's Investigation of the Psalms Scrolls," in Weis and Carr, eds., *A Gift of God in Due Season* (Sheffield: JSOT Press, 1996), 65–83. See also VanderKam, *The Dead Sea Scrolls Today*, 30. Fragments of Psalms scrolls have been found in Caves 1–2, 4–6, and 11). Two manuscripts were found at Masada and one at Naḥal Ḥever.

10. The *editio princeps* of this scroll is J. A. Sanders, *The Psalms Scroll of Qumran Cave 11 (11QPsª)*, DJD 4 (Oxford: Clarendon Press, 1965); see also his *The Dead Sea Psalms Scroll* (Ithaca, N.Y.: Cornell University Press, 1967).

11. Flint, "The Psalms Scrolls from the Judaean Desert," 46–47.

12. For a review of the various proposals, see G. H. Wilson, "The Qumran Psalms Scroll Reconsidered: Analysis of the Debate," *CBQ* 47 (1985): 624–42.

13. See the excellent account in VanderKam, *Enoch and the Growth of an Apocalyptic Tradition*.

14. J. T. Milik, *The Books of Enoch: Aramaic Fragments of Qumran Cave 4* (Oxford: Clarendon Press, 1976).

15. See my "Sons of Cain," in *A Word in Season: Essays in Honour of William McKane*, JSOTS 42 (Sheffield: JSOT Press, 1986), 35–56.

16. Norman Golb, *Who Wrote the Dead Sea Scrolls?* (New York: Charles Scribner's Sons, 1995).

17. Proponents of this view are too numerous to list; this is the view of the major older authorities: F. M. Cross, *The Ancient Library of Qumran and Modern Biblical Studies* (London: Duckworth; rev. ed., Garden City, N.Y.: Doubleday, 1961); 3d ed., *The Ancient Library of Qumran* (Sheffield: Sheffield Academic Press, 1995); J. T. Milik, *Ten Years of Discovery in the Wilderness of Judaea* (London: SCM Press, 1959); R. de Vaux, *Archaeology and the Dead Sea Scrolls* (Oxford: Oxford University Press, 1973); G. Vermes, *The Dead Sea Scrolls: Qumran in Perspective* (London: Collins, 1977).

18. VanderKam, *The Dead Sea Scrolls Today.*

19. Hartmut Stegemann, "The Qumran Essenes—Local Members of the Main Jewish Union in Late Second Temple Times," in J. Trebolle Barrera and L. Vegas Montaner, *The Madrid Qumran Congress: Proceedings of the International Congress on the Dead Sea Scrolls, Madrid 18–21 March 1991,* 2 vols. (Leiden: E. J. Brill, 1992), 1:83–166; *The Library of Qumran: On the Essenes, John the Baptist and Jesus,* with a Foreword from Emanuel Tov (Kampen: Kok Pharos/Grand Rapids: Eerdmans, 1993).

20. Stegemann, "The Qumran Essenes," 165.

21. I have developed this suggestion in "Redaction and Sectarianism in the Qumran Scrolls," in F. García Martínez, A. Hilhorst, and C. J. Labuschagne, eds., *The Scriptures and the Scrolls* (Leiden: Brill, 1992), 152–63 (= *Sects and Scrolls: Essays on Qumran and Related Topics* [Atlanta: Scholars Press, 1996], 151–61).

11. Holy Books

1. Jacob Neusner, "Rabbinic Judaism: History and Hermeneutics," in J. Neusner, ed., *Judaism in Late Antiquity,* 2 vols. (Leiden: Brill, 1994), 2:161–225 (177).

2. M. Haran, מבעיות הקנוניזציה של המקרא (Some Problems of Canonization of Scripture), in S. Z. Leiman, *The Canon and Masora of the Hebrew Bible* (New York: Ktav, 1974), 224–53; האסופה המקראית (The Biblical Canon) (Jerusalem: Magnes Press/Mossad Bialik, 1996), 201–6.

3. Beckwith, "Formation of the Hebrew Bible," 44–45.

4. H. E. Ryle, *The Canon of the Old Testament* (London, 1892, 1904).

5. S. Z. Leiman, *The Canonization of Hebrew Scripture: The Talmudic and Midrashic Evidence* (Hamden, Conn.: Archon Books, 1976).

6. Beckwith, "Formation of the Hebrew Bible," 39–86.

7. Barton, *Oracles of God,* 78–79.

8. W. S. Green, "The Hebrew Scriptures in Rabbinic Judaism," in Jacob Neusner, *Rabbinic Judaism: Structure and System* (Minneapolis: Fortress Press, 1995), 31–44.

9. This has been clearly demonstrated by Jacob Neusner in his analysis of the Mishnah. See his *Judaism: The Evidence of the Mishnah* (Chicago: Chicago University Press, 1981).

10. Green, "The Hebrew Scriptures," 37.

11. A. D. Nock, *Conversion* (Oxford: Clarendon Press, 1933).

12. D. Schwartz, *Studies in the Jewish Background of Christianity* (Tübingen: Mohr, 1992), 11. See also Hengel, *Judaism and Hellenism,* 95ff.

13. Such as that of Ezekiel the Tragedian; see Carl R. Holladay, *Fragments from Hellenistic Jewish Authors,* vol. 2: *Poets* (Atlanta: Scholars Press, 1989), 301–529.

14. E. Tov, *The Greek Minor Prophets Scroll from Naḥal Ḥever,* DJD 8, 1994.

15. J. Hughes, *Secrets of the Times: Myth and History in Biblical Chronology,* JSOTS 66 (Sheffield: JSOT Press, 1990), 234–35; the calculation is also discussed by T. L. Thompson, *The Historicity of the Patriarchal Narratives,* BZAW 133 (Berlin: De Gruyter, 1974), 15 and John H. Hayes, *An Introduction to Old Testament Study* (Nashville: Abingdon Press, 1979), 24–25.

16. This is due mainly to the work of Sundberg, *The Old Testament of the Early Church.*

17. R. Beckwith, *The Old Testament Canon of the New Testament Church* (London: SPCK, 1985), 30–46. For the conclusion, see 385–86.

Bibliography

Ahlström, G. *The History of Ancient Palestine*. JSOTSup 146. Sheffield: JSOT Press, 1993.

Alexander, P. S. "How Did the Rabbis Learn Hebrew?" Unpublished lecture, 1966.

Assman, J. "Egyptian Literature." *ABD* 2:386.

Attridge, H., et al. *Qumran Cave 4 VII. Parabiblical Texts Part 1*. DJD 13. Oxford: Clarendon Press, 1994.

Auld, A. G. "Prophets through the Looking Glass: Between Writings and Moses." *JSOT* 27 (1983): 3–23.

———. *Kings without Privilege: David and Moses in the Story of the Bible's Kings*. Edinburgh: T. & T. Clark, 1994.

Auld, A. G., and Margreet Steiner, *Jerusalem I: From the Bronze Age to the Maccabees*. Cities of the Biblical World. Cambridge: Lutterworth Press/Macon, Ga.: Mercer University Press, 1996.

Avigad, N. *Bullae and Seals from a Post-Exilic Jewish Archive*. Qedem 40. Jerusalem, Israel Exploration Society, 1976.

Baines, J. "Literacy and Ancient Egyptian Society." In *Man*. London: Royal Anthropological Institute of Great Britain and Ireland, 1983.

Baldermann, I. et al., eds. *Zum Problem des biblischen Kanons*. Jahrbuch für Biblische Theologie 3. Neukirchen: Neukirchener Verlag, 1988.

Barr, J. *Holy Scripture: Canon, Authority, Criticism*. Philadelphia: Westminster Press, 1983.

Barstad, H. "No Prophets? Recent Developments in Biblical Prophetic Research and Ancient Near Eastern Prophecy." *JSOT* 57 (1993): 39–60.

Barton, J. *Oracles of God: Perceptions of Ancient Prophecy after the Exile*. London: Darton, Longman & Todd, 1986.

———. *The Spirit and the Letter: Studies in the Biblical Canon*. London: SPCK, 1996.

Beckwith, R. T. *The Old Testament Canon of the New Testament Church*. London: SPCK, 1985.

———. "Formation of the Hebrew Bible." In M. J. Mulder, ed., *Mikra*, 39–86.

Berquist, J. L. *Judaism in Persia's Shadow: A Social and Historical Approach*. Minneapolis: Fortress Press, 1995.

Biran, A., and Naveh, J. "An Aramaic Stele Fragment from Tel Dan." *IEJ* 43 (1993): 81–98.

Blenkinsopp, J. *Prophecy and Canon: A Contribution to the Study of Jewish Origins*. Notre Dame, Ind.: University of Notre Dame Press, 1977.

————. *A History of Prophecy in Israel: From the Settlement in the Land to the Hellenistic Period.* Philadelphia: Westminster Press, 1983.

————. "Temple and Society in Achaemenid Judah." In P. R. Davies, ed., *Second Temple Studies,* 1:22–53.

————. *Sage, Priest, Prophet: Religious and Intellectual Leadership in Ancient Israel.* Library of Ancient Israel. Louisville, Ky.: Westminster John Knox Press, 1995.

Bloom, H. *The Western Canon: The Books and School of the Age.* New York and London: Harcourt Brace, 1994.

Brenner, A. *The Israelite Woman: Social Role and Literary Type in Biblical Narrative.* Sheffield: JSOT Press, 1985.

————. *The Song of Songs.* Old Testament Guides. Sheffield: JSOT Press, 1989.

————. *A Feminist Companion to the Song of Songs.* Sheffield: JSOT Press, 1993.

Brett, M. G. *Biblical Criticism in Crisis? The Impact of the Canonical Approach on Old Testament Studies.* Cambridge: Cambridge University Press, 1991.

Brettler, M. "How the Books of the Hebrew Bible Were Chosen." In H. Minkoff, ed., *Approaches to the Bible,* 108–12.

Brooke, G. J., ed. *New Qumran Texts and Studies: Proceeding of the First Meeting of the International Organization for Qumran Studies, Paris 1992.* STDJ 15. Leiden: E. J. Brill, 1994.

Broshi, M., ed. *The Damascus Document Reconsidered.* Jerusalem: Israel Exploration Society, 1992.

Brueggemann, W. "Bounded by Obedience and Praise: The Psalms as Canon." *JSOT* 50 (1991): 63–92.

Bruns, G. L. "Canon and Power in the Hebrew Scriptures." In R. von Hallberg, ed., *Canons,* 5–83.

Budde, K. *Das Hohelied.* Tübingen: Mohr, 1923.

The Cambridge History of Classical Literature, vol. 1, part 4: The Hellenistic Period and the Empire. Cambridge: Cambridge University Press, 1989. "Books and Readers in the Greek World," 154–97.

Carr, D. M. "Canonization in the Context of Community." In R. D. Weis and D. M. Carr, eds., *A Gift of God in Due Season,* 22–64.

Carroll, R. P. "Textual Strategies and Ideology." In P. R. Davies, ed., *Second Temple Studies,* 108–24.

————. "Manuscripts Don't Burn—Inscribing the Prophetic Tradition: Reflections on Jeremiah 36." In M. Augustin and K.-D. Schunck, eds., *"Dort ziehen Schiffe dahin . . . ": Collected Communications to the XIVth Congress of the International Organization for the Study of the Old Testament, Paris 1992,* 31–42. Frankfurt: Peter Lang, 1996.

Carter, C. E. "The Province of Yehud in the Post-Exilic Period: Soundings in Site Distribution and Demography." In T. C. Eskenazi and K. H. Richards, eds., *Second Temple Studies,* 1994.

Childs, B. S. *Introduction to the Old Testament as Scripture.* Philadelphia: Fortress Press/London: SCM Press, 1979.

Clines, D.J.A. *The Esther Scroll: The Story of the Story.* JSOTSup 30. Sheffield: JSOT Press, 1984.

Cohen, S.J.D. *From the Maccabees to the Mishnah.* Library of Early Christianity. Philadelphia: Westminster Press, 1987.

Crenshaw, J. "Education in Ancient Israel," *JBL* 104 (1985): 601–15.

Cross, F. M. *The Ancient Library of Qumran and Modern Biblical Studies*. London: Duckworth, 1961. 3d ed.: *The Ancient Library of Qumran*. Sheffield: Sheffield Academic Press, 1995.

———. *Canaanite Myth and Hebrew Epic*. Cambridge: Harvard University Press, 1973.

Crown, A. "Some Traces of Heterodox Theology in the Samaritan Book of Joshua." *BJRL* 50 (1967):178–98.

Davies G. I., ed. *Ancient Hebrew Inscriptions*. Cambridge: Cambridge University Press, 1991.

Davies, P. R. *The Damascus Covenant*. JSOTSup 25. Sheffield: JSOT Press, 1982.

———. *A Word In Season: Essays in Honour of William McKane*. JSOTS 42. Sheffield: JSOT Press, 1986.

———. *What Does Eve Do To Help? and Other Readerly Questions to the Old Testament*. JSOTS 94. Sheffield: JSOT Press, 1990.

———. *Second Temple Studies 1: Persian Period*. JSOTSup 117. Sheffield: JSOT Press, 1991.

———. *In Search of 'Ancient Israel': A Study in Biblical Origins*. JSOTSup 148. Sheffield: JSOT Press, 1992.

———. "Redaction and Sectarianism in the Qumran Scrolls." In F. García Martínez, A. Hilhorst, and C. J. Labuschagne, eds., *The Scriptures and the Scrolls,* 152–63. Leiden: Brill, 1992.

———. "Reading Daniel Sociologically." In A. S. van der Woude, ed., *The Book of Daniel in the Light of New Findings,* 345–61. BETL 106. Louvain: Peeters, 1993.

———. *Whose Bible Is It Anyway?* JSOTSup 204. Sheffield: Sheffield Academic Press, 1995.

———. *Sects and Scrolls: Essays on Qumran and Related Topics*. SFSHJ 134. Atlanta: Scholars Press, 1996.

Demsky, A. "Writing in Early Israel and Early Judaism: The Biblical Period." In M. Mulder, ed., *Miqra,* 2–20.

Edelman, D. V., ed. *The Triumph of Elohim*. Contributions to Biblical Exegesis and Theology. Kampen: Kok Pharos, 1995.

Eskenazi, T. C. *In an Age of Prose: A Literary Approach to Ezra-Nehemiah*. SBLMS 36. Atlanta: Scholars Press, 1988.

Eskenazi, T. C., and Kent H. Richards, eds. *Second Temple Studies,* vol. 2: *Temple and Community in the Persian Period*. JSOTSup 175. Sheffield: JSOT Press, 1994.

Fiandra, E., G. G. Fissore, and M. Frangipane. *Archives before Writing*. Rome: Ministero per i culturali e ambienti and Ufficio Centrale per i beni archivistici, 1994.

Fishbane, M. "Revelation and Tradition: Aspects of Inner-Biblical Exegesis." *JBL* 99 (1980): 343–61.

———. *Biblical Interpretation in Ancient Israel*. Oxford: Clarendon Press, 1985.

Flint, Peter W. "The Psalms Scrolls from the Judaean Desert: Relationships and Textual Affiliations." In G. J. Brooke, ed., *New Qumran Texts and Studies,* 31–52.

———. "Of Psalms and Psalters: James Sanders's Investigation of the Psalms Scrolls." In R. D. Weis and D. M. Carr, eds., *A Gift of God in Due Season,* 65–83.

Foster, B. R. *Before the Muses: An Anthology of Akkadian Literature*. 2 vols. Bethesda, Md.: CDL Press, 1993.

Fox, M. V. *The Song of Songs and the Ancient Egyptian Love Songs*. Madison, Wis.: University of Wisconsin Press, 1985.

Freedman, R. E. *The Creation of Sacred Literature*. Berkeley and Los Angeles: University of California Press, 1981.

Gammie, J. G., and L. G. Perdue, eds. *The Sage in Israel and the Ancient Near East*. Winona Lake, Ind.: Eisenbrauns, 1990.

Gardiner, A. *Hieratic Papyri in the British Museum*. Vol 1. London: British Museum, 1935.

————. *Ancient Egyptian Onomastica*. Oxford: Oxford University Press, 1947.

Golb, N. *Who Wrote the Dead Sea Scrolls?* New York: Charles Scribner's Sons, 1995.

Goldin, J. "The End of Ecclesiastes: Literal Exegesis and Its Transformation." In A. Altmann, ed., *Biblical Motifs: Origins and Transformations,* 135–58. Cambridge, Mass.: Harvard University Press, 1966.

Golka, F. "Die israelitische Weisheitsschule oder 'des Kaisers neue Kleider.'" *VT* 33 (1983): 257–70.

Gorak, J. *The Making of the Modern Canon*. London and Atlantic Highlands, N.J.: Athlone Press, 1981.

Goulder, M. *The Psalms of the Sons of Korah*. JSOTSup 20. Sheffield: JSOT Press, 1982.

————. *The Song of Fourteen Songs*. JSOTSup 36. Sheffield: JSOT Press, 1986.

Grabbe, L. L. *Judaism from Cyrus to Hadrian*. 2 vols. Minneapolis: Fortress Press, 1992.

————. *Priests, Prophets, Diviners, Sages: A Socio-Historical Study of Religious Specialists in Ancient Israel*. Valley Forge, Pa.: Trinity Press International, 1995.

Green, W. S. "The Hebrew Scriptures in Rabbinic Judaism." In Jacob Neusner, *Rabbinic Judaism: Structure and System,* 31–44. Minneapolis: Fortress Press, 1995.

von Hallberg, R., ed. *Canons*. Chicago: University of Chicago Press, 1984.

Hallo, W. W. "The Concept of Canonicity in Cuneiform and Biblical Literature: A Comparative Appraisal." In K. L. Younger et al., eds., *The Biblical Canon in Comparative Perspective: Scripture in Context,* 4:1–19.

Haran, M. מבעיות הקנוניזציה של המקרא (Some Problems of Canonization of Scripture). In S. Z. Leiman, *The Canon and Masora of the Hebrew Bible,* 224–53.

————. "Book-Scrolls in Israel in Pre-Exilic Times." *JJS* 33 (1982): 161–73.

————. "Book-Scrolls at the Beginning of the Second Temple Period: The Transition from Papyrus to Skins." *HUCA* 54 (1983): 111–22.

————. "More Concerning Book-Scrolls in Pre-Exilic Times." *JJS* 35 (1984): 84–85.

————. "On the Diffusion of Literacy and Schools in Ancient Israel," In J. A. Emerton, ed., *Congress Volume Jerusalem 1986,* 81–95. VT Supplements 40. Leiden: Brill, 1988.

————. האסופה המקראית (The Biblical Canon). Jerusalem: Magnes Press/Mossad Bialik, 1996.

Hayes, J. H. *An Introduction to Old Testament Study*. Nashville: Abingdon Press, 1979.

Heaton, E. W. *The School Tradition of the Old Testament*. Oxford: Oxford University Press, 1994.

Hengel, M. *Judaism and Hellenism*. 2 vols. London: SCM Press, 1974.

Hoglund, K. G. "The Achaemenid Context." In P. R. Davies, ed. *Second Temple Studies,* vol. 1: *Persian Period*. JSOTSup 117. Sheffield: JSOT Press, 1991.

————. *Achaemenid Imperial Administration in Syria-Palestine and the Missions of Ezra and Nehemiah*. SBLDS 125. Atlanta: Scholars Press, 1992.

Holladay, C. R. *Fragments from Hellenistic Jewish Authors.* Vol. 2: *Poets.* Atlanta: Scholars Press, 1989.

Hughes, J. *Secrets of the Times: Myth and History in Biblical Chronology.* JSOTSup 66. Sheffield: JSOT Press, 1990.

Jackson, B. S. "Ideas of Law and Legal Administration: A Semiotic Approach." In R. E. Clements, ed., *The World of Ancient Israel,* 185–202. Cambridge: Cambridge University Press, 1989.

Jamieson-Drake, D. W. *Scribes and School in Monarchic Judah.* JSOTSup 66. Sheffield: JSOT Press, 1991.

Kellermann, U. "Erwägungen zum Esragesetz." *ZAW* 80 (1968): 373–85.

Kessler, R. *Staat und Gesellschaft im vorexilischen Juda. Vom 8. Jahrhundert bis zum Exil.* VT Supplements 47. Leiden: Brill, 1992.

Kippenberg, Hans G. *Religion und Klassenbildung im antiken Judäa.* Göttingen: Vandenhoeck & Ruprecht, 1978; 2d ed. 1982.

Kraemer, D. "The Formation of the Rabbinic Canon: Authority and Boundaries." *JBL* 110 (1991): 613–30.

———. "On the Relationship of the Books of Ezra and Nehemiah." *JSOT* 59 (1993): 73–92.

Kreissig, H. *Die sozialökonomische Situation in Juda zur Achämenidenzeit.* Berlin: Akademie Verlag, 1973.

Lambert, W. G. "Ancestors, Authors and Canonicity." *JCS* 11 (1957): 1–14.

———. "Literary Style in First Millennium Mesopotamia." In E. Bender, ed., *Essays in Memory of E. A. Speiser,* 123–32. American Oriental Series 53. New Haven, Conn.: American Oriental Society, 1968.

Lang, B. *Wisdom and the Book of Proverbs: An Israelite Goddess Redefined.* New York: Pilgrim Press, 1986.

Leiman, S. Z. *The Canon and Masora of the Hebrew Bible.* New York: Ktav, 1974.

———. *The Canonization of Hebrew Scripture: The Talmudic and Midrashic Evidence.* Hamden, Conn.: Archon Books, 1976.

Lemaire, A. *Les Écoles et la formation de la Bible dans l'ancien Israel.* OBO 39. Fribourg: Éditions Universitaires, 1981.

Lemche, N. P. "From Patronage Society to Patronage Society." In V. Fritz and P. R. Davies, eds., *The Origins of the Ancient Israelite States,* 106–20. JSOTSup 228. Sheffield: Sheffield Academic Press, 1996.

Lenski, G. E. *Power and Privilege: A Theory of Social Stratification.* New York: McGraw-Hill, 1966.

Lewis, J. P. "What Do We Mean by Jabneh?" *Journal of Bible and Religion* 32 (1964): 125–32.

Lieberman, S. *Greek in Jewish Palestine.* New York: Jewish Theological Seminary, 1942.

———. *Hellenism in Jewish Palestine.* New York: Jewish Theological Seminary, 1950.

Lightstone, J. N. "The Formation of the Biblical Canon in Judaism of Late Antiquity: Prolegomena to a General Reassessment." *Studies in Religion* 8 (1979): 135–42.

———. *Society, the Sacred, and Scripture in Ancient Judaism: A Sociology of Knowledge.* Waterloo, Ont.: Wilfrid Laurier University Press, 1988.

Maier, J. "Zur Problem des biblischen Kanons im Frühjudentum im Licht der Qumranfunde." In I. Baldermann, ed., *Zum Problem des biblischen Kanons,* 135–46.

Marrou, H. I. *A History of Education in Antiquity.* Translated by G. Lamb. London: Sheed & Ward, 1956.

McKane, W. *Proverbs.* Old Testament Library. Louisville, Ky.: Westminster Press/London: SCM Press, 1970.

——. *Jeremiah.* Vol. 1. ICC. Edinburgh: T & T Clark, 1986.

McKenzie, S. *The Trouble with Kings.* Leiden: Brill, 1991.

Meade, D. *Pseudonymity and Canon.* WUNT 39. Tübingen: Mohr, 1986.

Mendels, D. "Hecataeus of Abdera and a Jewish 'patrios politeia.'" *ZAW* 95 (1983): 96–110.

Mettinger, T.N.D. *Solomonic State Officials.* Lund: Gleerup, 1971.

Michalowski, P. *Letters from Mesopotamia.* SBL Writings from the Ancient World. Atlanta: Scholars Press, 1993.

Milik, J. T. *Ten Years of Discovery in the Wilderness of Judaea.* London: SCM Press, 1959.

——. *The Books of Enoch: Aramaic Fragments of Qumran Cave 4.* Oxford: Clarendon Press, 1976.

Millar, F. "The Jews of the Graeco-Roman Diaspora between Paganism and Christianity AD 312–438." In J. Lieu, J. North, and T. Rajak, eds., *The Jews among Pagans and Christians in the Roman Empire,* 97–123. London: Routledge, 1992.

Millard, A. "An Assessment of the Evidence for Writing in Ancient Israel." In *Biblical Archaeology Today,* 301–12. Jerusalem: Israel Exploration Society.

Miller, J. M. "The Korahites of Southern Judah." *CBQ* 32 (1970): 58–68.

Miller, J. W. *The Origins of the Bible: Rethinking Canon History.* Mahwah, N.J.: Paulist Press, 1994.

Minkoff, Harvey, ed. *Approaches to the Bible: The Best of Bible Review,* vol. 1: *Composition, Transmission and Language.* Washington, D.C.: Biblical Archaeology Society, 1994.

Mulder, M., ed. *Miqra.* CRINT 2:1. Assen: Van Gorcum, 1988.

Müller, H.-P. "Märchen, Legende und Enderwartung: Zum Verständnis des Buches Daniel." *VT* 26 (1976): 338–50.

Neusner, Jacob. *Judaism: The Evidence of the Mishnah.* Chicago: University of Chicago Press, 1981.

——. "Rabbinic Judaism: History and Hermeneutics." In J. Neusner, ed., *Judaism in Late Antiquity,* 2:161–225. Leiden: Brill, 1994.

Niditch, S. *Oral World and Written Word.* Library of Ancient Israel. Louisville, Ky.: Westminster John Knox Press, 1996.

Niemann, H. *Herrschaft, Königtum und Staat: Skizzen zur soziokulturellen Entwicklung im monarchischen Israel.* Tübingen: Mohr, 1993.

Nock, A. D. *Conversion.* Oxford: Clarendon Press, 1933.

Noth, M. *Überlieferungsgeschichte des Pentateuch.* Stuttgart: Kohlhammer, 1948; ET, *A History of Pentateuchal Traditions.* Translated by B. W. Anderson. Englewood Cliffs, N.J.: Prentice-Hall, 1973.

——. *Überlieferungsgeschichtliche Studien: Die sammelden und bearbeitenden Geschichtswerke im Alten Testament.* Tübingen: Niemeyer, 1943; ET, *The Deuteronomistic History.* Translated by H.G.M. Williamson. JSOTSup 15. Sheffield: JSOT Press, 1981.

Olmstead, A. T. "Darius as Lawgiver." *AJSL* 51 (1935): 247–9.

——. *History of the Persian Empire.* Chicago: University of Chicago Press, 1948.

Oppenheim, L. "The Position of the Intellectual in Mesopotamian Society." *Daedalus* 104/2 (1975): 34–46.

———. *Ancient Mesopotamia: Portrait of a Dead Civilization.* 2d ed. Chicago: University of Chicago Press, 1977.

Paul, S. *Studies in the Book of the Covenant in the Light of Cuneiform and Biblical Law.* Leiden: Brill, 1970.

Pettinato, G. *The Archives of Ebla.* Garden City, N.Y.: Doubleday, 1981.

Pfeiffer, R. *History of Classical Scholarship.* Oxford: Clarendon Press, 1968.

Pope, Marvin K. *Song of Songs: A New Translation with Introduction and Commentary.* Anchor Bible. Garden City, N.Y.: Doubleday, 1977.

Porten, B. *Archives from Elephantine: The Life of an Ancient Jewish Military Colony.* Berkeley and Los Angeles: University of California Press, 1968.

Posner, F. *Archives in the Ancient World.* Cambridge, Mass.: Harvard University Press, 1972.

Qimron, E., and J. Strugnell. *Qumran Cave 4, V: Miqṣat Maʿaśe Ha-Torah.* DJD 10. Oxford: Clarendon Press, 1994.

Rabin, C. "The Song of Songs and Tamil Poetry." *Studies in Religion* 3 (1973–74): 205–19.

Rendtorff, R. *Canon and Theology: Overtures to an Old Testament Theology.* Overtures to Biblical Theology. Minneapolis: Fortress Press, 1993.

Rofé, A. "The Editing of the Book of Joshua in the Light of 4QJosh[a]." In Brooke, ed., *New Qumran Texts and Studies,* 73–80.

Rogerson J. W., and P. R. Davies. "Was the Siloam Tunnel Built by Hezekiah?" *BA* 59 (1996): 138–49.

Ryle, H. E. *The Canon of the Old Testament.* London, 1892.

Safrai, S. "Education and the Study of the Torah." In S. Safrai and M. Stern, eds., *The Jewish People in the First Century,* vol. 2, 947–70. Assen: Van Gorcum, 1976.

Salters, R. "Qoheleth and the Canon." *ET* 86 (1975): 339–42.

Sanders, J. A. *The Psalms Scroll of Qumran Cave 11 (11QPsᵃ).* DJD 4. Oxford: Clarendon Press, 1965.

———. *The Dead Sea Psalms Scroll.* Ithaca, N.Y.: Cornell University Press, 1967.

———. *Torah and Canon.* Philadelphia: Fortress Press, 1972.

———. "Adaptable for Life: The Nature and Function of Canon." In F. M. Cross, W. E. Lemke, and P. D. Miller, eds., *Magnalia Dei: The Mighty Acts of God: Essays on the Bible and Archaeology in Memory of G. E. Wright,* 531–60. Garden City, N.Y.: Doubleday, 1976.

———. *Canon and Community: A Guide to Canonical Criticism.* Philadelphia: Fortress Press, 1984.

———. *From Sacred Story to Sacred Text: Canon as Paradigm.* Philadelphia: Fortress Press, 1987.

Sarna, N. "The Order of the Books." In C. Berlin, ed., *Studies in Jewish Bibliography, History and Literature in Honor of I. Edward Kiev,* 407–13. New York: Ktav, 1971.

Sasson, J. M. "Some Comments on Archive Keeping at Mari." *Iraq* 34 (1972): 55–67.

Schäfer-Lichtenberger, C. "Sociological and Biblical Views of the Early State." In V. Fritz and P. R. Davies, eds., *The Origins of the Ancient Israelite States,* 78–105. JSOTSup 228. Sheffield: Sheffield Academic Press, 1996.

Schaper, J. "The Jerusalem Temple as an Instrument of the Achaemenid Fiscal Administration." *VT* 45 (1995): 528–39.

Schiffman, L. H. *The Halakhah at Qumran*. Leiden: Brill, 1975.

Schürer, E. *The Jewish People in the Age of Jesus Christ*, 3 vols. Revised by G. Vermes, F. Millar, and M. Goodman. Edinburgh: T. & T. Clark, 1979.

Schwartz, D. *Studies in the Jewish Background of Christianity*. Tübingen: Mohr, 1992.

Shavit, Y. "The 'Qumran Library' in the Light of the Attitude towards Books and Libraries in the Second Temple Period." In M. O. Wise, N. Golb, J. J. Collins and D. G. Pardee, eds., *Methods of Investigation of the Dead Sea Scrolls and the Khirbet Qumran Site*. New York: New York Academy of Sciences, 1994.

Sheppard, G. T. "The Epilogue to Qoheleth as Theological Commentary." *CBQ* 39 (1977): 182–89.

Sievers, J. *The Hasmoneans and Their Supporters*. Atlanta: Scholars Press, 1990.

Skehan, P. W., E. Ulrich, and J. E. Sanderson. *Qumran Cave 4, IV: Palaeo-Hebrew and Greek Biblical Manuscripts*. DJD 9. Oxford: Clarendon Press, 1992.

Smelik, K.A.D. *Writings from Ancient Israel*. Edinburgh: T. & T. Clark, 1991.

———. *Converting the Past: Studies in Ancient Israelite and Moabite Historiography*. OTS 28. Leiden: Brill, 1992.

Smith, M. *Palestinian Parties and Politics That Shaped the Old Testament*. New York and London: Columbia University Press, 1971.

Smith, Wilfred Cantwell. *What Is Scripture? A Comparative Approach*. London: SCM Press, 1993.

Sprinkle, J. M. *"The Book of the Covenant," A Literary Approach*. JSOTSup 174. Sheffield: Sheffield Academic Press, 1994.

Stegemann, Hartmut. "The Qumran Essenes—Local Members of the Main Jewish Union in Late Second Temple Times." In J. Trebolle Barrera and L. Vegas Montaner, eds., *The Madrid Qumran Congress. Proceedings of the International Congress on the Dead Sea Scrolls Madrid 18–21 March 1991*. 2 vols. Leiden: E. J. Brill, 1992. Vol. 1, pp. 83–166.

———. *The Library of Qumran: On the Essenes, John the Baptist and Jesus,* with a Foreword by Emanuel Tov. Kampen: Kok Pharos/Grand Rapids: Eerdmans, 1993.

Stemberger, G. "Jabne und der Kanon." In Baldermann, ed., *Zum Problem des biblischen Kanons*, 163–74.

Stern, M., ed. *Greek and Latin Authors on Jews and Judaism,* vol. 1: *From Herodotus to Plutarch*. Jerusalem: Israel Academy of Sciences and Humanities, 1986.

Sundberg, A. C., Jr. *The Old Testament of the Early Church*. Harvard Theological Studies 20. Cambridge, Mass., and London: Harvard University Press, 1964.

Tcherikover, V. *Hellenistic Civilization and the Jews*. Philadelphia: Jewish Publication Society, 1959.

Thompson, T. L. *The Historicity of the Patriarchal Narratives*. BZAW 133. Berlin: Walter de Gruyter, 1974.

———. *The Origin Tradition of Ancient Israel*. JSOTSup 55. Sheffield: JSOT Press, 1987.

———. *Early History of the Israelite People: From the Written and Archaeological Sources*. Studies in the History of the Ancient Near East 4. Leiden: Brill, 1992.

Tov, E. *The Greek Minor Prophets Scroll from Naḥal Ḥever*. DJD 8. Oxford: Clarendon Press, 1994.

Trebolle-Barrera, J. "Redaction, Recension and Midrash in the Books of Kings." *Bulletin of the International Organization for Septuagint and Cognate Studies* 15 (1980): 12–35.

————. "Authoritative Functions of Scriptural Works." In E. Ulrich and J. C. VanderKam, eds., *The Community of the Renewed Covenant*, 95–110.

Ulrich, E., and J. C. VanderKam, eds. *The Community of the Renewed Covenant: the Notre Dame Symposium on the Dead Sea Scrolls*. Notre Dame, Ind.: University of Notre Dame Press, 1994.

Ulrich, E. "The Bible in the Making." In E. Ulrich and J. C. VanderKam, eds., *The Community of the Renewed Covenant*, 77–93.

————. "The Canonical Process, Textual Criticism, and Later Stages in the Composition of the Bible." In M. Fishbane, E. Tov, and W. W. Fields, eds., *Sha'arei Talmon*. Winona Lake, Ind.: Eisenbrauns, 1992.

Ulrich, E., and F. M. Cross, eds. *Qumran Cave 4, VII: Genesis to Numbers*. DJD 12. Oxford: Clarendon Press, 1994.

Van Seters, John. *In Search of History*. New Haven and London: Yale University Press, 1983.

VanderKam, J. C. *Enoch and the Growth of an Apocalyptic Tradition*. CBQMS 16. Washington, D.C.: Catholic Biblical Association, 1984.

————. *The Dead Sea Scrolls Today*. Grand Rapids: Eerdmans/London: SPCK, 1994.

————. "Ezra–Nehemiah or Ezra and Nehemiah." In E. Ulrich, J. W. Wright, R. P. Carroll, and P. R. Davies, eds., *Priests, Prophets and Scribes: Essays on the Formation and Heritage of Second Temple Judaism in Honour of Joseph Blenkinsopp*, 55–75. JSOTSup 149. Sheffield: JSOT Press, 1992.

de Vaux, R. *Archaeology and the Dead Sea Scrolls*. Oxford: Oxford University Press, 1973.

Vermes, G. *The Dead Sea Scrolls: Qumran in Perspective*. London: Collins, 1977.

Waltke, B. "Superscriptions, Postscripts, or Both." *JBL* 110 (1991): 683–96.

Washington, Harold. *Wealth and Poverty in the Instruction of Amenemope and the Hebrew Proverbs*. SBLDS 142. Atlanta: Scholars Press, 1994.

Weeks, S. *Early Israelite Wisdom*. Oxford Theological Monographs. Oxford: Clarendon Press, 1994.

Weinberg, J. *The Citizen-Temple Community*. JSOTSup 151. Sheffield: JSOT Press, 1992.

Weinfeld, M. *Deuteronomy and the Deuteronomic School*. Oxford: Clarendon Press, 1972.

Weis, R. D., and D. M. Carr, eds. *A Gift of God in Due Season*. JSOTSup 225. Sheffield: Sheffield Academic Press, 1996.

Westbrook, R. *Studies in Biblical and Cuneiform Law*. Paris: Gabalda, 1988.

————. *Property and the Family in Biblical Law*. JSOTSup 113. Sheffield: JSOT Press, 1991.

White, J. *A Study of the Language of Love in the Song of Songs and Ancient Egyptian Love Poetry*. Missoula, Mont.: Scholars Press, 1978.

Whitelam, K. *The Just King: Monarchical Judicial Authority in Ancient Israel*. JSOTSup 12. Sheffield: JSOT Press, 1979.

Whybray, R. N. *The Intellectual Tradition in the Old Testament*. BZAW 135. Berlin: De Gruyter, 1974.

————. *The Making of the Pentateuch*. Sheffield: JSOT Press, 1987.

————. *The Composition of the Book of Proverbs*. JSOTSup 168. Sheffield: JSOT Press, 1994.

————. *Reading the Psalms as a Book*. JSOTSup 222. Sheffield: Sheffield Academic Press, 1996.

Williams, R. J. "The Sages of Ancient Egypt in the Light of Recent Scholarship." In J. M. Sasson, ed., *Oriental Wisdom, JAOS* 101 (1981):1–19.

————. "The Sage in Egyptian Literature." In J. G. Gammie and L. Perdue, eds., *The Sage in Israel and the Ancient Near East*, 19–30.

————. "Writing and Writing Materials." *IDB* 4: 909–21.

Wills, Lawrence M. *The Jew in the Court of the Foreign King*. Minneapolis: Fortress Press, 1990.

Wilson, G. H. *The Editing of the Hebrew Psalter*. SBLDS 76. Chico, Calif.: Scholars Press, 1985.

————. "The Use of Royal Psalms at 'Seams' of the Hebrew Psalter." *JSOT* 35 (1986): 85–94.

————. "The Shape of the Book of Psalms." *Interpretation* 46 (1992): 129–42.

————. "'The Words of the Wise': The Intent and Significance of Qoheleth 12:9–14." *JBL* 103 (1984): 175–92.

————. "The Qumran Psalms Scroll Reconsidered: Analysis of the Debate." *CBQ* 47 (1985): 624–42.

Younger, K. L., Jr. *Ancient Conquest Accounts: A Study in Ancient Near Eastern and Biblical History Writing*. JSOTSup 98. Sheffield: JSOT Press, 1990.

Younger, K. L., W.W. Hallo, and B. F. Batto, eds. *The Biblical Canon in Comparative Perspective: Scripture in Context IV*. Ancient Near Eastern Texts and Studies 11. Lewiston, N.Y.: Edwin Mellen Press, 1991.

Index of Ancient Sources

APOCRYPHA AND PSEUDEPIGRAPHA

DEAD SEA SCROLLS

RABBINIC SOURCES

CLASSICAL SOURCES

Index of Names and Subjects